The First Letter from New Spain

Joe R. and Teresa Lozano Long Series
in Latin American and Latino Art and Culture

THE *First Letter* FROM *New Spain*

THE LOST PETITION OF CORTÉS AND HIS COMPANY, JUNE 20, 1519

By John F. Schwaller

WITH HELEN NADER

UNIVERSITY OF TEXAS PRESS

Austin

Copyright © 2014 by the University of Texas Press

First paperback edition, 2015

Requests for permission to reproduce material from this work should be sent to:
Permissions
University of Texas Press
P.O. Box 7819
Austin, TX 78713-7819
http://utpress.utexas.edu/index.php/rp-form

♾ The paper used in this book meets the minimum requirements of
ANSI/NISO Z39.48-1992 (R1997) (Permanence of Paper).

LIBRARY OF CONGRESS CATALOGING-IN-PUBLICATION DATA

Schwaller, John Frederick.
The first letter from New Spain : the lost petition of Cortés and
his company, June 20, 1519 / by John F. Schwaller ; with Helen Nader.
pages   cm. — (Joe R. and Teresa Lozano Long series in
Latin American and Latino art and culture)
Study in English; letter in English accompanied
by a facsimile of the original in Spanish.
Includes bibliographical references and index.
ISBN 978-0-292-75671-7 (cloth : alk. paper)
ISBN 978-1-4773-0763-2 (paperback)
1. Cortés, Hernán, 1485–1547. Carta del cabildo de Veracuz.   2. Mexico—History—
Conquest, 1519–1540.   3. Veracruz (Veracruz-Llave, Mexico)—History—16th century.
I. Nader, Helen, 1936–   II. Cortés, Hernán, 1485–1547. Carta del cabildo
de Veracruz.   III. Cortés, Hernán, 1485–1547. Carta del cabildo
de Veracruz. English.   IV. Title.
F1230.S37   2014
972'.02—dc23
2013030491

doi:10.7560/756717

Contents

Preface

ON WHAT I REMEMBER AS A BRIGHT, SUNNY, BUT COLD DAY IN early 1977, I was sitting in the reading room of Spain's Archivo General de las Indias (AGI), which in those days was located on the interior of the second floor of the Lonja, the stock exchange designed by Juan de Herrera on a contract from Phillip II. I was there in Seville for the purpose of writing my doctoral dissertation on the secular clergy in sixteenth-century Mexico.

That quest had already occupied me for a full year in Bloomington, Indiana, where I was a PhD candidate in colonial Latin American history. I had used original materials held in the Lilly Library as well as the large collection of printed materials in the Graduate Library. From Bloomington I had traveled to Mexico, thanks to a Benito Juárez–Abraham Lincoln Fellowship of the Mexican government. I had begun my research in the Cathedral of Mexico, where I was allowed only an hour a day, and in the Archivo General de la Nación (AGN). A year later, I received a Training Fellowship from the Organization of American States, and was able to continue my research in Mexico for a second year. I expanded my investigation to also study in the Archivo General de Notarías of the Departamento del Distrito Federal. In order to augment my income beyond the fellowships, I had begun to teach English to Mexican businessmen and became a radio announcer on XEVIP, the English-language, CBS affiliate, which served Mexico City in those days. In 1976 I received a Fulbright-Hays graduate research fellowship, which allowed me to travel to Seville and Madrid for a third year of research.

At the AGI, my goal was to read all correspondence and other files which might conceivably have content relating to the secular clergy. Throughout the fall I consulted bundles of letters from ecclesiastical persons, files of priests seeking royal appointments, letters from bishops, and the records of several juicy lawsuits. By the spring I had moved on to correspondence to the Crown from private individuals, the viceroys, royal *audiencia*, and, finally, cities. I called up the first volume of letters from cities of New Spain to the Crown.

JOHN F. SCHWALLER

The first item in the bundle was damaged, and written in what was clearly a hand from early in the colonial period. As I read the first few lines, I simply could not believe what I saw. Here was a document that had been written in Veracruz, on the island of Ulúa, and it was dated 1519. Quite simply, I realized at that moment that this was probably the oldest original document written from the mainland of North America. All of the other documents relating to the conquest were copies—many of them made in the sixteenth century, true, but nevertheless copies.

I asked several friends to take a look at this find to confirm my initial evaluation, and they did. I then contacted the professional staff of the archive. I suggested that the document be moved from the *sección Gobierno, subsección México*, to a more appropriate part of the archive, logically the *sección Real Patronato*. *Real Patronato* is an "artificial" section of the archive. Materials housed there have been removed from the natural sections because of their historic importance. The real jewels of the AGI are in *Real Patronato*. After much consultation and deliberation, the archivists decided that it should stay where it was. It was, after all, a letter from a *cabildo municipal* in New Spain, and that particular *legajo* was for letters from towns and cities to the Crown.

Although this document was probably the find of a lifetime, I had a dissertation to complete. I had already written several chapters. The end was in sight. In order to properly study this document I would have needed to begin all over again. So I had a photocopy made, and filed it away for future reference. It stayed filed away until the mid-1980s.

After I had written two books on the Church in sixteenth-century Mexico, I turned to the Veracruz petition. I began to decipher the signatures, and to explore the lists of conquerors in the traditional sources. At about that time, Helen Nader published her book on towns and cities in early modern Spain. I invited her to join the project, both to have her investigate the role of the town in the conquest of Mexico and also to seek her paleographic skills with the signatures. For the next twenty years we worked on the project. In the late 1990s she began to insist, rightly, that we finish the project. Unfortunately, by that time I had become a university administrator and had much less time to spend on scholarly research.

Finally, by 2009, I had cleared away all other projects and began to focus my limited free time on the Veracruz petition. Fortunately, by that time two scholars, Hugh Thomas and Bernard Grunberg, had completed extensive and detailed studies of the conquest and of the conquerors. The works of these men provided necessary background research that would assist me immeasurably in completing the study of the Veracruz petition and the biographies of the conquerors. Relying heavily on their work to assist me in piecing together the biographies of the signatories of the Veracruz petition, I began to work bit by bit on identifying the conquerors. By this time Nader had retired and had more time to devote to the project. Consequently, in 2010 and 2011 we were able to make the final push to complete the project which had begun decades before on that bright, crisp day in Seville. Now, as we are only a few years from the five-hundredth anniversary of the landing of the Cortés expedition at Veracruz, this work has come to fruition.

Early versions of the research in this book were presented at annual meetings of the Rocky Mountain Conference of Latin American Studies and of the American Historical Association.

As I have indicated, this project has relied heavily on the assistance of many people and organizations. The necessary funding for the project began with the Fulbright-Hays program of the Department of Education, which supported my research in Spain twice: once as a graduate student, and then in the 1980s as an associate professor. Some funding was also provided by the Tinker Foundation, which supported me on a two-year research project for a biography of don Luis de Velasco the younger. I have benefited from the largess and indulgence of colleagues and administrators at Florida Atlantic University, the Academy of American Franciscan History, the University of Montana, the University of Minnesota, Morris, and the State University of New York at Potsdam.

Several people have been instrumental to this project from the very first day. María Antonia Colomar was a young archivist in the AGI when I began my research there. She continues to work in the archive, serving as the assistant director of that historic and important institution. She has helped me in more ways than I can express. I am always grateful for her friendship and assistance after all of these years.

G. Douglas Inglis was another young scholar in the archive in those days. He and I became friends the first week I was living in Seville, since he too had a Fulbright-Hays grant. He and his lovely wife, Pilar, and my wife, Anne, forged a friendship which has lasted nearly thirty-five years. Most recently he secured all of the paperwork to receive permission for the publication of the document in this book. I cannot begin to thank him enough for all of the countless kindnesses which he has provided to me and my family.

I also want to profoundly thank Matthew Restall and Stuart Schwartz for their wonderful suggestions and pithy comments on the first draft of this work. They provided me with great inspiration in their critiques. It is good to have supportive colleagues who are generous with their time.

Helen Nader, my colleague and friend, has had great faith in this project since I first ran it by her several decades ago. She has been tireless in her support. Helen and I first met as I was finishing my dissertation at Indiana University, where she had taken a position in the History Department. Although we overlapped briefly at IU, I did not take coursework with her. I have always respected the high quality of her scholarship. I am so grateful to have had her as a partner on this project.

My family has provided me with more joy and support than I can begin to describe. My parents, Henry and Juliette Schwaller, were responsible for my love of Mexican history. From my early childhood we traveled the length and breadth of the republic. Eventually they retired, purchasing a home in Cuernavaca, where the final draft of this book was written. They also took me to Seville when I was a young person, to see the glory of the Giralda and the Torre de Oro. It is their love of Mexico, and of all things Hispanic, which inspired me to pursue the history of that country. Both of my parents passed away as I was finishing the first draft of this work and thus never got to see it in its entirety. I know that she is now proud that my efforts have finally reached fruition.

My wife, Anne, was with me from the very beginning of this project. She was probably the first person I asked to look at the document, since she has always assisted me in the archive. She has been my copy editor, advisor, and sounding board throughout the process. Our two sons, Robert and William, have heard the story of this document more times than they can remember and are probably pleased that it is now over and they don't have to hear anymore about how someday I will finish it. Our older son, Robert, even got involved in the project, while he was doing his own doctoral research at the AGI. At some point I had him call up the document to check some details for me. He also found a *relación de méritos* for one of the signatories and assisted me in a last-minute check of the paleography of the manuscript. To all of them go my undying love and thanks.

The First Letter from New Spain

CHAPTER I

Introduction

ON GOOD FRIDAY OF APRIL 1519, HERNANDO CORTÉS AND HIS company of supporters landed on a beach in what is now Mexico. On that beach, he and his companions resolved to found a town, named La Villa Rica de la Vera Cruz (the rich town of the True Cross), in commemoration of their landing on that holy day. This event provides an important signpost in the conquest of Mexico, a dividing point from the prior activities of the Spaniards in the New World. Cortés had sailed from Cuba with some five hundred men under the auspices of and with a license from Diego Velázquez, governor of Cuba. That license, however, allowed Cortés only to conduct trade and to explore the coasts of what would become Mexico.

In resolving to establish a town, Cortés and his men symbolically broke away from the supervision of Velázquez and sought to place themselves under the direct control of the Spanish king. That act and its legality have generated much debate ever since it occurred. The event became famous in legend and history, and is mentioned prominently in all histories of the conquest. Yet other than a description by Cortés, by Bernal Díaz del Castillo (a member of the company), and in subsequent documents, the original record of this dramatic event — the actual petition to the Crown requesting royal recognition, the First Letter in this book's title — remained unknown and undiscovered. The absence of this document from the historical record represents a large and important lacuna in our knowledge of the conquest of Mexico.

In spite of efforts by historians over the past five centuries to find it, the petition was hiding in plain sight, in the Archives of the Indies, in Seville, in a bundle of other documents, letters, and petitions directed to the king from cities and towns in New Spain. The petition of the Veracruz town council (AGI, Mexico, 95, Carta del cabildo de Veracruz [1519]), signed by all the members of the company, provides the ultimate legal justification for the actions of Cortés and his expedition. This petition is one of the first documents written from the mainland of North America by any European. It is the only original document from this early in the conquest: other reports and letters have survived only in incomplete sixteenth-century copies. It is unique in that it provides details about the dramatic events related to the founding of Veracruz and illuminates our understanding of the early chronology of the conquest of Mexico. But what is most impressive is that the document was meant to carry the signatures of all the members of the company who participated in this historic event.

Lamentably, the letter has suffered damage over the last five hundred years, and as much as one-third of the bottom part of several pages is missing. Conservators have stopped further damage and replaced the paper of those pages, but the information those lost shreds held is irretrievably gone. Nevertheless, what does remain provides an invaluable glimpse into what is unquestionably one of the most stirring and exciting moments of the conquest.

The book presented here reproduces the Veracruz petition, along with other materials, in order to place this unique document in its historical context, clarify the chronology of the event, describe how that moment figured in the conquest of Mexico, and shed light on the lives of the men who participated in it.

James Lockhart's landmark study of events in Peru, *The Men of Cajamarca*, provided a solid basis upon which to proceed.[1] Just as Lockhart was able to use the roster from the distribution of booty at Cajamarca both to identify the members of the Pizarro expedition and to give us thumbnail biographies of the participants, so this document can provide us with the names of the members of the Cortés company at a point within a matter of weeks of their departure from Cuba. Yet not only does the petition of the town of Veracruz provide the names of the participants, but it is also an important document essential to an understanding of the legal bases of the expedition itself.

The petition demonstrates quite clearly that the expeditions of conquest were true companies: that is, organizations in which participants pooled their resources to achieve a common end, the benefits of which were then distributed share-wise to the members of the company. Although Díaz del Castillo refers to his colleagues as "soldiers" (*soldados*), they were not soldiers in the strict sense of the word, since they did not receive a salary (*sueldum*). They were not employed by a government nor even by Cortés, their leader. Rather, they were more like investors. Each man invested his own equipment and matériel in return for a portion of whatever treasure the company might gain. Similarly, each man had a voice in the direction of the expedition, while also recognizing that there was an established command structure, with Cortés at the top. Cortés was also the major investor, risking his own fortune in the purchase of ships, food, and supplies for the company. As a result he also expected a larger portion of whatever treasure they might acquire.[2]

Along the same lines as James Lockhart's work, this study further reinforces what we know about the social composition of the early Spanish expeditions.

It illuminates the role the conquest played in the lives of the men involved, following them through the period of the conquest and into their lives afterward. The men who took part in the conquest of Mexico were somewhat different from the participants in the conquest of Peru. Far more men on horseback fought in South America, as compared to the Cortés expedition, for example.

The petition of the Veracruz town council and residents is not the only document of its kind generated by the Cortés company. Just over a year later, when the expedition regrouped in the town of Tepeaca—renamed Segura de la Frontera by the Spanish—a second letter was sent to the Crown, and it too was signed by the members of the company, some 420 men (see the appendix for a list of the signatories). While that document has been known for some time, the original has been lost. Since the late nineteenth century scholars have had to rely on a contemporary transcription.[3] Unfortunately, it seems that the colonial secretary who transcribed the signatures was faced with the same problem as modern scholars: the names are devilishly hard to decipher. To compound matters, when the transcription was published, additional errors entered in, as the nineteenth-century scholars had difficulty reading the sixteenth-century scribal hand. This later document has assisted many historians in trying to identify the members of the company, and has served as a useful guide in this study as well.

This present study fits into a broad category of works characterized as the "New Conquest History" by Matthew Restall.[4] In his analysis of the historiography of the conquest, Restall sees a watershed in the late years of the twentieth century, when scholars began to ask new questions of old sources, to discover unknown sources, and to focus on individuals and groups of individuals who had been excluded from earlier studies of the conquests of the Americas. He recognizes that each generation will return to the traditional primary sources and probe them with new questions in mind. At the same time, improved archival and paleographic capabilities have allowed researchers both to discover new sources and to mine unexpected sources for important details to round out our understanding of the conquest. Since Lockhart, many historians have begun to look at the other conquerors, not just the famous men, like Cortés and Pizarro, or even their captains, but the rank-and-file members of their expeditions, and at people who were largely overlooked even at the time, such as women and servants. Lastly, whole groups of people, such as the native auxiliaries, were traditionally consigned to a few words, or even a footnote, but now are the protagonists of new histories of the conquest. It is in this vein that this book continues.

Historians over time have invested considerable time in studying the various conquests of the New World. As part of the New Conquest History, new meta-analyses are beginning to emerge; these examine the studies done in previous eras in order to extract new meaning and new conclusions from them. Excellent examples of these involve the various expeditions into what is now Colombia. In 1995, José Ignacio Avellaneda Navas investigated the studies of the conquest of New Granada.[5] Once he had extracted the essential data concerning the social composition of the conquering bands, he then compared them closely to the findings of Lockhart for nearby Peru. In 2007, Michael Francis returned to the original accounts of the conquests of Colombia, extracted the essential data regarding the conquerors, and then analyzed it in light of the many studies which had been conducted prior to his, including that of Avellaneda Navas.[6]

In keeping with this aspect of the New Conquest History, this book takes a new look at the traditional sources: the accounts of conquerors such as Díaz del Castillo and of Cortés himself. It also draws heavily from several important collective biographies of the conquerors of Mexico: works by Hugh Thomas, Bernard Grunberg, Victor Alvarez, and Robert Himmerich y Valencia.[7] Through the utilization of the earlier studies of the conquest, it continues a tradition of nearly five hundred years, and extracts the most significant findings from those studies both to better illuminate the moment in which the Cortés expedition legally severed its ties to Velázquez, and to produce detailed biographies of the conquerors themselves.

The second aspect of the New Conquest History is the discovery of new sources, or the utilization of previously underused materials, to inform our understanding of the period. In the case of New Spain, access to native documents, both pictorial manuscripts and texts written in native languages using European characters, has provided new insights into the conquest. Stephanie Wood, for instance, worked with both pictorial and textual manuscripts to discern the Nahua view of the conquest.[8] Drawing on a similar corpus of materials, but looking more at the impact on the psyche of native peoples, José Rabasa has also provided a reinterpretation, specifically analyzing the effects of the conquest and colonization.[9] Looking at the use of Nahua auxiliaries in the conquest of Guatemala, Florine Asselbergs drew heavily on a well-known pictorial manuscript to document that episode of the conquest.[10] A small contribution, which seeks clearer understanding of a particular text, is a new look at the iconic phrase "broken spears," which was attributed to a native observer of the conquest. To one looking closely at the original Nahuatl, it seems that the phrase was actually "broken bones."[11]

This book furthers this aspect of the New Conquest History through the use of a completely unknown manuscript as its central contribution to the literature. Scores of unknown manuscripts housed in Spanish and Mexican archives are waiting to be discovered by historians and so to add new data to our understanding of these events. One of the significant contributions made by Bernard Grunberg in his collection of biographies of the conquerors is the use of the many *relaciones de méritos* drawn up by conquerors and their heirs to document their participation in episodes of conquest. Prior to his work they had largely been unexplored, except for the occasional scholar who was focused on one or another conqueror and so consulted the account of his services as documented in the colonial archives.

Flowing from this reexamination of new sources of documentation is the prioritizing of the study of participants in the conquest whom historians previously ignored. In particular, the contributions of native auxiliaries, who played a crucial role in the Spanish success, are now being studied, as in the case of Asselbergs's book, mentioned above. Laura Matthew and Michel Oudijk edited an important collection of essays which looks at the contributions of native auxiliaries, and exemplifies this aspect of the New Conquest History.[12] Others, such as the native translator doña Marina, also known as La Malinche, are now the subject of significant scholarship.[13] Our study of the Veracruz petition also conforms to this feature of the New Conquest History in that it opens a window into the lives of the "foot soldiers" of the conquest, the unheralded men who fought alongside the better-known captains of the expedition. Unfortunately, the political reality of the moment in which the petition was created left women and natives excluded, and so even in this revision of the story they are relegated, yet again, to the background.

The focus of this work is one particular moment in time — June 20, 1519 — and an event which was to prove to be crucial in the time line of the conquest of Mexico. As with Cajamarca in Peru, the happenings in Veracruz have the potential to draw attention from the long processes of history in which many individuals act on a daily basis to bring about change. This reification of a particular event is an unfortunate by-product of our focus on this unique document. Nonetheless, by looking at this particular long-lost text, gaining an understanding of the broader context within which it was created, and analyzing the lives of the men who participated in the actions it describes, we are faithful to the New Conquest History. The goal is to return our focus to the members of the company and the long-term processes at work, as evidenced in the document, not to concentrate on the actions of the leaders and the impact of big, brash actions.

This book begins with a general synopsis of the conquest of Mexico. It outlines the major events of the conquest, in order to better place the foundation of the town of Veracruz in its historical context. Moreover, the events described in this chapter provide the signposts for understanding the accomplishments of the men who signed the letter. After the conquest, many men had an opportunity to recall their participation, and they tended to best remember the major events when they themselves had been present. In this way the synopsis can also help one understand the trajectory of the stories of the individual conquerors.

The third chapter considers the historiography of the Veracruz petition itself. The founding of Veracruz figures prominently in nearly every history of the conquest of Mexico. This section of our book will compare the histories of the conquest with the understanding of events as gleaned from the Veracruz petition, to enable a discussion of the value of primary sources and corroboration for historians. Specifically, the previously known narrative of the town (erroneously known as the "First Letter of Cortés") and the account of Díaz del Castillo will be analyzed, along with other major histories. This chapter will look at the chronologies of the conquest surrounding the foundation of Veracruz, since the date of the Veracruz petition provides a crucial new data point. Moreover, the chapter will consider the different perspectives of authors with regard to the true leadership structure of the expedition. Some writers have seen the Cortés company as a fairly egalitarian group, exercising broad consultation on issues of importance. Others see it as being firmly under the control of Cortés himself at all times. The petition of the town helps to illuminate this debate.

The next two chapters (chapters 4 and 5) include a detailed description of the document itself, along with a transcription and translation, and a facsimile reproduction of the original.

One of the truly unique features of the Veracruz petition is that it preserves the names of more than three hundred members of the Cortés expedition. Contemporary documents indicate that as many as five hundred persons participated in the Veracruz landing. Consequently this document provides a rare insight into the composition of the company that engaged in the conquest of Mexico. For historians it has all of the importance of the Cajamarca roster, which outlined the membership of the expedition to Peru led by Pizarro. Chapter 6 consists of the collective biography of the men who signed the letter: their origins and what happened to them during and after the conquest, as gleaned from numerous and varied sources. Many men do not appear in the historical record after this event, and so it is assumed that they died in the conquest or shortly thereafter. Most of the men have been identified, and some biographical information does exist for them, providing insight into their social status, occupations, and places of origin. This chapter also looks at what the Veracruz petition can illuminate about the internal structure of the company and relationships among the men who fought alongside Cortés. Many comparisons are made to the findings of studies which have focused on the conquests of Panama, Colombia, Peru, and Chile.

Chapter 7 contains thumbnail biographies of all the men who signed the letter. For several centuries now, scholars have attempted to identify the participants in the conquest. Even in the decades immediately following the conquest some authors took great pains to recall who those men were. Díaz del Castillo, a participant himself, devoted several chapters of his history to describing his fellow conquerors. By the nineteenth century, more and more historians were focused on recovering the names and biographies of the members of the Cortés company. Just within the last twenty-five years, two scholars, Hugh Thomas and Bernard Grunberg, have published what seek to be definitive collections of the biographies of the conquerors.[14] These men spent many years combing through all of the accounts of the conquest, and through scores of other histories, to compile a list of names and biographies. These works, and others, have greatly assisted in the writing of our thumbnail biographies.

In this book we have opted to use the common form of the conqueror Cortés's name — Hernán Cortés. In reality the name he used was variously Fernando or Hernando. At some point this was abbreviated to Hernán, and has remained as such ever since. Rather than continually refer to "La Villa Rica de la Vera Cruz," we have opted to use the simpler form "Veracruz." The ruler of the Mexica (Aztecs) is commonly known in English as "Montezuma," and "Moctezuma" in Spanish. His true name was closer to "Moteuczoma," the spelling preferred here.

FROM THE TIME OF CHRISTOPHER COLUMBUS'S FIRST VOYAGE in 1492, Spaniards had eagerly come to the Caribbean to seek their fortunes. Except for 1497, when the return fleet gathered in Hispaniola was destroyed by a hurricane, ships traveled between Spain and the Americas every year following 1492. Europeans completed dozens of transatlantic voyages before Columbus's death in 1506. In 1508 alone Spaniards made forty-five such journeys.[1] By 1520 they were undertaking annual transatlantic voyages of commerce and colonization, which were financed and organized by Spanish merchants who were shipping European textiles, implements, food, wine, and medicines to the colonists.[2] Already the House of Trade (Casa de Contratación) and the royal Council of the Indies (Consejo de Indias) in Seville were testing the qualifications of sea pilots, maintaining the ever-expanding navigation charts and coastal maps, establishing policy for the Indies (the name for the New World preferred by the Spaniards at that time), auditing the cargo brought from the colonies, collecting the royal one-fifth of gold and silver, and adjudicating civil and criminal cases involving persons in the colonies as well as those merchants involved in the crossings.[3]

Despite tragic losses at sea resulting from hurricanes and piracy, this well-oiled commercial and colonizing machine was so efficient that by 1518 Spaniards had established twenty-seven Spanish towns and cities in the Caribbean.[4] The robust success of Spanish colonization and commerce is evident in the fact that most of these early cities and towns — such as Santo Domingo, San Juan, and Havana — still exist and flourish.

Voyages of exploration, in contrast, followed a different protocol. Their purpose was to find a western passage to southeast Asia, so that Spaniards could participate in the spice trade. These exploratory expeditions were not organized for the purpose of settlement. They were planned and financed by the kings of Castile. King Fernando and Queen Isabel had sponsored Christopher Columbus's first three voyages for this purpose. In the years 1495 to 1500, the monarchs adopted a new method, allowing investors in Seville to organize companies that sent fleets to South America loaded with cargo they hoped to sell in Asia.[5] These ships followed the South American coast as far south as modern Venezuela's Orinoco River delta, but found no passage to Asia.

After Isabel died in 1504, Fernando acted as regent for their daughter, Queen Juana. He energetically committed royal resources to the search for a sea passage. In 1505 he ordered that all exploratory expeditions must not only record navigational and mapping information but also send reports of the terrain, climate, fauna and flora, and native peoples and their languages, customs, religions, and political systems. During his brief regency, Fernando sent three voyages in search of a passage to Asia. Two explored Central America, and a third ventured as far south as the Río de la Plata in South America — all without the desired results. One ship from that last voyage returned empty-handed after their captain, who had gone ashore, was killed, dismembered, cooked, and eaten by the natives.[6]

None of the voyages underwritten by the Castilian treasury succeeded. After Fernando's death in 1516, his Habsburg grandson Charles came from the Netherlands to rule Spain and revitalized his grandfather's search for a sea passage. Royal officers in the Caribbean sent exploratory voyages west and north into the Gulf of Mexico: Juan Ponce de León explored the coast of Florida and found nothing but swamp, while Diego Velázquez, lieutenant on the island of Cuba, sent two expeditions west to the Yucatan Peninsula, with the same results.[7]

For the next ten years, royal officials in the Caribbean under the leadership of Columbus's son Diego Colón, governor of Hispaniola, and his lieutenant on Cuba, Diego Velázquez, organized voyages of exploration to the west, which systematically examined the east and west coasts of Central America and established ill-fated towns there, such as Darién in the Isthmus of Panama, whose colonists perished from hostile native attacks and tropical diseases. Exploration of the shores around the Gulf of Mexico encountered swamps, tropical forests, and hostile natives, but the Spanish expeditions succeeded in mapping the coast. Fernando's systematic, scientific exploration had not, however, found the all-desired sea route to Asia. In 1516 Diego Colón was replaced as governor of the Indies by a triumvirate of three Jeronymite friars, appointed by the regent, Bishop Cisneros. These friars ruled until 1519, when they were replaced by members of the local royal court (*audiencia*). Eventually, in 1520, Diego Colón regained his office as governor, but only served for some three years. What is crucial here is that during the period of the Cortés expedition and its planning there was a relative power vacuum in the New World.[8]

Although, as noted above, the nominal rulers of the region were three friars who collectively served as governor of the Indies, it is clear that Velázquez, who had recently completed the conquest of Cuba, was potentially the most powerful person in the area. He wanted to begin expeditions to explore the islands and mainland in the immediate area around Cuba.

King Charles concluded that continuing to explore northward would not yield the desired results, because the east coast of Florida, just recently explored, curved back toward Europe instead of to the west. He next sponsored two futile voyages to the southernmost parts of South America and then signed a contract with a Portuguese sea merchant, Ferdinand Magellan.[9] By coincidence, Magellan and his five ships left Spain just two months before the Cortés expedition left Cuba. Both would succeed in reaching the Pacific Ocean: Magellan by sea around the tip of South America and Cortés on foot across Mexico. Diego Velázquez wanted to determine the contours of the oceans and landmasses near Cuba. This could be accomplished only by voyages of discovery and exploration.

The conquest of Mexico occurred some twenty-five years after Columbus first landed in the Antilles. The participants in the conquest saw it as the culmination of Spanish efforts to explore, conquer, and settle the New World. Many of the men who sailed with Hernán Cortés were newly arrived in the Indies, while others had already participated in many expeditions of discovery and conquest.[10]

Although Columbus left nearly one hundred men from his first expedition in 1492 to settle on the island of Hispaniola, by the time he returned on his second voyage they had all perished. Columbus then founded the city of Santo Domingo, in the southeastern part of the island. This would become the base of Spanish operations throughout the circum-Caribbean region. The settlement of the New World followed a sequence which repeated itself: a voyage of exploration would find a new place, and Spaniards would then settle that new place and spread out from there to neighboring islands or parts of the mainland.

In the period between 1504 and 1512, as seen above, explorations set out from Santo Domingo to what are now Florida, Puerto Rico, Panama, and the island of Cuba. The earliest of these focused on nearby islands and the north coast of South America. Early in the sixteenth century, Juan Ponce de León led an expedition to explore the islands near Hispaniola, landing on and eventually conquering Puerto Rico. In 1510 the Spaniards—most notably Vasco Núñez de Balboa—created a town, Santa María la Antigua, in what is now Panama, making it the first permanent European settlement on the American mainland; Pedrarias Dávila was later active in this region.[11] In 1512 Juan Ponce de León was removed as the governor of Puerto Rico. He then mounted an expedition, sailing to the north and landing in what is now Florida. At roughly the same time, Diego Velázquez, also sailing out of Santo Domingo, went to the west and north to land on the island of Cuba. He led an armed conquest of that island. These voyages established a pattern of exploration, conquest, and settlement that originated from Santo Domingo. Each new settlement then became the point from which new explorations could be mounted. From Cuba, Diego Velázquez organized a series of expeditions into the Gulf of Mexico and the Caribbean Sea. From Panama, expeditions moved north into Central America and south into South America.[12]

Starting in 1513, the Crown required expedition leaders to secure permission from local royal officials before any voyage of discovery or conquest. As a result, Diego Velázquez received authorization from the governors of the New World in Santo Domingo both to organize expeditions and to license others in the exploration of the oceans and lands in the vicinity of Cuba. In 1517 Velázquez approved an expedition into the Gulf of Mexico proposed by Francisco Hernández de Córdoba. The company organized by Hernández de Córdoba was modest by contemporary standards: about three ships and perhaps one hundred men. The purpose was to explore nearby islands and to trade with whatever natives were found.

Sailing in February 1517 from Santiago de Cuba, on the southeast coast, Hernández de Córdoba proceeded easterly to the end of the island, then westerly to Havana, and then further west into the Gulf of Mexico. He ran into a storm and eventually sighted land at what is now the northeast tip of the Yucatan Peninsula. He sailed along the coast and discovered large groups of natives and some impressive cities. When he made landfall, however, he was greeted with hostility. With a dozen or more men wounded, the Spaniards retreated to their ships. They made landfall several more times, to take on fresh water and what provisions they could. In one of three landings, they were again met by fierce native opposition. Wounded himself, Hernández de Córdoba lost approximately half of his men. Faced with these losses, and a ship which also began to founder, he sailed back to Cuba, two or so months after his departure, and died shortly after his return.[13]

While the voyage proved fatal for Hernández de Córdoba, he had discovered a new territory which was densely populated and which had manifestly great wealth. This persuaded Diego Velázquez to outfit a new expedition, under Juan de Grijalva, his nephew. This second expedition set sail in May 1518. With about twice as many men, in four ships — one of which returned promptly to Cuba — Grijalva was prepared for hostile natives. He followed a route similar to that of Hernández de Córdoba, although he traveled further south along the eastern shore of the Yucatan Peninsula, stopping at the island of Cozumel. During the first phase of his voyage he avoided towns and villages when he needed to land for fresh water. Yet midway through, running desperately short of water, he had to land at Campeche, where Hernández de Córdoba had met with the least native resistance. Fully armed and bringing several light cannon, the Spaniards successfully took on fresh water, and fought back at least one attack. Thereafter Grijalva landed at many of the same places as Hernández de Córdoba, using his superior numbers and weapons to add a measure of protection. After just over seven months of exploration, he set a course for Cuba to report to Velázquez on his expedition. The expedition had lost fewer men than Hernández de Córdoba's and came back with a significant amount of gold and other precious goods.[14]

Even before Grijalva returned, Velázquez began to mount yet a third expedition to this newly discovered coastline, thinking that Grijalva had met with the same fate as Hernández de Córdoba. Velázquez continued to appoint leaders from his inner circle, this time selecting a man to whom he was related by marriage and who had served him as a secretary, Hernando (Hernán) Cortés. From the first moment, however, there were some serious misunderstandings between Velázquez and Cortés. Cortés and many of the men he recruited understood their charge to include settlement and conquest. Not only were they to discover new lands, both for trade with the natives and in order to pillage where necessary, but, they believed, they could also settle and populate the land. Nevertheless, in the papers which empowered Cortés to lead the expedition, Velázquez indicated that the voyage's purpose was to find Grijalva, who in fact was returning to Cuba. Furthermore, Cortés was to "discover" new and rich lands in the places already visited by Hernández de Córdoba and Grijalva. Velázquez commissioned Cortés to lead yet another expedition of discovery and trade, not one of colonization and conquest. Trade was restricted to formal activity through the expedition leaders. Private members of the expedition could not trade with the natives. All goods were to be formally recorded and put into the official coffers of the expedition and be kept in a chest with three locks, their keys held by three different officials. Yet at the same time Velázquez did grant to Cortés all the additional powers as he might need for the success of the expedition.[15]

While Cortés made arrangements for his expedition, Grijalva returned. Word of his adventures spread quickly through the Spanish population of Cuba. Veterans of the Hernández de Córdoba and Grijalva expeditions soon flocked to join Cortés, as did others who had sailed on other expeditions throughout the region, as well as men who were newly arrived from Spain and seeking opportunities. Cortés promptly arranged for ships and supplies, paying for most of this from his own pocket, and borrowing heavily on the basis of his license from Velázquez. As veterans of the previous expeditions flocked to Cortés, Velázquez began to have second thoughts. He finally revoked Cortés's license and attempted to halt the expedition. Cortés heard of Velázquez's plans

Map of Veracruz and surrounding region.
After Gerhard, A Guide to the Historical
Geography of New Spain.

and set sail from Santiago. The fleet stopped in Trinidad and Havana, also in Cuba, before departing on February 10, 1519.[16] The expedition had some eleven ships and possibly as many as five hundred men.[17]

The Cortés expedition took essentially the same route as Hernández de Córdoba and Grijalva, as had been suggested in the agreement between Velázquez and Cortés. In the Yucatan they picked up two shipwrecked Spaniards who had survived to live among the Maya. One, Gerónimo de Aguilar, chose to join his compatriots. The other, Gonzalo Guerrero, had married a Maya woman and had children, and therefore opted to remain in his adopted home.[18] In the Yucatan and sailing up to the Isthmus of Tehuantepec, the expedition engaged the natives on several occasions, a few of which involved pitched battles. In the wake of one of these, Cortés received a young native woman as a prize. She was baptized Marina, and became known as doña Marina among the Spaniards, and La Malinche among the natives.[19] She was one of the keys to the expedition's future success since she was bilingual in Maya and the Aztec language, Nahuatl. By also speaking through Gerónimo de Aguilar, who was bilingual in Maya and Spanish, Cortés could communicate with most of the native groups of the region.

On April 22, 1519, Good Friday, the expedition reached a promising harbor guarded by an island called Ulúa (sometimes Uluacan). They dropped anchor and went ashore. This location would become their base of operations for the next two months. They were met by a large contingent of natives sent by the *huey tlahtoani* (emperor) of the Aztecs, Moteuczoma. The Aztec emissaries collected information about the Spaniards, and the Spaniards learned more about the Aztecs. The Aztecs also supplied the Spaniards with food and other provisions. After two weeks of conversations, the Aztec emissaries invited the Spaniards to come to Tenochtitlan, their capital, an offer Cortés refused. At the conclusion of talks with the Aztecs, the local Totonac natives came offering their support to Cortés, if he were to oppose the Aztecs. This was an important moment, since it indicated to the Spaniards that not all of the native groups were mutually supportive of one another.[20]

Some members of the company became concerned about Cortés's intentions. The group was divided over the nature of the expedition. Many believed that conquest and settlement were the best course of action, in order to increase the wealth each could gain. Others believed that continuing to trade, and occasionally plunder, was best. Added to the debate was the lingering concern that Velázquez had authorized only trade, not settlement or conquest.[21]

Cortés sent off two expeditions. One sailed up the coast to the north to discover a better harbor. The other proceeded inland with a more vague charge, which was possibly to find a place suitable for a prolonged encampment or perhaps simply in search of food.[22] At the same time that Cortés was negotiating with local native groups, fighting some battles to subdue others, and building fortifications at Veracruz, some members of the company rose up in opposition to him, citing Velázquez's original intent to only explore. They also sought to return to Cuba. Cortés and his followers stopped the rebels from taking command of one of the ships.[23]

In reaction, Cortés's supporters within the company, probably acting in accord with Cortés's own wishes, proclaimed their autonomy from Diego Velázquez, established the town of La Villa Rica de la Vera Cruz, and drafted the petition which is the subject of this book. As the document itself notes, the members of the company then proceeded to elect city officials and eventually to name Cortés as the effective governor. The details of this action and an analysis of the event are further described and examined in chapters 3 and 4.

Encouraged by the offers of assistance from the Totonacs, the Cortés expedition moved inland to the city of Cempoalla. There Cortés negotiated with the local rulers regarding support and the delivery of food and provisions. He also began the effort to convert the natives to Christianity by destroying some of the religious objects in their temples and pyramids and replacing them with crosses and statues of the Virgin Mary. He also had the priest of the expedition, fray Bartolomé de Olmedo, begin to preach the Gospel, through the interpreters.[24]

After the stay in Cempoalla, the company moved further north to a new settlement and built their town of Veracruz at a place called Quiahuiztlan. This action was based on the report of the expedition sent to reconnoiter for a better harbor.[25] Cortés continued to negotiate with local native leaders for their support. This was a twofold process. First, the Spaniards needed the food and labor provided by the natives to build their town and supply their army. Second, they sought to pit one native group against another, namely, the outlying native polities against the power and control of the Aztecs. When the natives supported the Spaniards, they ran a calculated risk of offending the Aztecs, while at the same time they hoped to benefit from an alliance with the newly arrived Spaniards. The Aztecs, for their part, were well informed of the Spaniards' actions. Since the time of Grijalva regular messengers had been dispatched to report on the intruders. The Aztecs also sent several groups of ambassadors, merchants, and other officials both to meet with the Spaniards and to reassure themselves that their subject towns and cities remained loyal to the Aztecs.

In their newly built town, the Spaniards began to inventory all of the treasure they had collected up to that point. Once the whole of the treasure had been counted, they allocated portions to the Crown and to Cortés, with the rest divided up among the members of the company, according to a document dated July 6, 1519.[26] The town council met and drew up a long set of instructions for the men whom they had selected to serve as representatives of the town in the royal court.[27] They also wrote a long historical narrative of the expedition—from the first efforts to organize in Cuba until the building of the town of Veracruz—dated July 10, 1519.

Cortés then sent to Spain two members of the company who had been empowered to be agents at court, along with the pilot Antón de Alaminos. They carried at least four documents: the narrative of the voyage, the instructions for the representatives to the royal court, an inventory of the treasure, and the petition of the town council, the latter dated June 20, 1519, which is the document being presented in this book. In spite of express orders to the contrary, the representatives of the expedition stopped in Cuba for provisions and water, thereby notifying Velázquez of their actions. Velázquez, in turn, mounted a punitive expedition, under the leadership of Pánfilo de Narváez, to capture Cortés and stop him from proceeding further inland.

With the departure for Spain of the agents who were to seek recognition of the town of Veracruz and reject the authority of Velázquez, some of the supporters of Velázquez attempted to commandeer a ship to return to Cuba. Cortés got word of their efforts, and after having punished the rebels, he ordered that the ships be run aground and dismantled. All of the metal fittings, anchors, lines, sails, and other valuable appurtenances were saved. The hulks were then broken and possibly eventually burned.[28] This had the psychological effect of cutting the company off from any hope of easy return to Cuba. In reality the ships were beginning to deteriorate because of the effects of tropical borers and other pests which attacked the wood hulls; they probably were no longer seaworthy.[29] Nonetheless, the act of dismantling the ships took on an almost mythical stature as the definitive moment in the conquest, when all possible routes for retreat were closed off and the expedition was compelled to inexorably move inland. By comparison, the founding of the town of Veracruz also had a similar effect in terms of the legal status of the expedition. By having revolted against Velázquez, the members of the company could be charged with treason. Consequently, unless the town received royal recognition, the members of the company were in fact rebels.

Leaving a small company of men to guard the settlement at Veracruz, Cortés then took the main body of his forces and native allies inland toward the central highlands. There he soon encountered forces from the native state of Tlaxcala. The first military engagement was nearly disastrous for the Spaniards, with many men being injured, several dying, and the Spanish forces sorely tested. Yet the Spaniards did escape. Over the next few days the Tlaxcalans would attack several more times, by day and by night. The Spaniards could at best adopt a defensive position and use their cannons, harquebuses, and crossbows to keep the native army at bay. Cortés sought to make peace with the Tlaxcalans, but his offers were rebuffed. Had the natives encircled the Spaniards and laid siege, the battle would have been theirs. But such a strategy ran counter to Mesoamerican practices. Meanwhile Cortés was steadily losing men, and his supplies were beginning to run out. He took the offensive, sending out armed, mounted companies to pillage nearby towns and villages for supplies. In the end, the Tlaxcalans relented and accepted the peace overtures.[30]

In all likelihood the Tlaxcalans decided to accept peace with the Spaniards because they recognized that they could be beneficial as allies. Mesoamerica had a long history of conflict among city-states and ethnic polities. Within the decades prior to the arrival of the Spaniards the balance of power had shifted toward the Aztecs and their allies. Tlaxcala increasingly found itself surrounded by members of the Aztec alliance. The arrival of the Spaniards inserted a new element into the power politics and military balance of the region. The newcomers had technologies unknown to the Mesoamericans and thus could be effective allies for Tlaxcala against other city-states.

In making the peace, each side pledged mutual support. Gifts were exchanged, and Cortés made his standard speech seeking the conversion of the natives to the Christian religion. For their part, the Aztecs were fully aware of what had happened in the field and sent emissaries to discourage Cortés from the alliance, asserting that the Tlaxcalans were known for treachery. In evaluating his options, Cortés realized that it was more important to resolve the issues locally, make peace with the Tlaxcalans, and save discussions with the Aztecs for another day. He was in a very tenuous position, surrounded on all sides by larger native armies and dependent on other native groups for food and other supplies. He was mostly concerned with day-to-day survival and eagerly sought anything which could offer him a means of eventually reaching the Aztec capital. Cortés entered the city of Tlaxcala in late September 1519.

While in Tlaxcala, the Spanish forces recovered from their wounds, acquired supplies for their army, and enjoyed a respite from battle and the march. Nevertheless, in a matter of days Cortés and his captains began to prepare for the next leg of their journey. The next-most important city-state of the region was Cholula, a center of the cult to the god Quetzalcoatl. The city had been a very powerful force up until recent decades. Cortés indicated that his purpose in going to Cholula was strategic. Yet it made more sense to go directly to the Aztec capital of Tenochtitlan, or even to Huexotzingo, near Tlaxcala and on a more direct route. Thus, in spite of Cortés's comments, we may infer that his detour to Cholula was political. Cholula was an important state, had a proud history, and might prove to be yet another powerful ally for the Spaniards, although it was nominally antagonistic to Tlaxcala.

Cortés traveled to Cholula with several thousand Tlaxcalan warriors. Upon arriving at the city, the Spaniards and their immediate native servants and porters were allowed to enter, with the main force of native allies remaining outside the city. The Spaniards were fed and entertained for two days. Most accounts indicate that the Cholulans had planned to attack the unprepared Spaniards and massacre them in collusion with their allies, the Aztecs. Cortés received word of the impending massacre, ordered a preemptive attack that killed hundreds of Cholulans, toppled the local ruler, and replaced him with someone more amenable to the Tlaxcalans. The Spaniards repeatedly claimed that the plots of the Cholulans were evidence that the Aztecs, and their allies, were not trustworthy. The end result of the events at Cholula was that the city went from being allied with the Aztecs to being allied with the Tlaxcalans.[31]

From Cholula, Cortés, his company, and the force of Tlaxcalan fighters set out for Tenochtitlan. There are two main passes into the Valley of Mexico from Cholula. The one to the north was lower, but heavily forested, and dropped into the valley near Texcoco, a powerful ally of the Aztecs and one of the three city-states in their Triple Alliance. The alliance was headed by the Aztecs of Tenochtitlan and included Texcoco in the east along with Tlacopan in the west. The southern route passed between the two snow-capped peaks of Iztaccihuatl (White Woman) and Popocatepetl (Smoking Mountain). It was steeper and slightly less forested, because it was also higher, but it entered the valley in the southernmost corner, near Amecameca and Chalco. This southern region had only recently been incorporated into the Aztec sphere of influence, having maintained a fierce independence for centuries. Given this, Cortés might have believed, based on information from his Tlaxcalan allies, that he would be greeted with less hostility in the south than in the north.[32]

Once the Spaniards entered the Valley of Mexico they were accompanied by a changing retinue of Aztec nobles. The Aztec capital of Tenochtitlan was built on human-made islands in the middle of Lake Texcoco. There had originally been two small natural islands in the lake. Over the course of two hundred years the Aztecs had reclaimed hundreds of acres of land surrounding the islands and then used them as their capital. The city was connected to the lake shore by a series of causeways, which were in turn pierced by covered bridges so that water could flow from one part of the lake to the other. In early November 1519, Cortés met Moteuczoma[33] on a causeway leading from the shore into the city of Tenochtitlan. The meeting is described in some detail by both the Spaniards and the natives who left testimony and accounts of the conquest. The greetings were cordial, and Moteuczoma invited the Spaniards into the city. He lodged them in one of the palaces in the center of the city. He made certain that they were well fed and well treated, and presented them with elegant gifts.[34]

While Cortés and the main force of the army penetrated ever deeper into the Aztec empire, accompanied by an army of Tlaxcalan warriors, the Aztecs began to reassert their control back on the Gulf Coast, bringing the erstwhile allies of the Spaniards back into the Aztec fold. The small contingent of Spaniards in Veracruz was threatened frequently. The Spaniards and their allies attacked the Aztec forces, keeping them at bay, but the situation was clearly tenuous. Spanish messengers exchanging news traveled regularly between the Veracruz camp and the main force. In the Aztec capital, Cortés found himself in an equally difficult position. He was surrounded by hundreds of thousands of potentially hostile natives.[35] Tenochtitlan was one of the largest cities in the New World at the time, with possibly as many as two hundred thousand inhabitants, far greater than the largest European cities of the day.[36] Even with several thousand Tlaxcalan allies, the Spaniards were badly outnumbered.

There is debate about the role of the Spaniards during their residency in Tenochtitlan. Spaniards later recalling the conquest indicated that after a week as a guest of the *huey tlahtoani*,[37] Cortés took a calculated risk and captured Moteuczoma and held him as a prisoner in his own palace.[38] From that point on, the Spaniards ruled through Moteuczoma. Because of the uncertainty caused by the arrival of the Spaniards, some of the outlying provinces began to withhold tribute and to rebel against Aztec central authority. The rulers of the other two member states of the Triple Alliance, especially Texcoco, began to distance themselves from Moteuczoma and to plot against the Spaniards.[39] Meanwhile the Spaniards were able to live in moderate comfort and security in Tenochtitlan.

Back in Cuba, as noted, Velázquez had begun to mount yet another expedition to Mexico, under Pánfilo de Narváez, to capture Cortés and restore Velázquez's own authority. It was a mammoth undertaking, dwarfing even Cortés's sizeable company. The Narváez expedition consisted of some nineteen ships and some eight hundred men, nearly double the size of the Cortés expedition. Mounting an expedition of this size took a considerable amount of time and money. This fact and the weather conditions did not allow the company to sail until the spring of 1520. They landed in Veracruz in late April, a full year after Cortés's arrival. A few other ships sailed even later, arriving in the following weeks. In the end the contingent led by Narváez might have numbered as many as twelve hundred men.[40]

When Cortés received news of the arrival of Narváez, he made the decision to split his forces. It is at this point, some believe, that the Spaniards captured Moteuczoma. While some of the company remained in Tenochtitlan, under the command of Pedro de Alvarado, Cortés himself took the main body of the army and proceeded to the coast. Most if not all of the native allies remained in Tenochtitlan. Holding the Aztec emperor hostage while the Spaniards were at their most vulnerable made great sense. The ranks of the Cortés company had dwindled, due to early encounters with hostile natives and some deaths from natural causes. As a result, the army which Cortés led against Narváez probably was not even 250 men. There was little expectation that Cortés could defeat the larger Narváez expedition in an open battle.[41]

Cortés and Narváez began negotiating with one another through emissaries. Cortés wanted the members of the Narváez expedition to understand that confrontation was not necessary. They could abandon Narváez and join Cortés. Cortés decided to attack the Narváez camp by night, to inflict the maximum damage and cause confusion at the same time. The attack was completely unexpected by Narváez and his followers. It is possible that many had anticipated the onslaught and had already decided to throw their lot in with Cortés. Whatever the behind-the-scenes situation, Cortés and his company won the battle. Narváez was imprisoned, and his men overwhelmingly accepted the leadership of Cortés. While many of them were pleased to have been given the opportunity to possibly gain riches and the other fruits of war, others were not so enthusiastic.[42]

Back in Tenochtitlan, Pedro de Alvarado was in control. Although holding Moteuczoma captive, the Spaniards had barricaded themselves into a palace, converting it into a fortress. During native celebrations, Alvarado had ordered his men to fire on a large contingent of Aztec nobles as they participated in the public ceremonies. Scores of native leaders were killed in the massacre, and the event stirred up deep resentment toward the presence of the Spaniards in the city. Cortés received word of the massacre and rushed back to the city with his now much-larger army. When he arrived he found the city in turmoil. While many of the Aztec nobles had begrudgingly supported the Spaniards when they were operating through Moteuczoma, the massacre eroded their loyalty.

While the Aztecs allowed Cortés and his native allies to return to the city, once they were inside, all possible avenues of retreat were cut off. The Aztecs, in essence, laid siege to the Spaniards in their own capital.[43]

Cortés attempted to use Moteuczoma to appease the natives, but when the ruler emerged to address his nobles and people, he was struck by a stone. The injury proved fatal. With the death of Moteuczoma, the Spaniards no longer had any hope of negotiating with the Aztecs, and resolved to leave the city. Alvarado had made various attempts to flee, as well as to negotiate and bully his way out, before Cortés's return, but to no avail. Consequently, on the night of June 30, 1520, the Spaniards and their native allies formed into companies and began the flight from the city. The route chosen for the escape should have taken them quickly to the mainland, but native opposition forced them on a several-hundred-mile march through hostile territory. The Spaniards were discovered as they retreated and were attacked by the Aztecs. Bridges on the causeways were removed and the Spaniards were harassed from the lake by boats filled with archers. Hundreds of Spaniards died in the flight from the city, known as the Noche Triste, or "sad night." The bulk of the dead were from the Narváez expedition. These newcomers had made up the majority of the rear guard.[44]

Once they were out of the city, the Spaniards could count on greater assistance from their native allies. Several of the communities of the Valley of Mexico were willing to aid the Spaniards, or at least to allow them free passage. Nevertheless, forces loyal to the Aztecs continued to harry the Spaniards, until they reached the northeastern passes out of the valley and once more entered into territory controlled by Tlaxcala. It is estimated that the Spaniards lost upwards of two-thirds of their men, and at least a thousand native allies. Much of the booty collected during the months of living in Tenochtitlan was lost, as were all of the cannon and many of the crossbows and harquebuses.

After two weeks, during which the Spaniards recovered from their wounds and regrouped in Tlaxcala, Cortés began a process of challenging numerous communities and polities in the valleys surrounding the Valley of Mexico. The first major engagement was at Tepeaca, to the south and east of Tlaxcala. His now-diminished army, without cannon but with native allies, defeated the forces of Tepeaca. To symbolically mark the initiation of a new phase of the conquest, yet another Spanish town was created there by the men of the company and called Segura de la Frontera.[45] Again, a letter was written to the Spanish king that explained recent events and sought recognition for their foundation as an independent city. This letter, from October 1520, was also signed by all the members of the company, about 420 men (see the appendix).[46]

During the period in which Cortés and his men rested and recuperated in Tepeaca, several small expeditions arrived in Veracruz, bringing additional supplies and men. Three of these were sent by the governor of Jamaica, Francisco Garay, and have been conflated in most histories. The relief forces sent by Garay were led by Diego de Camargo, Miguel Díez de Aux, and Francisco Ramírez. Taken together, the Garay relief forces added about 240 men to the Cortés company.[47]

As Cortés moved his army to the south, he encountered troops sent by the Aztecs to reinforce their outlying allies. The combined Spanish and native armies, however, were victorious on the field, and Cortés continued to take control of the whole region to the east of the Valley of Mexico. During this period additional supply ships arrived from Cuba and other places in the Caribbean, bringing in more men and additional war materiel, including guns and cannon. At this point disease began to grip the Aztec capital of Tenochtitlan. In all likelihood this was smallpox, which had been brought originally by Spanish shipwrecks several years earlier and spread inexorably through the native population thereafter.[48]

The Spaniards also used their time in Tlaxcala in late 1520 and early 1521 to build a set of small ships known as brigantines. They used the hardware salvaged from the original ships of the expedition, along with other hardware from the Narváez ships and planks cut from the nearby forests. By the early months of 1521, the Spaniards had expanded their operations back toward the Valley of Mexico. Several of the city-states of the Valley of Mexico had fallen into political disarray. Between the repercussions of the death of Moteuczoma, followed by the death of two new rulers in the next eight months, and the devastation from smallpox, local leaders were reevaluating their position.

In returning to the Valley of Mexico, their goal was to establish a headquarters in Texcoco. From Tlaxcala-Tepeaca they reentered the valley at Amecameca, from the south, and began to both conquer and establish treaties with the city-states to the south and east, ultimately reaching their goal of Texcoco by late April 1521. In a series of major battles, the Spaniards also ventured further afield, to Yautepec, Cuauhnahuac (Cuernavaca), and other communities. In Texcoco, dynastic infighting had beset that city-state, as a result of the death of the traditional ruler some six years earlier. One of the leading claimants for the throne sensed the political advantage of an alliance with the Spaniards and seized the opportunity to take control. Through this maneuver Cortés gained an important ally on Lake Texcoco, just a few miles from Tenochtitlan. Cortés then ordered that the brigantines be brought up from Tlaxcala into the Valley of Mexico. They were reassembled in Lake Texcoco, and Cortés began the final siege of Tenochtitlan.[49]

The siege of Tenochtitlan demanded a few specific actions on the part of Cortés and the Spaniards. They had to control most of the shoreline of Lake Texcoco. They had to either defeat all of the valley city-states in battle or win them over into a political alliance. Even if the Spaniards controlled the entire shore, it would still be possible for native canoes to slip through and continue to supply the city. Much of the early fighting concentrated on the few causeways which linked the city to the shore. The Spaniards sought to control these roads, but were constantly beset by native archers in boats.

The Spaniards were never able to gain control of all of the shore, but with the use of the brigantines they could better interdict supplies going into the city. In addition, the Spanish boats could be used to attack the flotillas of canoes filled with native archers. In response, the natives laid traps for the boats by placing obstacles just under the waterline to damage or to destroy them. As the Spaniards tightened their grip around the city, additional supplies of men and weapons arrived from Veracruz. The Spaniards mounted cannons on the brigantines and began to use the boats as floating gun platforms, aiming their fire at the city and destroying large areas, which native allies would then clear — all of which opened up flattened areas where Spanish horses could be used effectively. In this way the Spaniards slowly conquered the city.[50] By early August the Spaniards had captured Tlatelolco, the market district of Tenochtitlan. Then, on August 13, 1521, the Spaniards broke through the last Aztec defenses and reached their major temple. Shortly thereafter they captured the emperor, Cuauhtémoc, and the hostilities slowly came to an end.

Tenochtitlan had fallen. Thousands of corpses filled the city, and its major structures had been destroyed. On the Spanish side hundreds of men had died. Perhaps just under a thousand Spaniards survived the last battle, augmented by as many as two hundred thousand allied native forces.

Following the defeat of Tenochtitlan, Cortés established a headquarters in the town of Coyoacan, on the south shore of the lake. The booty captured in the conquest was distributed to the men of the company, but it was insufficient to satisfy their demands for recompense. In response, Cortés allocated the labor from the natives of villages throughout the region to members of the company. This grant of Indian labor was called an *encomienda*, from the Spanish word "to entrust" (*encomendar*), since the villages were entrusted to the conquerors.

Although Cortés continued to lead other expeditions — to the west, through Michoacan and on to Colima, and south toward Guatemala — many Spaniards remained behind in the Valley of Mexico. In 1524 the Spaniards decided to re-enter Tenochtitlan. On top of the rubble of the Aztec temples and palaces, they established a new city, Mexico-Tenochtitlan. They assigned house and garden plots to the citizens (*vecinos*) of the city.

After establishing his capital of Mexico-Tenochtitlan, Cortés led an expedition into southern Mexico and Honduras, and Pedro de Alvarado spearheaded the conquest of Guatemala. While Cortés was absent from Mexico, many of his detractors began to complain to the Crown. In late 1525 he returned to

Mexico to take up his power as governor of the territory, having been recently confirmed by the Crown. His government did not last long. He was soon replaced by a series of royal appointees, and by April 1527 he had been forced to return to Spain to protect his privileges. Later that year the First Audiencia, or royal court, took over the government of the region, which by then was called New Spain (Nueva España). The judges of the court undid many of the actions taken by Cortés, stripping many conquerors of their *encomiendas* while granting *encomiendas* and other privileges to more recent arrivals to the territory. Complaints from aggrieved conquerors began reaching the Crown. Eventually the king removed those justices of the court from their offices and dispatched a second group of judges, known as the Second Audiencia. Cortés returned to Mexico in the spring of 1530, and the judges of the second court arrived in the waning days of that year.[51]

Although Cortés engaged in further explorations, he was never able to recover control of the government of New Spain. He was eventually granted a title of nobility, Marquis of the Valley, in recognition of his singular services to the Crown. He established noble estates in the Valley of Mexico, based in Coyoacan; in the Toluca Valley, immediately to the west of Mexico; in the Cuernavaca Valley, immediately to the south; and in the Oaxaca Valley, in the far south of the territory.[52] The other members of the company settled in the various Spanish cities which sprang up across the land. They enjoyed grants of native labor, some received stipends from the royal treasury, and others received grants of coats of arms and other trappings of nobility. Many, however, received nothing and merely became farmers, miners, and merchants in the new society.

THE FOUNDING OF THE TOWN OF VERACRUZ WAS A CRITICAL
point in the conquest of Mexico. The events at Veracruz changed the direction
and nature of the Cortés expedition, marking the shift from a mission of trade
and discovery to one of settlement and conquest. One modern scholar has referred to this event as "crossing the Rubicon,"[1] comparing it to the famous moment when Julius Caesar entered Roman territory not as a returning general
but as a conqueror. The men who participated in the events understood them
to be daring. Historians looking back have also recognized their significance.

The founding of a town on the coast of what would be Mexico linked the
Cortés expedition to the Reconquest of Spain, the seven-century process
whereby the Christian kingdoms of the north reclaimed the peninsula from
Muslim occupation. An important part of that effort was the founding of
Christian towns and cities in newly conquered regions. These served as centers
from which Christian law and traditions could be applied to the newly conquered lands. The Christian rulers recognized the importance of these settlements by granting them special privileges (*fueros*) which regulated the political
relationship between the town and the monarch.[2]

In late medieval Spain, the town existed politically as part of a patchwork
quilt of jurisdictions which also included the dominions of local nobles, lands
owned by the Church and military-religious orders, and other entities that also
claimed authority over the countryside. In receiving a royal charter and grant
of privileges, the town established its own autonomy from these other, compet-
ing jurisdictions. In just the same way, Cortés and the members of his company
sought to establish the autonomy of their expedition from that point forward,
arguing that their mission was now separate and distinct from the jurisdiction
of Velázquez. They could achieve this end in one of two ways. Cortés could
gain his own license from the Crown, and it would supersede the license from
Velázquez, or the town could establish itself as an independent entity, directly

subservient to the Crown, thus bypassing all intermediate authorities. In many ways, the actions of Cortés and the company sought to do both of these.

Nevertheless, scholars have lacked one of the key documents of the event: the petition of the town council which sought the legal recognition of the town by the Crown. The various eyewitness accounts which have survived discuss the petition in general, but none reproduces or even paraphrases it in any detail. In order to better understand the importance of the document we are presenting in this book, the Veracruz petition, we must look at how the events of Veracruz have been described in contemporary documents and by subsequent scholars.[3]

This chapter will focus on the four months in 1519 during which the Cortés company landed at Veracruz, engaged with local native tribes, rebelled against the authority of Diego Velázquez, and then sent off their agents to press their case at the royal court in Spain. Many historians have focused on this period of the expedition because of the crucial role it played in the subsequent history of the New World. Several documents generated by the expedition have survived to the present day, although most of these have come to light only in the last hundred and fifty years or so.

A cornerstone for the study of the foundation of La Villa Rica de la Vera Cruz (Veracruz) is a narrative of the exploits of the company from the time of the preparations in Cuba until July 10, 1519, when the agents of the new town of Veracruz prepared to return to Spain. Often called the "First Letter," it was written by the officials of the town of Veracruz and it frequently appears with the four letters of Cortés to the Crown.[4] The narrative of the town occupies this place of prominence because the similar letter written by Cortés himself has been lost to history.

In addition to the narrative, the town officials ordered an accounting of the treasure collected by the company. The town council remitted the king's portion back to Spain with their agents. That inventory is dated July 6, 1519.[5] It does not shed too much light on the events of the foundation of the town of Veracruz but does corroborate details found in other accounts.

Two other documents of the period also help to illuminate the actions of the company. In early July the town council prepared the instructions for their agents at court.[6] The copy of the instructions is not dated. Nevertheless, it helps to further explain the actions of the company and of Cortés in founding the town of Veracruz. Lastly, there is an anonymous letter, the original of which has been lost; a copy translated into German survives. This letter contains a brief description of the expedition and was dated June 28, 1519, from the town of New Seville, which is the name given to Cempoalla, a large native city not too far from Veracruz.[7] While modern historians have come to rely on these sources to gain an understanding of the events of the late spring and early summer of 1519 in Veracruz, by and large they were unknown for centuries.

If one accepts the widely reported observation that the company landed at what would become Veracruz on Good Friday of 1519, these documents can be used to provide a very rough chronology of events:

April 22, Good Friday[8]	Expedition lands at San Juan de Ulúa
April 24, Easter Sunday	
June 20	Petition of the town council at San Juan de Ulúa [*the subject of this study*]
June 28	Anonymous letter sent while expedition in New Seville (Cempoalla)
July 6	Treasury inventory
July 10	Town narrative — "First Letter"
Mid-July	Agents sail to Spain

Following the conquest, and separated from it by several decades, a number of authors tackled the task of writing comprehensive histories of the period, working from the records and eyewitness accounts of many of the participants. These texts are roughly contemporaneous with one another. One was written by Cortés's personal secretary, Francisco López de Gómara.[9] It should be noted that López de Gómara did not participate in the conquest, but did have access to Cortés and his papers. When his book appeared it created a deep sense of outrage in at least one of the participants of the conquest, Bernal Díaz del Castillo (signature 181), a resident of Guatemala by that time. He was so incensed by Cortés's secretary's account that he wrote his own history of the conquest as a rebuttal to it.[10] In addition to Díaz del Castillo, a few conquerors wrote chronicles of their adventures, only a small number of which have been preserved.[11]

Also writing in the sixteenth century was a canon of the Cathedral of Mexico and professor at the University of Mexico,[12] Francisco Cervantes de Salazar.[13] Cervantes had access to the history written by López de Gómara, as well as to various chronicles compiled by early missionaries. He seems to have also interviewed veterans of the conquest who were still living in Mexico City in the mid-sixteenth century.

The leading advocate for the native peoples of the Americas, fray Bartolomé de las Casas, also wrote a history which included a section on the conquest of Mexico.[14] Las Casas was the bishop of Chiapas, in New Spain, and had spent time in Mexico. He certainly had access to many people who were eyewitnesses to the events depicted in his history, and he also consulted the many documents available to him in the royal court and elsewhere.

Juan Suárez de Peralta was a creole,[15] born in Mexico, son of Diego Suárez de Peralta, Cortés's brother-in-law. Toward the end of the sixteenth century, Suárez wrote a history of the discovery of the Indies, the conquest of Mexico, and the development of the colony of New Spain. He also was able to consult with many people who were witnesses to the events he described.[16]

Finally, Antonio de Herrera y Tordesilla, the official chronicler of Phillip II, wrote several histories for the Crown, including one which traced the history and development of the Spanish discovery and conquest of the New World. This volume was popularly known as the "Decades," from the organization of his work into ten-year periods covering from 1472 until 1554.[17] Herrera included an account of the landing and foundation of the town of Veracruz.

TAKEN AS A WHOLE, THEN, THE SIXTEENTH CENTURY GENER-ated several accounts of the history of the conquest. Nearly all of them were written by men who did not participate in the event, but who, acting like modern historians, sought documents and testimonies from eyewitnesses to develop their chronicles. At the same time, some of the chronicles were firsthand, eyewitness accounts by men who also sought to preserve their recollections for posterity. This created a tension between those who had lived the experience of the conquest and those who merely wrote about it: a distinction between personal testimony and official authority. The eyewitness could not possibly know everything about the event in which he participated. Similarly, he would be unable to attain objectivity, having lived through the episodes he narrated. The historian, drawing upon a range of sources, had a better chance of depicting the breadth of the events of history and could strive for objectivity, although, as will be seen, the authors of the sixteenth century did not prize objectivity as a guiding principle of their writing.[18]

The petition of the town council of Veracruz, the document presented in this book, helps to clarify two major issues related to the early phase of the conquest of Mexico. First, the document clearly describes the foundation of the town of Veracruz, and the expectations of the members of the company with regard to what this action would accomplish, especially in the Spanish royal court. Second, the document allows scholars to better understand the chronology and sequence of events between Good Friday and mid-July 1519.

The "First Letter": The Narrative of the Town Council of Veracruz

The first historical account of the foundation of the town of Veracruz is the narrative written by the town council. It provides only a bare-bones description of the events of the period through early July, since it is dated July 10, 1519.[19] Recall that the expedition landed at San Juan de Ulúa on April 22, 1519.

The narrative describes the richness of the territory, cataloguing the gold and silver already collected. The authors, the town officials, note that the gentlemen and nobles of the company, desirous of increasing the realms and rents of the Crown, discussed matters with Cortés. It was the town officials' opinion that since the land was rich and wealthy and that the natives in the neighborhood in which they were currently stopped were friendly, they should no longer follow the instructions given to them by Diego Velázquez in Cuba — namely, that the expedition be one simply to trade, collect treasure, and corroborate the earlier voyage of Juan de Grijalva.[20] Instead, they suggested, they should populate the land and found a town there in order to provide "justice"[21] to the territory. The members of the company all came together and with one accord unanimously implored Cortés to appoint officers for the town, so that the town officials, in turn, might request recognition and empowerment from the Crown.

The town narrative then notes that Cortés had promised to mull this offer over and to report back the next day. When Cortés replied, he said that he wished to serve the king in all ways, and, in spite of any personal interest he might have in the affair, his own inclination was to continue collecting treasure, in order to defray his own costs of the expedition. Nevertheless, Cortés was willing to accede to the desires of the group. He therefore began with all solemnity to create the town. It was given the name "The Noble Town of the True Cross" (La Villa Rica de la Vera Cruz) because the expedition had landed there on Good Friday. By virtue of his role as captain general of the expedition, Cortés then proceeded to appoint the justices, councilmen, and other officers for the town.

With the town formally constituted, the town officials then met as a council and asked Cortés to attend on them. They requested that he present to them all of the instructions and powers of attorney he had received from Velázquez. These documents constituted the legal basis for the expedition up to that point. Having examined them, the town council members concluded that Cortés lacked any current authority since, in their opinion, all of his powers had expired with the founding of the town. Consequently, they recommended that the king appoint Cortés as the leader of the expedition and also that he serve as the chief justice of royal law in the new territory.

In the interim, exercising their authority as municipal officers under the power of the monarch, they appointed Cortés to be chief justice and captain (*justicia mayor y capitán*). With great ceremony, Cortés took the appropriate oaths before them, and they in turn received him in the name of the king. Following these formalities, the town council resolved to send one-fifth of all the treasure collected up to that point to the Crown as its portion, the royal fifth (*quinto real*).

Next they elected two members of the company to serve as their agents (*procuradores*) in the Spanish court, to present their petition and the gift of the royal fifth. These agents were Alonso Hernández Portocarrero (signature B) and Francisco de Montejo (signature C). The councilmen noted that in their specific instructions, or power of attorney, to their agents they outlined in greater detail the specific rights and privileges which they sought from the Crown. They noted that the agents would present a petition from the town council requesting specific privileges, which were then outlined in some detail in the instructions. The petition to which the council members make reference is the document presented in this study. Thus we see that there were three separate and distinct documents: the narrative, the instructions, and the petition.

In the narrative, the town councilors explained that in the petition they requested that no further grants or privileges be made to Governor Diego Velázquez of Cuba regarding the territory in which they themselves were now settled. They demanded that Velázquez be prohibited from granting *encomiendas* to colonists, and asserted that he should not be permitted to exercise justice or any other function of government in their region. The town council recommended that if any such privilege or authority had been granted to Velázquez, it should be revoked. Moreover, they asserted, the officers of the town council were prepared to and would arrest and impede any officer of Velázquez who came into their district and who attempted to exercise any governmental function.[22] The councilors then proceeded to characterize Velázquez in the most negative terms possible. In support of these privileges and requests, we are told, the whole population of the town assembled and signed their names to the town's petition.[23] The town leaders requested that a formal investigation be opened against Velázquez so that the truth of their accusations might be known. Lastly, the town council asked that Cortés be appointed judge and captain of the company until such time as the whole territory might be pacified, or for however long the king might choose.[24] The town narrative thus provides a rough synthesis of the petition — the document, again, which is the focus of this book.

The town narrative, which describes the founding of Veracruz and all of the events related to it, is one of only two documents contemporary to the petition of the town council. It provides the framework for understanding the points the town council members believed were most important. The central issue was that Velázquez had authorized only an expedition of discovery and trade. Cortés was not authorized to settle or conquer the territory, yet he and his men found themselves poised and ready to launch an expedition of conquest into the interior of the continent and thus to establish settlements. For these reasons, and in the tradition of the Spanish Reconquest, they founded a town, which, as an independent political entity under the Crown, could then authorize the conquest and settlement of the territory.

The Instructions to the Agents

After the town council had selected two members to represent the interests of the expedition to the Crown and lobby for recognition of the town, a series of instructions was drafted to guide these agents. Unfortunately the original of that document is no longer extant. The best copy can be found among documents which were copied in 1526–1533 and included in a series of charges leveled against Cortés by the members of the First Audiencia.[25] The copy included in the larger suit is also damaged, and lacks the introductory material. It begins in the midst of a series of admonitions from the town council to their agents.

The first request embodied in the instructions was that the monarchs confirm the town's appointment of Cortés as "captain and chief justice" of the territory. Following that, the agents were to request that the Crown appoint Cortés governor for as long as the Crown might wish once the conquest and pacification of the region was complete. The agents were to continue to oppose any efforts to grant privileges to Diego Velázquez and especially to deny him any form of control or authority over the lands they were to conquer. In a curious premonition of later conditions, the town council officials asked their agents to ensure that the grants of Indian labor put forth by Cortés would be made permanent by the Crown. The agents also were to request that the offices of councilmen in the town council be made permanent and that the town be granted a royal coat of arms and banner.

The list of petitions then begins to focus on very specific issues, such as the appointment of town officials, an entreaty that the royal tax on gold, silver, pearls, and rare gems be reduced to only 10 percent, and a request that the conquerors be allowed to sell lands received from the town after having held them for two years. The instructions continue to focus on local issues until the end, when the town council requests that a high-level investigator (*pesquisidor*) be appointed to look into the government of Diego Velázquez. In all, the instructions detail thirty-three different requests dealing with the recognition of the town and government of the territory.

While the instructions of the town council cover a fairly broad range of issues, many of the essential points from the narrative of the town appear therein: that Cortés be appointed captain and chief judge, later governor, of the newly conquered territory, and that Velázquez be prohibited from benefiting in any way from their conquest, be punished for opposing them, and be subjected to a high-level investigation. Consequently, one can appreciate that the narrative of the town, the instructions issued by the town, and the petition of the town all correspond with one another on these essential details, which serves to further corroborate the veracity of all three documents. The caveat is that all three documents suffer from the same shortcoming, namely that they are self-serving to the members of the expedition, as represented by the leaders of the town and Cortés himself.

The Account of Francisco López de Gómara

Chronologically the next contribution to the historiography of the landing at Veracruz came from the pen of Francisco López de Gómara, Cortés's personal secretary. As noted, López de Gómara did not participate in the conquest, but did have access to Cortés, his collection of documents, and interviews with some of the other conquerors. The history of the conquest of Mexico written by López de Gómara obviously presented his employer, Cortés, in a good light.[26] The explanation for the founding of Veracruz presented by López de Gómara differs from that suggested in the narrative of the Veracruz town council. López de Gómara indicates that Cortés had been planning all along to populate and conquer the land, in direct contravention of Velázquez's orders. According to López de Gómara, after having sent Montejo and two brigantines up the coast to find a better harbor, Cortés loaded the remaining ships and sailed up the coast about three leagues from their base, at what is now the Papaloapan inlet, to a broad but shallow river.

López de Gómara writes that the larger expedition came upon an abandoned native village filled with food and supplies. In the surrounding region they found several other villages, also well-stocked but empty of people. López de Gómara has Cortés meditate on the wonder of this place: abundant food, well-populated, well-built towns, all richer than anywhere else in the Indies. Cortés believed it would be a good place to settle. By setting up a fort they could protect themselves from the natives yet provide an entrepôt for trade with the other Spanish settlements in the Indies, perhaps even with Spain. In order to do that, Cortés established a local town and appointed officers for the town. He then took possession of the land in the name of the king of Spain. The royal scribe, Francisco Fernández, witnessed the act. Next, Cortés named the members of the town council (*regidores*), judges (*alcaldes*), and other officers. He called the place Veracruz, because they had first landed on Good Friday. In Cortés's next step, he convened the town council and formally renounced the licenses granted to him by Diego Velázquez, who took his own authority from the governors of the Indies, the Jeronymite friars who ruled in Hispaniola. He chose to ignore the powers granted to him by Velázquez because they called on him only to explore and trade in the new territory.[27]

Describing the sequence of events, López de Gómara writes that the newly appointed town officials took possession of their offices and began meeting. In turn they appointed Cortés as captain and chief justice in the district, assignments which he accepted. The town council noted that all of the supplies for the expedition had been provided by Cortés. It was just and reasonable that these supplies should be evaluated for their cost and that the company should pay him fairly for what had been consumed or, alternatively, pay him from the treasure they had collected. The town council offered to purchase more guns and other supplies, using the common portion of this treasure. The councilors also asked that the ships and cannon be evaluated for price so that the company could reimburse Cortés for the cost, although Cortés protested that when he prepared the supplies for the expedition he did not do so with an eye toward resale. He ordered the men to unload, inventory, and then distribute everything equitably among the company members. Similarly, even though he still owed seven thousand ducats for the ships to various persons back in Cuba, he would not charge the company. Moreover, he would consult the town council before he did anything with the ships themselves. López de Gómara indicates that Cortés did this in order to gain the support of the men through their mouths and stomachs.[28]

This account of the founding of Veracruz offered by López de Gómara differs somewhat from the narrative of the town. Cortés clearly takes a central role. He did all of the thinking and all of the acting. The narrative of the town council and the history by López de Gómara do correspond to one another in general terms. Both accounts indicate that everyone recognized that the land was fertile, well populated, and potentially wealthy. Many people wanted to stop simply trading for gold and treasure and begin settling these lands, conquering them if needs be. Nevertheless, both accounts recognized that this goal was in direct contravention of the license Cortés had from Diego Velázquez. Thus the founding of the town, based on the traditions of Reconquest Spain, provided them with a legal basis for doing what they wanted to do: settle and conquer. The López de Gómara account depicts Cortés as a fair and magnanimous leader, except in his dealings with the supporters of Velázquez, with whom he had no patience. Rather than the men of the company coming up with the notion of settling a town to address their own needs, as suggested in the town narrative, López de Gómara indicates that Cortés had intended all along to revolt from the supervision of Governor Velázquez. That Cortés was the author of the plan to establish the town and rebel is a contradiction of the town's narrative of the events.

One event occurred well after the foundation of Veracruz, but was inevitably linked to that action: Cortés's decision to dismantle the ships on which they had sailed from Cuba, prior to the expedition turning inland. According to López de Gómara, Cortés had the ships destroyed in order to force everyone, supporters and opponents, to join the march toward Tenochtitlan. Cortés negotiated with the captains and pilots to either run the ships aground or to declare that they were too badly rotten to sail further, thus closing off any hope of return to Cuba.[29] Cortés did order that all the iron fittings, lines, blocks, sails, and other appurtenances be saved, in order for them to be used on the march inland. In this way López de Gómara paints the event as yet another critical moment in which Cortés unequivocally set his sights toward Tenochtitlan and closed off any possible retreat from that course of action, just as the founding of Veracruz had inevitably broken off ties to Velázquez, leaving the expedition no option but to go forward.

The Testimony of Bernal Díaz del Castillo

The history written by López de Gómara triggered a violent reaction in Bernal Díaz del Castillo (signature 181), a veteran of the conquest who eventually settled in Guatemala. He was so angered that he resolved to write his own "true" history of the conquest. When he composed his history, he was an elderly man attempting to recall events which had occurred more than forty years earlier. As will be seen, there are some discrepancies between his recollections and the accounts we have already examined.

Díaz del Castillo begins his description of the founding of Veracruz by noting that shortly after the company landed at San Juan de Ulúa, Cortés sent an expedition—under the command of Francisco de Montejo and the two pilots, Antón de Alaminos (signature 243) and Juan Alvarez, *el manquillo* (signature 37)—to explore the coast farther north. Montejo had served on the Grijalva expedition and knew the coast. The expedition was gone about ten days. On the voyage they encountered a river beyond which they could not sail because of the powerful currents. On the return voyage, they found a village, Quiahuiztlan, which could be fortified and which had a good harbor, located several leagues to the north of Veracruz.[30]

Díaz del Castillo notes that at about this time the company began to suffer from a shortage of food. The natives had stopped bringing supplies to the Spanish, and what they did deliver was practically inedible. The amount of treasure previously collected began to decline significantly as they used some of it to trade for food. At that point, the native chief they called "Tendile" arrived with a retinue of other native leaders. He presented Cortés with many precious gifts.

During the meeting, the native lords took Cortés aside and told him that the treasure was for the Spanish king. They also made it clear that it would be impossible for Cortés to meet with the Aztec ruler, Moteuczoma. The members of the company with Díaz del Castillo said that they were ready to move inland and that someday they would go meet that great lord. When it was time for the praying of the Ave María, Cortés had his chaplain, fray Bartolomé de Olmedo, explain the rudiments of the Christian faith to these lords. The members of the company traded for gold with the Indians in Tendile's retinue. The gold they received was of little value, and they ended up using it to pay the sailors of the company for the fish they had been catching. Without the sailors' fish, Díaz del Castillo confesses, they would have been very hungry. As a result of their hardships, many of the men who were loyal to Velázquez began to complain. Some even threatened to return to Cuba on their own, by commandeering the ships of the expedition.[31]

One afternoon Díaz del Castillo and some companions were scouting the perimeter of their camp near some sand dunes. They spied five natives approaching. Wary that this might be a trap, the Spaniards engaged the natives, but no one was able to understand them. Díaz del Castillo and his platoon brought the natives to the Spanish encampment. There they learned that they were from another native group, the Totonaca. These ambassadors invited Cortés and the company to come to their city, Cempoalla. They proclaimed that they were enemies of the Aztecs and that they sought an alliance with the Spanish. Hearing this, Cortés ordered that the entire company move first to Cempoalla and then on to the village and bay sighted by Montejo and Alaminos at Quiahuiztlan.[32]

Meanwhile, the Velázquez supporters within the company, according to Díaz del Castillo, were complaining about individual members of the company who were trading for gold. They argued that Cortés should not have given them his permission to do that, and that Cortés personally should supervise the trade and that he should appoint a treasurer to keep track of the gold. They suggested naming Gonzalo Mexía for this role. Cortés declined their suggestion. He said that he had already prohibited individuals from trading for gold for themselves. But beyond that, if individuals did not engage in some trade, it would be hard to imagine where the food for the company would come from.

Díaz del Castillo writes that some of the members of the company, especially those who had *encomiendas* in Cuba, began to express their desire to return to the island. They were joined by other supporters of Velázquez. The detractors argued that it was senseless to move to Cempoalla and Quiahuiztlan when what they properly should do was return to Cuba. Already thirty-five men had been killed in the expedition, they noted, asserting that it would be better just to leave with the treasure they had already collected. Cortés replied that deaths always occurred in wars and adventures such as theirs. He argued that they needed to continue to explore the country. At the very least they could get some food from the local natives.[33]

In reaction to the complaints of the Velázquez supporters, according to Díaz del Castillo, Cortés began to discuss his options with his closest advisors, including Alonso Hernández Portocarrero, Cristóbal de Olid, Alonso de Avila, Juan de Escalante, Francisco de Lugo, and Pedro de Alvarado and his four brothers, Jorge, Gonzalo, Gómez, and Juan. Díaz del Castillo here tells us that he felt that he and Lugo were like kinsmen, since they came from the same place in Spain. One evening Lugo, Hernández Portocarrero, and Escalante visited Díaz del Castillo in his shack and asked him to pick up his weapons and join them. They told him that the men with whom Díaz del Castillo shared lodgings were Velázquez supporters. Lugo and the others wanted to confide a secret. They shared their opinion with him that Cortés had lied when he brought them there from Cuba. While in Cuba Cortés had told all the adventurers that he was going to conquer and settle, but his instructions and license from Velázquez allowed them only to explore the coast and trade for treasure. They knew that since this was Díaz del Castillo's third trip to the coast he would be ready to be part of a settlement. With Cortés, they said, there was a chance to settle the new land. Díaz del Castillo agreed that there was no sense in returning to Cuba. So they began to visit all the men of the company, arguing along these lines and also letting the supporters of Velázquez know that they were completely outnumbered.[34]

Contrary to López de Gómara's account, Díaz del Castillo writes that when the men came to Cortés and asked him to abrogate his license and instructions from Velázquez, he refused and in fact began to order the men to make ready to return to Cuba, forming up into squads, with each man boarding the ship on which he had set sail to Mexico. Díaz del Castillo and the others then protested that they had been brought to this new land under false pretenses, having been told they would conquer and settle. Finally, after much argument, Cortés acceded to the will of the company, on the condition that he be named chief justice and captain general of the expedition. For Díaz del Castillo the worst of it was that Cortés also demanded to receive a fifth of all the treasure, equal to the king's portion. Cortés asked for other extensive powers as well. Diego de Godoy, a royal scribe, was called forward to make a record of everything that had transpired.[35]

Díaz del Castillo asserts that it was at this point that the men of the company ordered the creation of a town, to be called La Villa Rica de la Vera Cruz. They elected the judges (*alcaldes*), councilmen (*regidores*), and other officials, including the officers of the military company: captain of the expedition, Gonzalo de Alvarado (signature A); field marshall (*maese de campo*), Cristóbal de Olid (signature G); sheriff (*alguacil*), Juan de Escalante; treasurer (*tesorero*),

Gonzalo Mexía; accountant (*contador*), Alonso de Avila (signature E); and standard-bearer (*alférez*), a fellow named Corral (signature 307); sheriffs of the camp were Juan Ochoa de Elejalde (signature 292) and Alonso Romero (signature 53). In his *True History*, Díaz del Castillo notes that López de Gómara had everything confused in his history. Díaz del Castillo insists that the prime movers of the creation of the town were the members of the company, who also elected the officials.[36]

Díaz del Castillo tells us that the supporters of Velázquez were angered by these actions. They began to arm themselves and to speak against Cortés. In response, Cortés shared with the whole company the actual instructions and powers which Velázquez had given him, to show them that he was permitted only to explore and trade. Even with this, the Velázquez supporters complained that they had not elected Cortés as their leader and that they should be allowed to return to their homes and estates in Cuba. In the end, Cortés ordered four men from the Velázquez camp be held for insubordination: Juan Velázquez de León; Diego de Ordaz; Escobar, the page; and Pedro Escudero. Díaz del Castillo emphatically reiterates his contention that López de Gómara had written lies regarding these events.[37]

According to Díaz del Castillo, it was at this point that Cortés sent Pedro de Alvarado inland to discover what he could and to trade for gold and food. Alvarado took more than half of the Velázquez supporters with him, allowing Cortés the opportunity to make peace with the remainder of the company. Cortés gave some trinkets to the dissidents and eventually released Velázquez de León and Ordaz from their prison. Alvarado's company came back with two native porters, who carried corn while the Spaniards brought poultry and vegetables. The whole company marched northward through the town of Cempoalla to the fort at Quiahuiztlan.[38]

In Quiahuiztlan, Díaz del Castillo explains, the men of the company then began to physically create the town of La Villa Rica de la Vera Cruz. They traced out the city blocks, established the location of the church, house plots, and the docks, and began construction. Cortés ordered that stone be brought in, and various buildings began to rise. They completed the church and part of the fort during this first phase of construction.[39] It was from Quiahuiztlan-Veracruz that a punitive expedition was sent to Tizapantzinco.[40] Upon their return to Quiahuiztlan the company encountered the relief expedition of Francisco de Salcedo as it was arriving from Cuba.[41]

According to Díaz del Castillo, Salcedo reported that Velázquez had received permission from the authorities in Spain to both trade and settle in the newly discovered lands. Velázquez's supporters rejoiced at this news. Díaz del Castillo writes that he and others in the company went to Cortés and said that after three months in the territory it would be good to go ahead inland to find the great Aztec lord, Moteuczoma. But before they did that, Cortés should send a letter to the king explaining everything which had transpired since they left Cuba. They should send a large shipment of gold and treasure as well. Cortés concurred. He called upon Diego de Ordaz[42] and Francisco de Montejo, both good businessmen, to go to those members of the company who might withhold a portion of the treasure they had collected and not want to give it up. Ordas and Montejo presented the men with a declaration they were to sign to indicate that they were giving up their portion on behalf of the king, with the hopes that they might benefit later on. Everyone signed. The men named their agents—Hernández Portocarrero and Montejo, along with the pilot, Alaminos—to accompany the gold and their petitions. The other document was a petition asking that the company be given permission to populate the land. The members of the company also named Cortés as the captain general, and everyone signed.

The treasure was inventoried and then the portions were extracted for the royal fifth. Díaz del Castillo summarizes the letter written by the town council, and the petition of the town, discussed here. He also notes that everyone signed the document.[43] These documents, along with the royal fifth, were sent to Spain with the two agents, Montejo and Hernández Portocarrero, with the pilot Alaminos. Unfortunately, the ship landed at Marién, in Cuba, ostensibly to put on fresh water before the transatlantic crossing, and thus Velázquez learned of the actions taken by the company.[44]

Needless to say, Díaz del Castillo also describes the scuttling of the ships quite differently from López de Gómara. He implies that the idea came up in a conversation between Cortés and the members of the company who were friendly to him. Their first thoughts were that if the expedition were to march inland, they would need all the men they could possibly muster, and it made no sense to leave nearly a hundred captains and seamen in Veracruz. Díaz del Castillo later found out that Cortés had already been discussing this option with the captains and mariners, but the captains wanted to be paid for their ships. Finally, Cortés empowered the sheriff of the expedition, Juan de Escalante, a bitter enemy of Velázquez, to force the captains to run their ships aground. Escalante would remain as leader of the Veracruz encampment, not Pedro de Ircio, as López de Gómara implies. Those seamen who were unfit for duty in the expedition to the interior were to remain in Veracruz to guard the stores left behind. It is here that Díaz del Castillo likens the moment to when Caesar crossed the Rubicon.[45]

THE ACCOUNT OF THE FOUNDING OF VERACRUZ BY DÍAZ DEL Castillo differs in a number of ways from the three examined thus far. Most important, in the Díaz del Castillo version, nearly every action is taken collectively, by all the members of the company. There was no rigid military command structure, but a very flat collective decision-making process. In addition, Díaz del Castillo has inserted himself into situations where he seems an unusual participant, such as when the various captains of the expedition come to him in the night seeking his guidance and assistance. If López de Gómara envisions a conquest in which everything depended on Cortés, then Díaz del Castillo sees the world only from his own perspective, implying that every important action was taken either as a result of his personal suggestion or as the collective assent of the whole company. Nevertheless, while Díaz del Castillo emphasizes the role of the men of the company, he does not belittle or lessen the importance of Cortés. He depicts Cortés as authoritative, if indecisive. From Díaz del Castillos's perspective, there were many occasions when Cortés made a decision, only to be cajoled by his men to take another course of action—such as when he first gave license to the Velázquez supporters, and then was convinced later, by the other men of the company, to revoke that order.

The Díaz del Castillo account is much longer, vastly more detailed, and filled with continual asides by the author about the various members of the company. While not every conquistador had a nickname, many did, and Díaz seems to have remembered them all. He also provides many details about a particular soldier's place of origin and frequently a physical description as well. Right before the company departed for the Tizapanzingo expedition, Cortés sent one of the harquebusiers out of sight, to fire off a volley to frighten and impress the local caciques with whom Cortés was meeting. The man was Alonso Heredia the elder. Díaz del Castillo describes him as "having a bad scar on his face, a long beard, his face was half-knifed, one eye blind, with a limp in one leg."[46] Díaz del Castillo also goes on at length in descriptions of occasions when Father Olmedo or Cortés was explaining Christian doctrine to the natives, or when Cortés was discussing political affairs with local chiefs.

There are several details on which López de Gómara and Díaz del Castillo seem to concur. One of these is the issue of supplies, which both imply were running low. Either Cortés was concerned about the cost of the supplies incurred up to that point and fearful that the treasure they had collected would not cover his costs or, as Díaz del Castillo interprets it, supplies were running low and they were using the treasure to buy food. Taken together, the accounts strongly suggest that one of the factors leading up to the dramatic break with Velázquez, and the abrogation of his licenses, was a shortage of resources. Similarly, Díaz del Castillo and López de Gómara follow roughly the same chronology. Obviously, this might be because they both narrated the events as they actually occurred, and thus should agree. Alternatively, Díaz del Castillo had the opportunity to read López de Gómara's account before he composed his own version, and thus might have followed the same sequence of events.

Both the narrative of the town and López de Gómara's version of its founding imply that this all occurred in a single series of events in the original camp at San Juan de Ulúa. Cortés founded the town, appointed the officials, and oversaw the collection and inventory of the treasury in the course of a few days. The narrative of the town, the petition, and the powers granted to the agents were all drafted about the same time. While Díaz del Castillo's text agrees that the town was founded at San Juan, he describes it as taking form at Quiahuiztlan. For Díaz the key event precipitating the legal foundation of the town was the arrival of the Salcedo expedition with news that Velázquez had himself received permission to conquer and settle the new territory. All of the documents, according to Díaz del Castillo, were written in the second camp.

Christian Duverger has recently posited that Cortés is the true author of the chronicle attributed to Bernal Díaz del Castillo. The crucial indicator for Duverger is the absence of Díaz del Castillo's name from any of the previously extant documentation of the conquest.[47] Cortés does not mention Díaz del Castillo in any of his letters. Most damning for many has been the absence of Díaz del Castillo's signature from the 1520 letter of Tepeaca–Segura de la Frontera, following the flight from Tenochtitlan during the Noche Triste. Given the chaotic nature of the events of the period, it should come as no surprise that his name is missing from much of the documentation of the conquest. Similarly, there are men whom we strongly believe were present in Veracruz, whose names do not in fact appear among the signatories of the petition studied here.[48]

Furthermore, as will be discussed, the original of the Tepeaca–Segura de la Frontera document has been lost, and so scholars have had to rely on copies made in the sixteenth century. Unfortunately, sixteenth-century scribes and notaries had tremendous difficulty deciphering the signatures of their near-contemporaries, and so Díaz del Castillo's signature might have been wrongly interpreted, or overlooked, although in reality his is one of the clearest signatures on the Veracruz petition.

As we shall see later, in direct contradiction to Duverger's theory, Bernal Díaz del Castillo's signature appears among the members of the company in the Veracruz petition under consideration here,[49] and thus Díaz del Castillo was assuredly at Veracruz in the spring of 1519, and did participate in the events surrounding the creation of the town. Further, when comparing Cortés's letters with Díaz del Castillo's history, one notices dramatic differences in narrative style. Cortés wrote unequivocally in the first-person singular. Díaz del Castillo generally preferred the first-person plural. Cortés describes events in a manner consonant with a military commander: roads are measured, and distances are stated; the numbers of opponents are articulated. Díaz del Castillo, on the other hand, offers colorful descriptions of everything from the landscape to his fellow conquerors.

SEVERAL OTHER CONQUERORS WROTE ACCOUNTS OF THE CON-
quest of Mexico. Most of these texts are very short and focus on the specific
moments in which the individual conqueror played an important role. Only a
few of these discuss the founding of the town of Veracruz, and fewer still refer
to the petition sent by the town to the king. These other eyewitness accounts
were discovered by scholars working largely in the nineteenth century and were
eventually published in collections of inedited documents. A few of these provide some discrete details about the founding of Veracruz and the chronology
of events.

The Writings of Andrés de Tapia

The narrative of the conquest written by Andrés de Tapia provides a unique insight into the events surrounding the founding of Veracruz. Tapia's signature
does not appear on the damaged 1519 petition, but he is known to have been a
member of the company from its very beginning. Díaz del Castillo considers
him one of the captains of the expedition. His narrative of the conquest covers
the period from the organization of the expedition in Cuba until the confrontation with Narváez. The account was written in about 1545, but only published in 1866.[50]

Tapia confirms that the expedition arrived at San Juan de Ulúa on Good
Friday of 1519. He writes that Cortés disembarked with most of the company
and proclaimed the creation of a town, which he named the Rich Town of the
True Cross. Tapia then describes Cortés speaking to the local natives through
the use of two interpreters. He relates that Cortés sent Montejo to sail further
north to look for a better harbor. In the meantime, Cortés received ambassadors from Moteuczoma, and they exchanged gifts. When Cortés became aware
of a possible mutiny among the supporters of Velázquez, he had the malefac-
tors arrested. Tapia then tells us that agents were selected for the town and they
were given the petition to the monarchs, along with the booty collected up to
that time. He further adds that the petition and narrative were signed by all
the members of the company.[51] The expedition then sailed on up the coast to
formally establish the town, which previously was founded legally at San Juan
de Ulúa.[52]

While Tapia leaves out many of the details included in the histories of Díaz
del Castillo and López de Gómara, he concurs with the general time line for
the events surrounding the creation of Veracruz. He gives Cortés primacy in
establishing the town. In keeping with the sequence presented by Díaz del Castillo, Tapia suggests that although the town of Veracruz had been proclaimed at
San Juan de Ulúa, it was formally erected at Quiahuiztlan.

SEVERAL OTHER AUTHORS OF THE SIXTEENTH CENTURY WROTE histories of the conquest that were based upon interviews with participants and on whatever documents they could consult. Two of these were a famous advocate for native rights, Bartolomé de las Casas, and a professor of rhetoric from the University of Mexico, Francisco Cervantes de Salazar. Their two accounts differ on the exact details of the events surrounding the establishment of Veracruz and in particular on the nature of Cortés's role.[53]

The HISTORY of Bartolomé de las Casas

In addition to his work defending the native peoples of the Americas from what he saw as exploitation by the Spanish, Bartolomé de las Casas was a historian. He had originally traveled to the New World as a young man on Columbus's second voyage, and so was a participant in much of the early history of the Indies. He traveled extensively in the New World and served as bishop of the southern Mexican diocese of Chiapas. He had ample opportunity to inform himself about the history of the Indies from a wide variety of people. He began to write his *History of the Indies* in the 1520s and continued to labor on it for most of the rest of his life. It was not published until the nineteenth century.

Las Casas displays an unalloyed dislike of Cortés. In describing the events leading up to the founding of Veracruz, Las Casas writes that Cortés was a usurper who had acted faithlessly against his superior, namely Diego Velázquez, governor of Cuba. Las Casas indicates that Cortés, because of personal ambition and jealousy, had secretly conspired with leading members of the expedition to have himself elected governor of the newly found lands. Following through on this conspiracy, Cortés unilaterally appointed the members of the town council. In turn the town council named the place La Villa Rica de la Vera Cruz. Cortés appeared before them and renounced his ties to Velázquez and placed that authority in the hands of the council. The town council appointed him chief justice and captain general. When the supporters of Velázquez protested, Cortés had them arrested and punished. Cortés ordered all of the ships save one to be dismantled and burned, to prevent disaffected members of the company from returning to Cuba. Cortés appointed the two agents who would travel to Spain and oversaw the allocation of the treasure. The ship, agents, and treasure sailed for Spain from the new location of Veracruz in July. Las Casas indicates that he himself was with the royal entourage in La Coruña when Cortés's agents reached the court.

Las Casas describes Cortés as unequivocally the man in charge. At the same time, Las Casas accuses López de Gómara of being a sycophant of Cortés. Las Casas denigrates him for having dared to suggest that the town council had to convince Cortés to accept their appointment. In Las Casas's opinion, Cortés had prearranged the entire affair.[54]

The CHRONICLE *of Francisco Cervantes de Salazar*

Francisco Cervantes de Salazar was a canon in the cathedral of Mexico, a professor of rhetoric at the university, and one of the leading humanists of the colony. He is most famous for three Latin dialogues which use walks in mid-sixteenth-century Mexico City as their point of departure.[55] Cervantes became the official historian of the city council of Mexico, and in 1558 the council charged him to write a history of the colony. He received a four-year salary for his efforts. The book remained in manuscript form until the twentieth century, when it was rediscovered and published. Cervantes seems to have taken advantage of his role as municipal historian and consulted old papers held by the council, and others, to write his history, as well as having conversations with veterans of the conquest.

Cervantes says that the Cortés expedition arrived at San Juan de Ulúa on Maundy Thursday, 1519, and landed the next day, Good Friday. While the main body of the expedition landed at San Juan de Ulúa, Montejo and two brigantines sailed up the coast in search of a better harbor. Upon landing, the Spanish were greeted by Tendile, the native governor of the province. When Montejo returned with news of a better harbor further north, at Quiahuiztlan, the expedition prepared to move overland via the important city of Cempoalla.

Before proceeding to the new site, several of the leaders of the expedition called upon Cortés to settle the land in the name of the king, and not simply to continue going about exploring as Grijalva had done. Since Cortés agreed with this plan he proceeded to name a town council, to renounce his jurisdiction as originally granted by Velázquez, and to ask the new town council to elect him captain general. According to Cervantes, the town also offered to pay Cortés for the value of the foodstuffs and war materiel he had acquired for the expedition. Cortés refused such payment. The expedition then set out for Quiahuiztlan via Cempoalla.[56]

Once the company had visited Cempoalla, and settled in Quiahuiztlan, they got around to formally establishing the town. Cortés distributed the house lots and set about constructing the public buildings, such as the church, town hall, port facilities, and plaza. Following the brief Tizapantzinco expedition, the town council appointed two agents to sail to the Spanish court with the king's portion of the treasure. The officials also composed the various documents to be sent to the king. Cervantes indicates that two petitions were written to ask that Velázquez be deprived of any authority over the newly discovered lands.

One of these was signed only by the town officials; the other was signed by all the members of the company. Another document drawn up at this time was the narrative of the town. The last document was the instructions — power of attorney — for the two agents being sent to court.[57]

Cervantes de Salazar offers a very rich account of the founding of Veracruz, full of dialogue and speeches. He grants primacy neither to Cortés nor to the members of the company, but rather presents a very balanced account of the adventure. Unlike the other authors, Cervantes does not create a point of dramatic tension, an event which forced either Cortés or the men of the company to act decisively or to break off from Velázquez. He clearly had a copy of López de Gómara's history, since he makes passing references to that work. He also mentions an account of the conquest by fray Toribio de Benavente, known as Motolinía, which unfortunately is no longer extant.

THE RECOUNTING OF THE CONQUEST OF MEXICO CONTINUED to be a topic of historical writing well into the seventeenth century. Two authors stand out as a result of their contributions to Mexican historiography. Each of these men served as royal chronicler: Antonio de Herrera, and Antonio de Solís y Ribadeneyra, a well-known poet, dramatist, and historian of the early seventeenth century. Both of their histories drew heavily on the earlier-known accounts of the conquest and did not depart from the general outline already established. Both accounts paint a far more balanced picture of Cortés and of the members of the company; neither party emerges from these histories as being dominant.[58]

Until additional documents could be uncovered, each succeeding generation of historians merely interpreted the known facts according to the historical perspective of the moment.

Nineteenth-Century Historians

The nineteenth century brought to light some additional documents relevant to the conquest of Mexico, thanks to the Positivist movement. The Positivists sought to acquire as much data as they could as a means to better understand the underlying patterns which govern humanity. Positivist historians focused on the collection and publication of reams of previously unknown documents. Two scholars in particular took advantage of this wealth of new information in studying the conquest of Mexico, William H. Prescott and Hubert H. Bancroft.

Prescott, son of a U.S. Revolutionary War hero, became fascinated by the rise of the Spanish American empire. He began to study the history of both Spain and her overseas colonies, first writing a history of the reign of Ferdinand and Isabella (1837), and then very successful histories of the conquests of Mexico (1843) and Peru (1847). His *History of the Conquest of Mexico* was a critical and popular success.[59] He drew heavily upon the traditional sources, López de Gómara and Díaz del Castillo. By the mid-nineteenth century some new materials were available, such as the manuscript of a history of central Mexico by the mestizo historian Fernando de Alva Ixtlilxochitl, the narrative of the town of Veracruz, and other newly discovered works. These accounts gave added richness to the original narratives, but did not change any of the details regarding the founding of the town. Prescott gave much colorful detail to his history—describing the sand dunes of San Juan de Ulúa, the heat, lack of food, and swarms of insects, to name a few—yet the general chronology remained the same. After the return of Montejo and the arrival of the Cempoallan Indians, the Velázquez supporters pressed to return to Cuba. Thus in Prescott's version the legal creation occurred in San Juan de Ulúa, but the physical settlement and the drafting of all the pertinent documents took place in Quiahuiztlan.

Hubert H. Bancroft was the leader of what he referred to as a "literary industry." He opened a bookstore in San Francisco in 1852. He then began to write a series of regional histories, which eventually grew to ninety-nine volumes. He eventually turned his attention to the history of the conquest of Mexico, as the first part of a multivolume history of the region. To assist him in his history writing, he amassed a huge library of books and manuscripts, including many rare items. As was the case for Prescott, while these newly available sources allowed him to present a thrilling story, in terms of the essential details of the establishment of Veracruz and the early phase of the conquest, he repeats much of what had been written by others.[60] His chronology does not differ in any significant manner from the one established by the long series of prior historians. Nonetheless, he does make reference to the petition of the town, although in many ways he confuses that document with the longer narrative. He believed that the longer of the two documents had been signed by the entire company. His description of the contents of the two documents does note that the narrative of the town contained numerous complaints against Velázquez while the petition was directed more specifically at both denying the governor any control over Mexico and recognizing the claim of Cortés and the company.[61]

Modern Historians

Over the last eighty years, several historians have studied the conquest of Mexico in great depth. Some wrote in English, and others in Spanish. Most put significant effort into trying to get the chronology right. These authors benefited from a wealth of additional documentation found in various archives as a result of the rise of professional historians trained in archival research. Each of these modern historians relied heavily on Díaz del Castillo and López de Gómara and other traditional chronicles, as well as recent archival finds.

Salvador de Madariaga, writing in the late 1930s, attempted to retell the old story in light of new critical analysis of the texts. He generally made use of previously published materials, but by that time a large number of the original documents from the Spanish archives had been published. In general Madariaga followed the same chronology as López de Gómara and Díaz del Castillo. He viewed the creation of the town of Veracruz in a curious light. Drawing on Díaz del Castillo, Madariaga describes the group of leaders as consulting with every member of the company in an early form of voting. He also proposes that one of the motivating factors behind the foundation of Veracruz was the fear of famine. Rations had become short, and the members of the company were bartering their gold back to the natives for food.[62] He posits that the election of the town officials occurred after Montejo and his small expedition had returned from their voyage up the coast. Once Cortés heard of the better harbor and site in Quiahuiztlan, he moved the expedition to that location, passing through Cempoalla along the way. Like earlier authors, Madariaga also placed in Quiahuiztlan all of the events related to the collection of the treasure, the appointing of agents, and the departure of the ships.[63]

Henry R. Wagner, an American historian writing in the 1940s and 1950s, also sought to create a unified narrative of the conquest of Mexico based on all the available information. He engaged in limited archival research, but relied heavily on the printed collections of documents and the traditional sources, as did Madariaga. Writing slightly later, Wagner recognized the difficulty of establishing the chronology of the period surrounding the founding of the town of Veracruz on the basis of the available documentation, which he characterized as contradictory. He accepted the notion that the expedition did land on Good Friday, April 22, 1519. He concluded that the town of Veracruz was legally founded around May 15–25 (about a month before the date of the petition, June 20, 1519, a document unknown to him). Wagner depicts the founding of the town along the lines first presented by López de Gómara.

In Wagner's view the idea of founding the town and everything associated with it was promoted by Cortés, who took a central role in the action. Moreover, Wagner separates the action of legally creating the town from the physical establishment of the town. He writes:

> [T]here was great confusion about the founding of Vera Cruz. Some writers speak of it as the town set up by Cortés at San Juan and others more correctly

as the one near Quiahuiztla. The latter was the only one founded; Cortés did not found any town at San Juan, but merely set up for ulterior purposes a *cabildo* for a town to be founded later on.[64]

Working from documents published in the 1920s, Wagner believed that the expedition left Veracruz for Quiahuiztlan via Cempoalla in early June. The company spent fifteen days in Cempoalla and arrived at Quiahuiztlan around June 18. A few days later, after establishing the new Veracruz and renaming a local Indian village, the company went to Cempoalla for a second time. Wagner found confirmation for that assumption in a letter supposedly written from Cempoalla, called New Seville, dated June 28, 1519. This letter also refers to the agents of the town and the collection of the treasure for the purpose of remitting the king's portion back to Spain.[65] This episode in the chronology fits with the details of the actual Veracruz petition under consideration here. In his reading, the treasury account and the town narrative would have been drafted in the new Veracruz, near Quiahuiztlan. It would have been from that place that the agents left on about July 16–25. By July 1, the company had returned from Cempoalla to the new site for Veracruz-Quiahuiztlan, around the same time that Francisco de Salcedo and his supply expedition are assumed to have arrived.

While the New Seville document used by Wagner helped in giving more detail to the activities of the Cortés expedition, his chronology cannot accommodate the petition signed by the town of Veracruz on June 20 (a document he did not know). His chronology can be made to come in line with the newly found petition, however, with only some minor changes. If one assumes that the expedition set out for Cempoalla and Quiahuiztlan immediately after the petition was signed, with part of the group going by sea and part by land, Wagner's chronology would hold. The Cempoalla letter dated June 28 would have to have been written at the end of the first stay in that city. The expedition then went to Quiahuiztlan, where the members of the company who arrived by sea had already begun to build houses. The arrival of the Salcedo expedition at the "new" Veracruz occurred at about the same time, around July 1.

Another document discovered in the 1930s represents part of the early correspondence of the town council. This document, which was analyzed earlier, is the set of instructions the town granted to their agents, Montejo and Hernández Portocarrero, for their mission of delivering the town's petition and the royal fifth to the king. This document, also housed in the Archive of the Indies in Seville, lacks a date, but clearly comes from late June or early July of 1519. The location in which it was drafted was noted as: "En la villa rica de la Vera Cruz."[66]

Manuel Giménez Fernández, an important Spanish historian of the early modern period writing at essentially the same time as Wagner, focused intently on what he saw as Cortés's revolt against Velázquez. In attempting to better understand the sequence of events of the discovery and conquest, Giménez created a chronology from the landing on Good Friday of 1519 until the departure for the interior of the continent, sometime in early August.[67] After piecing together the various accounts, namely those of Díaz del Castillo and López de Gómara, he came to the conclusion that the founding of Veracruz happened later than indicated by many scholars. He believed that the arrival of Salcedo was the critical moment for Cortés. The Salcedo expedition of men and materiel arrived — bringing with it the royal decree granting to Velázquez the right to discover and settle the vaguely defined region of Ulúa — precisely at the same time as Cortés was establishing his base of operations in the "new" Veracruz at Quiahuiztlan. From there he could surge into the interior to engage in a lucrative conquest.[68]

According to the chronology established by Giménez, Cortés finally resolved to break with Velázquez on July 6, 1519, after the expedition was already at Quiahuiztlan. At this point he ordered the inventory of the spoils of war and the setting aside of the king's portion. Thus, for Giménez, the election of leaders occurred on July 8. On July 9 the town council elected Cortés to his dual offices of judge and captain. Finally, on July 10, the declaration, dictated by Cortés, that the town would throw off the supervision of Velázquez and seek direct royal authority was signed by the members of the company. On July 26 the agents sailed for Spain.[69] It is unfortunate that despite his detailed archival research, Giménez was unaware of the June 20 petition, which demonstrates clearly that the town had been legally constituted several weeks before the actions of July 6–10, and that the petition was drafted and agents elected in late June.

Other aspects of Giménez's analysis bear scrutiny. He was of the opinion that the true author of the narrative of the town was Cortés himself. But perhaps most important, he believed that the actions of the expedition, whether instigated by Cortés or merely aided and abetted by him, were nothing short of a revolution that well exceeded the boundaries of the established political and juridical practice of the day. Because Cortés had acted so far outside of the normal legal process, Giménez held, he believed that it was absolutely necessary for the agents of the town to arrive first at the royal court, before any opposing counsel from Velázquez could appear and contradict their story. The plot and political maneuverings of Cortés were the by-products of a relative lack of centralized power in the Indies, since the government of the Jeronymites was largely perceived as ineffective. Yet if the legitimate government in Santo Domingo had given to Velázquez the full power and authority to explore and conquer the newly discovered territories, his hand would have been considerably strengthened in any conflict with Cortés.

Almost fifty years after Wagner, José Luis Martínez set out to write a definitive biography of Hernán Cortés, and to publish as many of the key documents of the conquest as possible. This work is unquestionably one of the most thorough treatments of Cortés in Spanish. Although he did obtain many documents from both the archives and printed editions, he was unaware of the petition of the town of Veracruz. The documentation he consulted led him to conclude that the town of Veracruz began on Good Friday of 1519. He calculated that the town achieved its legal standing sometime between May 15 and 25, when the municipal council was elected. Martínez did not deal with the thorny issue of who was responsible—Cortés or the men of the company—for the creation of the town. Nevertheless, Martínez at least implies that Cortés was the originator of the plan. In explaining the legal basis for the action, Martínez suggests that Cortés made use of knowledge gained during his time as a student at Salamanca.[70]

Martínez believed that the expedition left for Quiahuiztlan, via Cempoalla, after the legal founding of Veracruz, presumably at San Juan de Ulúa. The town of Veracruz was founded once again in Quiahuiztlan. He has the group then return to Cempoalla on about June 18, getting back to Quiahuiztlan around July 1, when Salcedo arrived. Martínez suggests that the documents narrating the history of the expedition and the inventory of the treasure were executed in the new Veracruz, and that it was from there, on July 26, that the agents sailed for the Spanish court.[71] Unfortunately, we now know that the chronology offered by Martínez is impossible, given that the company was still at San Juan de Ulúa, not Quiahuiztlan, on June 20, when the actual petition was dated and signed.

In a unique and powerful argument, Víctor Frankl, an Austrian Catholic who fled his homeland in 1938 and eventually settled in Colombia, holds that Cortés was not necessarily rebellious or a stickler for legalities but rather viewed the process of the conquest from a perspective very different from what later historians have attributed to him. Frankl considers the narrative of the town to be the best resource we have for an understanding of the events and ideas behind the Veracruz petition. He notes that many contemporary authors described Cortés's actions as growing out of a desire to uphold the common good, "el bien común." Working from this assertion and from the descriptions of the event, Frankl argues that Cortés operated out of his belief in the authority of the monarch, as embodied in Spain's medieval compilation of law, the Siete Partidas. As an individual who was to represent royal authority in a new territory, and especially as someone who brought the Gospel to those who had lived outside Christendom, Cortés carried with him the full authority of the monarch. Thus the actions of founding the town and having the council recognize him as captain and justice were a mere formality as the expedition entered a new and hitherto uncharted region. Moreover, the actions which the expedition took were to favor the common good and not the personal interests of one person, namely Velázquez. In Frankl's view, it was only in their support of the common good that the town council resorted to invoking the tradition of municipal sovereignty and direct authority under the Crown.[72]

Taking some of the ideas of Frankl, Beatriz Pastor Bodmer, a professor at Dartmouth College, turned them on their head. Looking at the narrative of the town and the letters of Cortés from a literary perspective, she interpreted the posturing of Cortés and the company as fictionalizations. Although Cortés was a rebel, he was characterized as a model conqueror; the rebellion itself was an act of service. The conqueror was seeking to circumvent the royal administrative system at the very same time that he was presenting himself as a most loyal servant of the Crown. Yet she too recognized that Cortés's criterion for action was "the service of the king."[73] Consequently, she confirms the essence of the argument made by Frankl, while offering a literary interpretation for the works.

Hugh Thomas, well known for his thoroughly researched studies of the Spanish Civil War and the history of Cuba, wrote the largest and most thorough analysis of the conquest of Mexico and biography of Cortés. While using the many published primary documents from the period, he also did research in Spanish and Mexican archives. His telling of the story of the foundation of Veracruz follows the general outlines seen in other writers. Unlike others, however, Thomas believed that Veracruz was formally established at San Juan de Ulúa during the time that Francisco de Montejo was absent, sailing further north. Thomas has Cortés leaving San Juan de Ulúa in early June for Cempoalla and eventually Quiahuiztlan. He believed that Veracruz was formally established, again, at Quiahuiztlan on June 28. He writes: "The *Caudillo* [Cortés] then decided to found Villa Rica de la Vera Cruz at the site, Quiahuiztlan, which had been recommended by Montejo."[74] This passage demonstrates two important points. First, Thomas follows the López de Gómara school in seeing the creation of the town of Veracruz as being an initiative of Cortés, and not as a collective action, as envisioned by Díaz del Castillo. Second, while this chronology falls well within the parameters established by other scholars, it cannot accommodate the fact that, as we now know, the actual Veracruz petition was written from San Juan de Ulúa on June 20.

Thomas also rejects Giménez's idea that the legal foundation of the town was prompted by the arrival of Salcedo with news of Velázquez having received royal authorization for conquest and settlement. Rather, Thomas believed that Cortés took advantage of the absence of many Velázquez supporters, who were sailing on the mini-expedition with Montejo, to simply overpower the rest. Thomas envisions Cortés as telling the members of the company who wished to journey inland in search of treasure that he simply could not do so, because of the strictures placed on him by the license from Velázquez. No one would be harmed more than he, Cortés, by abandoning the venture, he might have said, since he had not recouped his massive investment, but he was committed to serving the Crown ahead of his own personal interests (harking to the arguments made by Frankl). When the members of the expedition greeted this with outrage, since they too were interested in gaining the wealth of the land, Cortés reluctantly allowed for the town to be created, and himself to be appointed as leader.[75]

That Spaniards might choose to live in towns and villages seems evident to many scholars of the Iberian Peninsula. While recognizing the elements of rebellion within the acts of Cortés and his expedition, Helen Nader also makes clear that urban civilization was the touchstone of Spanish culture. Consequently, regardless of the political implications associated with the act of founding Veracruz, for Nader it is a simple instance of the expedition doing what was considered normal and usual.[76]

A Refined Chronology

On the basis of the available documentation, now enhanced by the discovery of the June 20 petition of the town of Veracruz, a more definitive chronology of the landing at and foundation of the town of Veracruz might be proposed.

Obviously the starting date for this phase of the expedition remains Good Friday, April 22, 1519. There is near-universal consensus that the Cortés company landed on that day. They may have arrived at San Juan de Ulúa the evening before, but they made landfall on Friday. By Easter Sunday, emissaries of the Aztec emperor had arrived to meet with the Spaniards.

There are no other generally accepted dates before June 20, when the petition of the town was written in San Juan de Ulúa. Given the extant documentation, it seems the company must have remained in San Juan de Ulúa until about June 21, when they set off for Quiahuiztlan by way of Cempoalla, a trip which took about two weeks. Just over a week later, on June 28, an anonymous letter was written from New Seville (Cempoalla). Around July 1, Salcedo arrived in Veracruz, which must have been at Quiahuiztlan, at about the time that Cortés and the main body of the expedition arrived from San Juan de Ulúa, via Cempoalla. Once all were in Quiahuiztlan, this new site was also christened Veracruz — a sequence which has caused a great deal of confusion over the history of the expedition. A few days after their arrival, the treasure was inventoried and the town council finished its narrative of the conquest. Those documents were dated July 6 and 10, respectively. Ten to fourteen days later, the single ship going to Spain was loaded and set sail around July 26.

The company was in Quiahuiztlan for only about two weeks between the arrival from Cempoalla and the departure of the agents to court. Given all of the activity undertaken in this period (unloading the treasure, inventorying it, setting up the town physically, and beginning construction of appropriate buildings), the punitive expedition to Tizapantzinco is unlikely to have been sent until after the departure of the agents, or possibly it set out from Veracruz–San Juan de Ulúa before the transfer to Quiahuiztlan.

Consequently, while the petition of the town council cannot reveal the intentions of the participants, it can help to clarify the chronology of events. This in turn provides greater information about the circumstances in which decisions were made.

Based upon the known documents, now illuminated by the June 20 petition, the following is a close approximation to the actual chronology of the Cortés expedition between April and August 1519.

April 22, Good Friday	Landing at San Juan de Ulúa
April 24, Easter	Meetings with Tendile
Early May	Montejo sails northward
Early May	Alvarado expedition into interior
Late May	Cortés orchestrates founding of the town
June 20	Petition signed at San Juan de Ulúa
June 28	Anonymous letter sent while expedition in Cempoalla (New Seville)
Early July	Instructions for agents sent to court
July 1	Salcedo expedition arrives, Quiahuiztlan renamed Veracruz
July 6	Treasury account written in "new" Veracruz
July 10	"First Letter"/narrative written in "new" Veracruz
July, third week	Ship sails to Spain

The landing at San Juan de Ulúa and the creation of the town of Veracruz remain two iconic moments in the conquest of Mexico, and of the entire settlement and conquest of the New World by the Spanish. For centuries scholars have attempted to come to grips with its implications, as well as to understand the events leading up to it and after it. It is impossible to relive the moment, to completely and accurately reconstruct the series of events. The extant documents simply do not provide a precise chronology. Nevertheless, as more documents become available, one hopes that scholars can lift the veil of the past and shine a light on some of the details which have been lost. The petition of the town of Veracruz is just such a document. It allows us to understand this exciting time, to piece together a more comprehensive picture of the events, and to learn more about the men who played such a decisive role in the conquest and settlement of Mexico.

Beyond enabling a more precise understanding of the dynamics of the early phase of the conquest of Mexico, the June 20 petition of the town of Veracruz provides something of unique importance: the names of the conquerors. In an act of solidarity, all of the members of the company signed the petition to the Crown. As a result, not only can modern scholars see the development of the political and legal underpinnings of the expedition, but they can also gain an idea of who these men were and what their individual contributions to the larger expedition were. The remainder of this study will focus on the men and their activities during and after the conquest.

CHAPTER 4
Description OF THE Veracruz Petition

ON APRIL 22, 1519, AS WE DISCUSSED IN CHAPTER 2, HERNANDO Cortés and his company landed on the eastern shore of what is now Mexico. On the sandy beach of the island they named San Juan de Ulúa, facing the broad expanse of the mainland, he and his companions founded a town they named La Villa Rica de la Vera Cruz, which was destined to become modern Mexico's major port. Despite the heat, humidity, and unrelenting mosquitoes, all of the men, including Cortés, worked to establish a toehold on the North American mainland. These events marked an important moment in the conquest of Mexico.

As we have seen, by establishing a town, Cortés and his men legally and symbolically broke away from the supervision of Diego Velázquez and attempted to place their town in the royal patrimony: that is, directly under the control of the Spanish king. Three months later, in open defiance of Velázquez, the expedition began its march west toward the Mexica capital Tenochtitlan (modern Mexico City).

Although the founding of Veracruz is mentioned prominently in histories of the conquest, and has become famed in legend and history, few extant documents describe this dramatic event. Bernal Díaz del Castillo and other participants who recorded their memories of the conquest state that the expedition wrote a petition to the king in 1519, but throughout years of searching the historical records no researcher had ever found the original. The paucity of documentary evidence from the first year of the conquest opened the way for long-lived controversies about the intentions of the founders, about the claims Cortés made for himself in his letters to the king, and about the veracity of Díaz del Castillo's chronicle. As seen earlier, for decades, if not centuries, scholars have combed the archives for original documentation relating specifically to the foundation of Veracruz and to the details of the conquest in general.

We can now state that the first petition exists, and that it carries the signature of Bernal Díaz del Castillo. The petition is the earliest extant original European document written from the mainland of North America. It is the only original document from the conquest; other reports and letters have survived only in sixteenth-century copies. While it is physically damaged, it is also the only structurally complete document from the expedition, because the sixteenth-century copyists did not bother to retain the opening and closing paragraphs of the other documents. It is unique in that it provides details about the dramatic events around the founding of Veracruz. But perhaps more importantly, the document carries the signatures of all the members of the expedition.

The document itself is eighteen pages (nine leaves, or folios, front and back [recto and verso]) long. In many regards it is identical to millions of other documents produced in the colonial period. The paper is made from mostly cotton rags. It measures approximately 22 by 31 cm, although, as noted, a portion as large as 10 cm has been torn from the bottom of several pages. Once the men had signed, the document was folded in half and then in half again, producing a packet of about 6 by 8 cm in size to be sent to the royal court.

It consists of three parts. The first three folios comprise two documents: a letter from the Veracruz town council to King Charles of Spain and his mother, Queen Juana, that is signed by the newly elected town councilmen (*regidores*), agents, and other important figures; and a petition presented to the town council by Francisco Alvarez Chico, advocate for the town citizens. The next fifteen pages contain the signatures of the members of the company, with the notary's certification. Lamentably, the paper suffered insect damage, a common problem with documents from this era. As much as one-third of the lower portions of many of the pages of signatures has been lost. Nevertheless, the letter and petition have survived nearly intact, and the surviving pages provide us with 318 signatures.

Although no effort has been made to scientifically authenticate the document, it seems to be exactly what it claims to be: a letter and petition composed and written in the town of Veracruz on June 20, 1519.[1] The paper and its watermarks are standard for the sixteenth century. The Veracruz town clerk followed the prescribed format, writing about thirty lines on each full page; and he certified the document's authenticity by signing it and enclosing his signature between two marks or flourishes, known in Spanish as *rúbricas*.

In the opening paragraph on folio 1, the person who wrote the documents describes himself as "Pedro Hernández, clerk of the queen, doña Juana, and of the king, don Carlos, her son, our lords, and their notary public in their court and in all their kingdoms and lordships, and public clerk of this town."[2] In order to become a royal notary, Pedro Hernández would have had to serve for several years as a clerk in the royal secretariat and then pass an examination that tested his knowledge of the law and his skill in drafting royal documents.

Once having passed the examination, he could draft and write royal documents anywhere in Spain and its territories. A royal notary held that license for life.

The office of clerk (*escribanía*) did not provide such wide powers, though the clerk (*escribano*) was much more than a scribe who simply wrote whatever a client dictated to him. Every town had a clerk, and cities usually had one clerk in each parish. This office could be held by anyone with a basic knowledge of the legal wording needed to compose such daily documents as contracts, pre-nuptial agreements, wills, loans, and inventories. A clerk could draft and certify documents only within his prescribed territory, whether that was the royal court, a town, or a parish. While the client received a copy of his document, clerks and notaries had to maintain bound registers (now called *protocolos*) containing all the original documents they had written. Clerks were appointed to their office by the city council or by the lord of a town; a few decades after the events discussed here, these offices came to be available through a process of bidding at auction.[3]

The wording and composition of the Veracruz documents have frequently been ascribed to Cortés by modern scholars, but these authors base their convictions on the letters of Cortés, which are sixteenth-century copies that lack the original prefaces and postscripts. The newly found first petition contains both the beginning and the ending paragraphs by Pedro Hernández, which clearly state that he, a royal notary as well as town clerk ("escrivano") of Veracruz, composed the text and certified the signatures.

The order of the three text sections is important. The first section is the introduction to the petition, written in the voice of the notary, Pedro Hernández. This initial section is structured like a record of the minutes of the town council, giving the date and place of the meeting. In it the notary recognizes that the agent of the town, Francisco Alvarez Chico, appeared before the town council and presented a petition to them for approval and action by the council.

The second section consists of the petition itself, written in the voice of Alvarez Chico, in which he outlines its purpose. He is serving as a representative (*procurador*) of the town council in the petition to the royal court. The council sought specific benefits from the Crown. These benefits were outlined in a set of instructions which they drafted for their agents at court; a version of this document was studied in chapter 3. In recognition of their support of these actions, all of the members of the company affixed their signatures to the document. Alvarez Chico then outlines some of the specific requests contained in the instructions to the agents: that Diego Velázquez not gain any benefit from the conquest and settlement of the new territory; and that Cortés be granted the offices of governor and chief judge for the newly discovered regions and be allowed to distribute Indians in *encomienda*. They requested these things out of the friendship and respect which they had for Cortés. In short, they sought confirmation of their actions by the Crown, including the creation of the town and their acquisition of all the privileges associated with that status.

The third text section, at the end of the document (folio 9, verso), is the ratification of the petition by the members of the town council. This action empowered Alonso Hernández Portocarrero and Francisco de Montejo, the two agents, to take the petition to the royal court and seek all that was requested.

The text of the petition helps to inform the sequence of the events related to the foundation of the town of Veracruz. Quite clearly the city was founded first, and then the members of the town council were elected. Following that, the council determined its course of action, named the two agents to go to court, and then wrote the set of instructions, or power of attorney, for the agents. Concurrent with the naming of the agents, the town council ordered the collection and inventory of the treasure, in order to separate the royal portion from the total. Once these issues were resolved, the town council then drafted the petition, which directly addressed the monarchs and outlined the specifics of the request. In signing this petition the members of the company ratified all of the actions of the town council.

Reviewing the several documents drafted by the town council, discussed in-depth in chapter 3, alongside the Veracruz petition, one can see their common origin. For example, the narrative of the town, the instructions to the agents, and the petition all focus on two essential points: that Velázquez no longer had authority over either the expedition or the territories recently explored and that Cortés should be named as captain general and chief judge of the expedition and territory for a period of time that best suited the monarchs. The wording of the requests is quite similar among the three documents. Regarding the opposition to Velázquez, the instructions to the agents stipulated they would request that "their royal majesties never appoint nor grant to Diego Velázquez any leadership in an expedition nor to be a governor nor any other office in these regions."[4]

The petition details the request in almost exactly the same way. It asks the monarchs "not to give Diego Velázquez any responsibility or profit at all from this region nor grant it [directly] to him."[5] This backwards construction has the effect of asking the monarchs both to deny to Velázquez the authority to name persons to offices and to deny him any office as well. It was not sufficient to break off from the authority of Velázquez. The town council also sought to limit his power by prohibiting him from appointing additional expeditions to anyplace, but particularly to where they were. If the Crown accepted this proposition, it would have the twofold benefit of limiting Velázquez's power to the island of Cuba and of giving the Cortés expedition the exclusive right to settle and conquer what would become New Spain.

Looking at the requests concerning Cortés and his leadership of the expedition, one finds the parallel situation, where the instructions and the petition frame the arguments in a very similar manner. Firstly, in the instructions the town noted that Cortés had served the Crown with great faithfulness and had already spent a considerable sum of money in outfitting the expedition: "[in] the duties and royal offices which in these islands he has held and in these regions has served he has given good account and service to your Majesties and besides he spent all that he had on the aforementioned armada in order to serve the Crown."[6] The petition is actually more wordy in this regard: "Fernando Cortés has come to these parts in the service of their highnesses in order to conquer them and spent large sums of maravedis and left the company that he had made with Diego Velázquez from which he could have profited a great deal, and as a vassal and loyal servant of their highnesses he tried to settle this land . . . , his majesty may be served to assign the office of conqueror and captain general and chief judge in these parts . . ."[7]

In both instances the town focuses on the great sums of money Cortés had already spent and on his loyal and faithful service to the Crown up until that point; these assertions function as precursors to his appointment as captain general and chief judge. In the tradition of the Reconquest in Spain, the Crown recognized exemplary service, including mounting military expeditions at one's own cost. Service and loyalty, in the social equation of the time, demanded recompense, which in this instance the town suggested should take the form of appointments for Cortés.

Both the instructions and the petition also require that the agents request that Cortés be granted authority not simply to grant Indians in *encomienda* but that such grants also be made perpetual. In the instruction the town fathers wrote: "Grant us the mercy that the Indians of these parts be [granted] in perpetuity and in order to accomplish this send orders to your royal officials and to Fernando Cortés that they perpetually distribute and entrust them among the conquerors and first settlers."[8] The petition states the request more succinctly, asking that Cortés be able to "distribute [the] Indians in perpetuity."[9]

While the *encomienda* was not an innovative institution, the Crown had demonstrated its concerns about making the grants perpetual as recently as 1512, in the Laws of Burgos. With this codified set of laws the Crown began a many-decades-long process of legally circumscribing the institution of the *encomienda* in order to better protect the natives. The issue of perpetuity of the grants was thus on the minds of the members of the company. At this crucial juncture in the conquest of the new territory, the members of the company wanted to establish an important precedent, one which they might need to use at some point in the future. In what would become their contract with the Crown, the conquerors wanted to make certain that they had outlined this particular privilege clearly.

In looking at the petition and the instructions, one sees that the similarity of the phrases and the structures of the arguments are such that the two documents are clearly linked. Moreover, throughout the petition there are constant references to the instructions wherein the town council had more fully outlined its requests. The overlap, the congruity of voice, and the many cross-references between the two documents helps to establish the authenticity of the petition.

The ratification was signed by the members of the town council. The petition was accompanied by the signatures of all the members of the company, of which some 318 legible signatures remain. Bernal Díaz del Castillo states that some 450 men were at Veracruz at the time of the drafting of these documents.[10] Consequently, it is possible that the ravages of time have destroyed not only some of the text of the document but as many as a hundred of the signatures. Nonetheless, the record of these signatures marks a signal moment in the history of the New World in general and of Mexico in particular. A fuller analysis of the signatures and the men they represent is found in chapters 6 and 7.

The petition and associated documents reflect an ancient tradition in the Hispanic world: a settlement at an outpost or frontier whose authority extends into the surrounding hinterland, offering political structure to the newly annexed region. This was accomplished through a contract with the Crown. Unfortunately for the Cortés expedition, the contract in force at the time they landed at Veracruz was the license Cortés had from Velázquez. In turn Velázquez had authority delegated from the Spanish governors of Hispaniola, at this moment the Jeronymite friars. The actions at Veracruz served to seek to abrogate the old authority, vested in Velázquez, and engage the monarch directly. But the other advantage Cortés and his followers sought was to rewrite the terms and conditions of their relationship to the Crown. They did not simply propose replacing Velázquez with royal authority, but rather they intended to create a new working environment. In the instructions, in particular, the members of the town council provided a detailed outline of what they expected from the Crown.

The petition, then, served the important purpose of clearly and simply outlining the salient points of the commission granted to the agents sent to court. It described the situation which gave rise to the action. It outlined the legal bases whereby the action was taken. It listed the major issues which the agents were empowered to discuss. Finally, the petition was ratified by the members of the town council. Their action was seconded by all the members of the company.

In many ways the signing of the petition by all the members of the company prefigures a moment from the American Revolution at the signing of the Declaration of Independence, when Benjamin Franklin is reported to have said: "We must all hang together, or assuredly we shall all hang separately." Quite simply, as in the case of Franklin, the conquerors recognized that the action they had taken could be considered *lèse-majesté*, a crime of treason committed against the sovereign. By throwing off the authority granted to them by Velázquez, the members of the company were committing an act of rebellion against a royal official, which was considered an act of rebellion against the sovereign himself. Only by securing approval of their actions from the sovereign could they avoid the charge of treason. That is precisely what the petition sought to accomplish. But in a daring and bold stroke, the town council of Veracruz not only sought recognition for their actions, but also attempted to significantly improve their lot and extract additional concessions from the Crown.

CHAPTER 5
Facsimile, Transcription, AND Translation
OF THE Veracruz Petition

AGI, Mexico, 95, Carta del cabildo de Veracruz (1519):
Facsimile and Transcription

HELEN NADER AND JOHN F. SCHWALLER

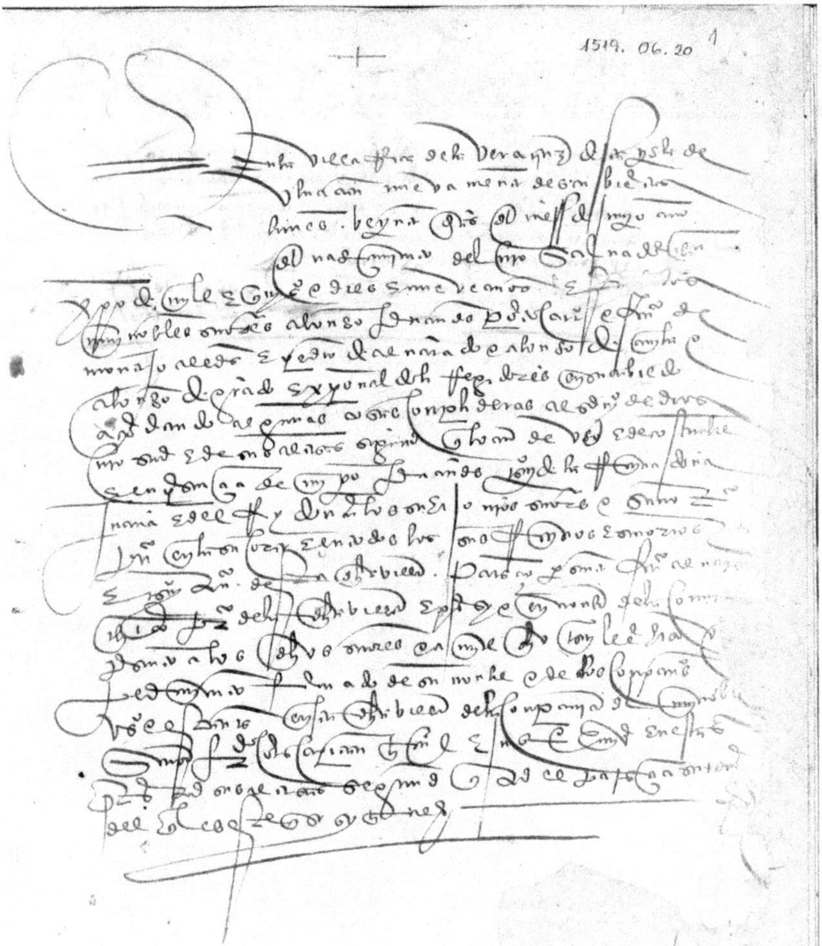

Petition of the town of Veracruz, folio 1, recto

En la villa rica de la Vera Cruz deEta ysla de
Uluacan nuevamente descubierta
lunes veynte dias del mes de junyo año
del nascimiento del nuestro salvador Jesu
Christo de mill e quinientos e diez y nueve a estando presentes los   5
muy nobles señores Alonso Hernandez Portocarrero e Francisco de
Montejo alcaldes e Pedro de Alvarado e Alonso de Martin e
Alonso de Grado e Christoval Doli rregidores en su cabildo
acordando algunas cosas conplideras al servicio de dios
nuestro señor e de sus altezas segund que lo an de uso e de costumbre   10
e en presencia de mi Pedro Hernandez escrivano de la rreyna
doña Juana e del rrey don Carlos su hijo nuestros señores e su notario
publico en la su corte e en todos los sus rreynos e señorios
e escribano publico de la dicha villa parescio presente Francisco Alvarez
Chico procurador de la dicha villa e por sy e en nombre de la com[unidad]   15
presento a los dichos señores e a mi el dicho escrivano leer hizo un
pedimiento firmado de su nonbre e de sus conpañeros
vecinos e estantes en esta dicha villa de la conpañia del muy noble
señor Hernando Cortes capitan general e justicia mayor en estas
partes por sus altesas segund que por el parescia su tenor   20
del qual es este que se sigue

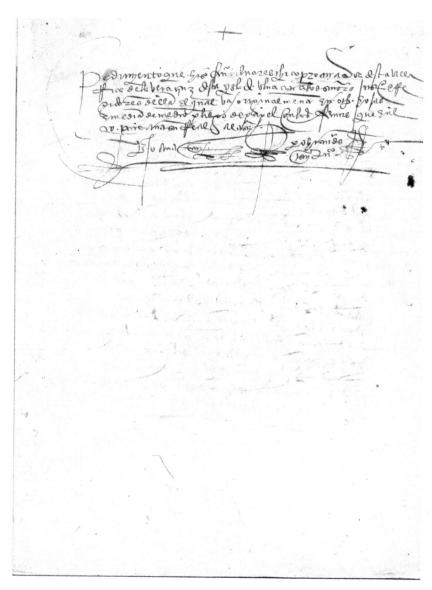

Petition of the town of Veracruz, folio 1, verso

Pedimiento que hiso Francisco Alvares Chico procurador desta villa
rica de la Vera Cruz desta ysla de Uluaca a sus señores Justicia e rre
gidores della el qual va originalmente en ocho hojas
e media de medio pliegos de papel con las firmas que en el
ay para ante su rreal altesa.   5
Paso ante mi Pedro Hernandes escrivano publico.

Petition of the town of Veracruz, folio 2, recto

Muy nobles señores,

Francisco Alvares Chico procurador de la villa rica de La Vera Cruz paresco
ante vuestras mercedes e digo que ellos bien saben como a mi como
a procurador desta dicha villa estando en su cabildo acordando las
cosas complideras al servicio de dios nuestro señor e de sus altesas   5
me hisieron saber que avian acordado de enbiar
a haser saber a su magestad por una instruccion
ciertas cosas cumplideras al servicio de dios nuestro señor e de
sus altesas la qual enbian con los señores
Alonso Hernandez Portocarrero e Francisco de Montejo a los quales dan poder e   10
entregan para que asi lo negocien como yo sea obli
gado de escribir las cosas que al servicio de sus altesas
o bien de esta villa converngan abiendolo acordado con
vuestras mercedes hacerse saber a las personas vecinos desta
villa lo contenido en la ynstruccion e dar les parte   15
del haser mercedes que a su magestad suplican les haga e
de hacer otras cosas que a su rreal servicio conviene probeer.
     E aviendo lo todo escrito por pedimiento de las dichas personas
he sido rrequerido que asi lo pidan e rrequierren a vuestras mercedes
lo enbien a haser saber a sus altesas para que asi lo   20
[m]anden probeer por ende yo en nonbre desta dicha villa e de los
vecinos della pido e requiero a vuestras mercedes que la dicha yns
trucion que asi tienen acordado de enbiar a su magestad
e firmado de sus nonbres la enbien e de para ello e para
lo negociar den poder a los dichos procuradores porques [. . .   25
. . .] e a servicio de su magestad e bien de toda la[. . .
. . .] conviene porquesto hecho sus altesas seran s[. . .
. . .] rreal corona aumentada e esta villa como s[. . .
. . .]tos e naturales favorescidos e honrrado[. . .
. . .] pido por es   30

Petition of the town of Veracruz, folio 2, verso

The diagonal lines at the top of the page were inscribed to prevent anyone from inserting unauthorized text into the document. The page begins with a strike-out: "otrosi digo que las."

En especial digo que ya vuestras mercedes saben como en la dicha ynstrucion
esta uno de los dichos capitulos en que a su magestad suplican
que a Diego Velazquez no haga merced de le encargar ni probeer
cosa ninguna en estas partes ni le hacer merced della asi por el
daño e perjuicio que todos los destas partes rescibiriamos como   5
porque como es notorio aviendo dexado de rescatar
e de hacer lo que el dicho Diego Velazquez queria e aviendo poblado
e en nonbre de su magestad se a abido justicia, e por su rreal
corona ofrecida la tierra de que cel dicho Diego Velazquez terna
harto cuidado e trabajara de dañar en todo lo que pudiera   10
a los que en ello entendieran e si el viniese a estas partes
ninguna persona quedara a quien no dañase e echase a
perder como personas que no quisieron haser lo que el quisiere
sino lo que a servicio de sus altesas como sus vasallos devian
hacer ha esto bien parece ser asi porque algunas personas   15
que señaladamente se mostravan ser amigos del
dicho Diego Velazquez quisiendo estorvar que no se hisiera
el servicio que a sus altesas se a hecho e como a personas que
estorvan el servicio de sus altesas e estorvan su rreal corona
estan presos para dellos hacer Justicia e viniendo el dicho Diego   20
Velazquez no solamente se quedaran los susodichos
delinquentes syn castigo pero aun todos los demas
que aqui estamos padeceriamos mucho daño en nuestras
personas e hasiendas segund que mas larga [. . .
. . .] magestad par la dicha ynstruycion firmada   25
. . .]asi mismo rrequiero a vuestras mercedes por lo que toca a ser[vicio]
de sus altesas e al bien procomun de todos que encargen a la [. . .
procuradores e juesces a . . . den poder señaladamente para [. . .]
e haciendo lo asi [de] lo se sigue el pro e servicio de sus
altesas ya dicho e sy necesario es asi lo pido por escrivano.   30

Petition of the town of Veracruz, folio 3, recto

Asi mismo digo que en la ynstrucion que vuestras mercedes dan a los
dichos procuradores de las cosas que a su magestad an de suplicar
esta un capitulo en que todas las personas desta villa e que en estas
partes estan viendo que el señor Hernando Cortes a venido a
estas partes en servicio de sus altesas para las conquistar   5
e gastado muchas sumas de maravedis e dexado la conpania
que el dicho Diego Velazquez con el avia hecho de que se pu
diera bien aprovechar e como vasallo e leal servidor
de sus altezas procuro que para que su rreal corona fuese
aumentada se poblase esta tierra e con su yndustria   10
y trabajo todo o la mayor parte ya conquistada e debaxo
de la servidumbre de sus altesas que asi por esto como que por
otras muchas cosas contenidas en el capitulo señalada
mente para esto en la ynstrucion contenido que su magestad
sea servido de le encargar el dicho cargo de conquistador   15
e capitan general e Justicia mayor de estas partes e hasta
el fin de la pacificacion desta ysla e que pueda rre
partir los yndios della perpetuamente e teniendola
conquistada e apaciguada le de la governacion della
por el tiempo que su al[tesa] fuere servido y como esto sea   20
cosa que tanto al servicio de su magestad e bien
de todos convenga asi por el dicho señor Hernando Cortes
. . .] hecho los servicios que a hecho como por que todos
. . .] de su conpania en [. . .
    . . .] tratado con todo amor [. . .   25
     . . .] como buen ca[. . .

Petition of the town of Veracruz, folio 3, verso

Asi paresce porque al tienpo que a estas partes vinieron ninguna
persona de las que de la cibdad de Santiago salieron
con el viniera sino por la mucha amistad e amor e buena
conversacion que de los tiempos pasados en cargos
avia tenido le como parecian segund que son testigos   5
e las dichas personas sabiendo que a su magestad enbian
a hacer rrelacion de esta tierra me an requerido a su al[tesa
suplicase a que fuese servido de lo dexar en el cargo
susodicho e no probeer a otra persona porque si a otra
persona probeyese su al[tesa] o enbiase a estas partes seria   10
no poblar en ella ni querer aver la voluntad que de permanescer
asi todos tienen por tanto de pedimiento de todos los com
pañeros vecinos estantes en esta villa que aqui firman sus nonbres les
pido e requiero una e dos e tres vezes e mas quantas
puedo e devo que asi mismo suplica a su magestad   15
haga esa merced aqui contenida e segun que por la dicha ynstru
cion se contiene encargando lo mucho a los dichos procuradores e
en esto tengan especial cuidado e sea lo primero que con su
magestad procuren para que asi lo confirme e haga e todo
como convenga lo enbian a su magestad e asi mismo   20
en estos pedimientos en publica forma para que mejor sus al[tesa]s
sean ynformados y sepan como el dicho se Hernando Cortes
conviene estar en estas partes para el servicio de su magestad e pro
e bien de todos [. . . . .] los [compañeros].
          ][A]Gonzalo de Alvarado[

Petition of the town of Veracruz, folio 4, recto

[1]Pedro [Alonso?] Morales Negros   [2]Antonio de Saldaña   [3]Alonso
Ximenez de Herrera (*or* Alonso Hernandez de Herrera)

[4]Alonso Rodriguez, piloto; Alonso Rico, piloto   [5]Miguel de Palma
[6]Rodrigo Cervantes

[7]Diego Suarez   [8]Sancho de Bretes; Gonzalo de Bretes   [9]Gonzalo Galindo;
Gonzalo Galdos

[10]Gonzalo de Arcos   [11]Juan de Sandes [Fandes?]   [12]Cristobal Vanegas

[13]Juan Jimenez   [14]Fernando Xuarez [Juarez]   [15]Pedro de Carmona
[16]Juan de Carmona

[17]Ochoa de Arcia; Ochoa de Arcos/Arce?   [18]Gonzalo Dominguez
[19]Ochoa de Veraza   [20]Juan Bono de Quepo   [21]Francisco de Ledesma

[22]Diego Lopez de Guadalupe   [23]Gaspar de Tarifa

[24]Bartolome Muñoz   [25]Gonzalo de Bonilla   [26]Juan Ruiz   [27]Pedro
Lopez   [28]Juan Juarez; Juan Alvarez

[29]Anton Quemado   [30]Juan de Camacho; Juan de Tamayo   [31]Martin de
Vergara   [32]Pedro de Maya   [33]Beltran (Belgran?) Rodriguez

[34]Feliche Napolitano   [35]Juan de Meco   [36]Benito de Vexer   [37]Juan
Alvarez, maestro   [38]Diego de Orrios; Diego de Lorros; Diego de Porras

[39]Juan Nizard   [40]Domingo Martin   [41]Diego Ruiz de Yllescas; Diego Perez
de Yllanes   [42]Maestre Diego   [43]Martin de Idiaquez; Martin Dircio [de
Ircio]   [44]Alonso[

[45]Juan Cervantes   [46]Juan de[

Petition of the town of Veracruz, folio 4, verso

[47]Francisco Maldonado   [48]Martin Vazquez   [49]Francisco Bonal
[50]Alonso del Alberca   [51]Pedro Martin Parra   [52]Pedro Garcia   [53]Alonso
    Romero
[54]Juan de Magallanes   [55]Alonso Garcia   [56]Fernan Blanco; Juan Blanco
    [57]Alonso Fernandez
[58]Juan Melgarejo   [59]Diego Gonzalez   [60]Gines Nortes   [61]Juan Catalan
[62]Melchor de Contreras   [63]Alonso de Salamanca   [64]Francisco de Medina
    [65]Alonso Perez
[66]Hernando de Escalona   [67]Marcos Ramirez [Reyes?]   [68]Cristobal Suarez
[69]Pedro Gallego   [70]Diego de Utrera   [71]Juan Lopez
[72]Diego de Peñalosa   [73]Juan de Trujillo   [74]Hernando Davila; Hernando de
    Avila   [75]Gutierre de ??? [Badajoz?]
[76]Diego Pizarro   [77]Miguel Navarro   [78]Alonso Mi[. . .
[79]Alonso de Vitoria   [80]Diego Anaya   [81]Pedro Gonzalez

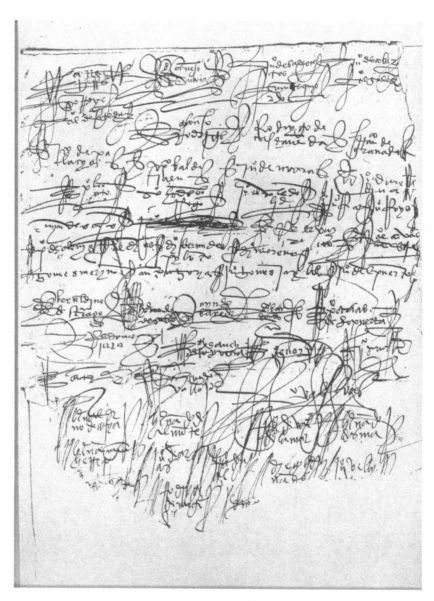

Petition of the town of Veracruz, folio 5, recto

[82]Hernando [de] Torres   [83]Pedro Cornejo de Vitoria   [84]Juan de Ballesteros
      [85]Juan de Escobar
[86]Pedro Ruiz   [87]Martin Izquierdo   [88]Alvaro Gallego
[89]Alonso de Ojeda   [90]Alonso Rodriguez   [91]Rodrigo de Castañeda
      [92]Francisco de Granada
[93]Juan de Palacios   [94]Cristobal de Jaen   [95]Juan de Mora   [96]Juan de
      Medina
[97]Pedro Lizato   [98]Diego Hernandez Borrego   [99]Juan de Valladolid
      [100]Juan Rico   [101]Juan Ruiz
[102]Martin de Solis   [103]Rodrigo de Lepuzcano   [104]Alonso Cav[. . . ; Alonso
      Alvarez, maestre
[105]Pedro de Alanis   [106]Alonso Diaz   [107]Diego Bermudez, piloto
      [108]Diego Moreno
[109]Gomez Merino   [110]Francisco Montoya   [111]Juan Gomez Jayolo
      [112]Juan del Puerto
[113]Bernaldino de Santiago   [114]Hernando de Solis   [115]Martin de Laredo
      [116]Diego Bardabo (Bardavo?)   [117]Pedro Arias de Sopuerta
[118]Rodrigo de Najera   [119][Diego?] Sancho (de) Sopuerta   [120]Diego Enos
      [121]Francisco Donal
[122]Antonio Xuarez   [123]Juan de Vallejo   [124]Cristobal (de) Flores
[125]Bernardino (Bernaldino) de Tapia   [126]Hernando de Almonte   [127]Juan de
      Valdelamar (Valdelomar)   [128]Hernando de Osma
[129]Hernan Martin Herrero   [130]Juan Darcos   [131]Fernando Donal
      [132]Diego Hernandez   [133]Juan Villa
[134]Rodrigo de Moguer

Petition of the town of Veracruz, folio 5, verso

[135]Alvaro del Grado   [136]Francisco Lopez   [137]Juan de Benavente

[138]Alonso Rodriguez   [139]Juan Muñoz   [140]Juan Larios

[141]Hernan de Arcos   [142]Hernan de Olid   [143]Francisco de Najera

[144]Juan Martinez Narices   [145]Francisco Hernandez

[146]Martin Lopez   [147]Alonso Garcia   [148]Pedro Rodriguez

[149]Juan Sastre   [150]Alonso Fernandez Pablos   [151]Miguel de Navarra

[152]Luis de Ojeda (Hojeda)   [153]Alonso de Navarra   [154]Francisco Marques/Marquez

[155]Gonzalo de Alaminos   [156]Alonso de Estrada

[157]Pedro Hernandez   [158]Andres de Mola

[159]Luis Ortiz

Petition of the town of Veracruz, folio 6, recto

[160]Miguel Gomez   [161]Sebastian Rodrigo   [162]Benito (de) Venegas

[163]Pedro Guzman   [164]Cristobal Cardenas   [165]Francisco de Terrazas

[166]Martin Diaz Peñalosa   [167]Melchor Dalava; Martin Lopez Dalava
    [168]Fernando Bargueño

[169]Mendo Xuarez (Suarez)

[170]Andres de Paredes   [171]Bartolome de Loja (Loxa)   [172]Santos
    Hernandez   [173]Anton de Veintemilla

[174]Hernando Alonso   [175]Francisco Lopez de Nambroca; Francisco Lopez de
    Marmolejo

[176]Domingo Hernandez   [177]Rodrigo Diaz

[178]Martin Bajerol; Martin Gonzalo Heroles   [179]Lorenzo Xuarez (Suarez)

[180]Cristobal Diaz   [181]Bernal Diaz   [182]Diego Ramirez

[183]Diego de ???   [184]Andres Farfan   [185]Arias de Ribera
    [186]Alonso de ???

Petition of the town of Veracruz, folio 6, verso

[187]Alonso Rodriguez   [188]Alonso de Argüello   [189]Juan de Alcantara
  [190]Anton Darco

[191]Juan Hedivo/Juan Sedeño   [192]Sebastian de Grijalva   [193]Blas (Pablo?) de
  Retamales   [194]Francisco Gutierrez Coguyos

[195]Alonso de Monroy

[196]Juan Mendez   [197]Sebastian de Porras   [198]Juan Gango   [199]Miguel de
  Anos (Llanos?)

[200]Gonzalo de Jaen   [201]Antonio Alonso   [202]Manuel Verdugo   [203]Juan
  Jimenez

[204]Gaspar de Polanco   [205]Rodrigo de Medellin   [206]Bartolome Garcia
  [207]Bartolome Sanchez   [208]Juan Castaño

[209]Gonzalo Garcia   [210]Luis de Frias   [211]Hernan Lopez Davila

[212]Alonso de Valencia   [213]Martin de Monjaraz   [214]Juan Ruiz Canias
  (Cangas?)

[215]Pedro de Solis   [216]Roman Lopez

[217]Martin de Xerez (Jerez); Martin Perez   [218]Juan (de) Sedeño   [219]Miguel
  de Losa   [220]Pedro Ponce

[221]Rodrigo Ronquillo   [222]Juan Gonzalez de Heredia   [223]Juan Enriquez

[224]Alonso Coronado

Petition of the town of Veracruz, folio 7, recto

[225]Rodrigo de Guevara [226]Francisco Martin [227]Juan de Espinosa
[228]Juan de Cardenas [229]Diego Perez [230]Andres de Monjaraz [231]Juan de la Pera
[232]Pedro de Alcantara [233]Gregorio de Monjaraz [234]Sebastian de la Peña
[235]Juan de Limpias [236]Juan Ramirez [237]Francisco de Manzanilla
[238]Juan Enriquez [239]Alonso Fernandez [240]Francisco de Horozco (Orozco)
[241]Anton Rubio

[242]Cristobal Bravo [243]Anton de Alaminos
[244]Hernan Martinez
[245]Juanes de Fuenterrabia

Petition of the town of Veracruz, folio 7, verso

[246]Rodrigo Alvarez Chico   [247]Francisco Flores   [248]Pedro Gutierrez de
Valdedueñas
[249]Juan Ramos de Lares   [250]Pedro Vizcaino
[251]Cristobal Rodriguez   [252]Pedro Montefrio   [253]Pedro Lopez de Belvas
[254]Alonso Muñoz   [255]Francisco Quintero   [256]Juan Ceciliano (Siciliano)
[257]Alvaro Velon
[258]Juan Diaz Carpintero   [259]Hernando Sanchez; B. Hernandez
[260]Francisco Alvarez   [261]Juan de Valdivia
[262]Arriego de Alva   [263]Luis de Cardenas
[264]Martin   [265]Sancho   [266]Juan Bautista Maestre

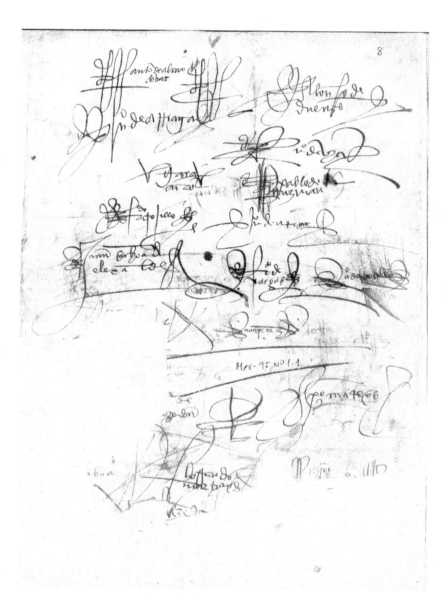

Petition of the town of Veracruz, folio 8, recto

[284]Antonio de Almodovar   [285]Alonso de Dueñas

[286]Juan de Arriaga   [287]Vasco de Via

[288]Garcia Coral   [289]Pablo de Guzman

[290]Francisco (Fernando?) Trujillo   [291]Juan de Artigas; Juan de Arteaga

[292]Juan Ochoa de Elejalde   [293]Fernando de Vargas   [294]Juan de

[295]Nuño Perez

[296]?? de Azedon   [297]Pedro Marcos

[298]Hernando Martinez   [299]Martin

[300]Francisco de Valdez

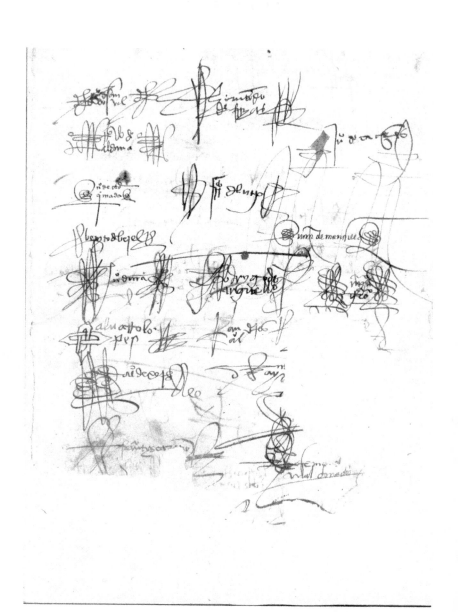

Petition of the town of Veracruz, folio 8, verso

FOLIO 8, VERSO

[267]Gonzalo de Sandoval   [268]Simon de Frias

[269]Fernando de Aldama   [270]Juan de Caceres

[271]Juan de Torre Quemada   [272]Francisco de Lugo

[273]Benito de Vejel   [274]Juan de Mancilla

[275]Juan Darias (Juan de Arias); Juan Duran   [276]Domingo de Argüello
     [277]Martin Nodeo

[278]Alvaro Lopez   [279]Andres de Alonso

[280]Alonso de Jerez   [281][*Signature too badly damaged to be read.*]

[282]Francisco de Scarano; Francisco Santos Scarano   [283][*Signature too badly
damaged to be read.*]

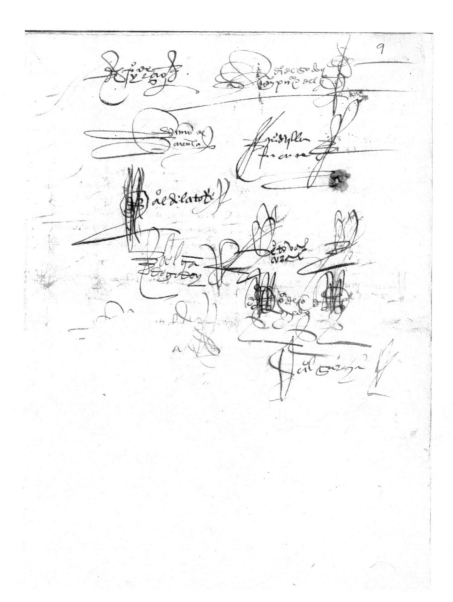

Petition of the town of Veracruz, folio 9, recto

[301]Pedro de Ircio [302]Diego de Godoy, escribano publico
[303]Simon de Cuenca [304]Pedro de Villafuente
[305]Alonso de la Torre
[306]Beltran de Godoy [307]Cristobal Corral
[308]Pedro de Toledo
[309]Alonso Garcia

Petition of the town of Veracruz, folio 9, verso

E asi presentado e leido a los dichos señores justicia e rregidores e leido segund
dicho es el dicho [H]Francisco Alvares Chico procurador susodicho lo pidio por
   escrivano.

Y luego los dichos se dixeron que ellos viendo que lo pedido e rre
querido por el dicho Francisco Alvares por si e en nonbre de la comunidad e asi
   mismo
como lo piden e rrequieren todos los vecinos estantes e conpañeros de esta   5
dicha villa segund paresce por el dicho rrequerimiento dixeron que ellos
estan prestos de encargar a los dichos señores Alonso Hernandez Puertocarrero e
Francisco de Montejo que negocien e procuren lo por el pedido e para ello
se lo encargan e dan poder porque esto es lo que cumple al servicio de sus altesas
e bien de toda la comunidad e que mandaran e mandaron a mi el dicho escrivano 10
que este rrequerimiento original lo de a la parte del dicho Francisco Alvarez
en forma publica para que mas deso sean ynformados sus altezas quedando en mi
   poder el traslado del segun que aqui se contiene e lo
firmaron de sus nonbres.
[B]Alonso Hernandez Portocarrero/alcalde   [C]Francisco de Montejo/alcalde
   [D]Pedro de Alvarado   [E]Alonso Davila   [F]Alonso de Grado   [G]Christoval
Dolid

E yo el dicho [I]Pedro Hernandez escribano de sus altesas e [. . .   15
   . . .]fe que las personas aqui conteindas d[. . .]firmaron s[. . .
    ] algunas personas que[. . .

Petition of the town of Veracruz, folio 10, recto

Pedimento hecho por los vecinos desta villa a quenta de la
qual va para dar a sus altezas y va cerrado y sellado con un
sello de quien es e paso ante mi Pedro Hernandez escribano de
camara de sus altezas escribano publico desta dicha villa. 4

Written in a different, later hand: Villa de la Veracruz.

Translation OF THE *Text*

In the noble town of Vera Cruz on this newly discovered island of Uluacan Monday, June 20, in the year of our Lord Savior Jesus Christ 1519, in the presence of the very noble lords Alonso Hernández Portocarrero and Francisco de Montejo, judges, and Pedro de Alvarado and Alonso de Martín and Alonso de Grado and Cristoval Doli[d], councilmen, in their town council considering those things most suitable to the service of God our Lord and Their Highnesses, according to their use and custom and in the presence of me, Pedro Hernández, clerk of the queen doña Juana and of the king don Carlos, her son, our lords, and their notary public in their court and in all their kingdoms and lordships, and public clerk of this town, there appeared Francisco Alvarez Chico, representative of this town and, for himself and in the name of the community, he presented to these lords, and to me the clerk in order to read it aloud, a request signed with his name and those of his companions who are citizens and residents in this town in the company of the very noble lord, Fernando Cortés, captain general and chief judge in these parts for their highnesses, the tenor of which request is the following:

FOLIO 1, VERSO

Petition made by Francisco Alvares Chico, representative of this noble town of Vera Cruz on this island of Uluacan, to its lords judge and councilmen, which comes originally on eight and one half folded folios of paper with signatures on it to be presented before his royal highness.

Verified by me, Pedro Hernandes, public notary.

FOLIO 2, RECTO

Very Noble Lords,

Francisco Alvares Chico, representative of the Noble Town of Vera Cruz, appears before your graces and says that you well know that, while in your council considering those things most suitable to the service of our lord God and of their highnesses, you informed me as representative of this town that in order to inform his majesty of those things most suitable to the service of our lord God and of their highnesses you decided to send a report with the lords Alonso Hernandez Portocarrero and Francisco de Montejo, whom you authorized to negotiate on your behalf, and because I am obligated to be informed of whatever is most suitable to serve their highnesses and the well-being of this town, I have agreed with your graces to inform the citizens of this town of the content of the report and so give them a share in the favors that you ask his majesty to give you and those things that it would be most suitable to provide for his royal service.

And having written all that has been required of me at the request of these persons, which they ask and require of your graces, they sent to inform their highnesses so that they might thus provide, to which end I in the name of this town and its citizens, ask and require your graces that the said instruction which thus you have decided to send to his majesty signed with their names and authorize the representatives to negotiate because it is . . .

And to the service of his majesty and welfare of all the . . .

Agrees because when this is done their highnesses will be . . .

royal crown increased and this town as . . .

. . . and naturals favored and honored . . .

I ask [in writing] . . .

FOLIO 2, VERSO

Especially, I say that your graces already know that in the report are some sections in which you ask his majesty not to give Diego Velázquez any responsibility or profit at all from this region nor grant it to him, both because the harm and prejudice that all of us here would receive and because it is obvious that having ceased to trade and do what Diego Velázquez wanted, and having settled, and chosen a judge in his majesty's name, and offered this land to his royal crown — land where Diego Velázquez would deliberately try to damage in any way possible those people involved in it, and if he were to come to this region no one would escape being hurt and thrown out, being persons who did not want to do what he wanted, rather what which would be to the service of their highnesses, as their subjects should do and in this it seems well, because some people who have demonstrably shown themselves to be friends of the said Diego Velázquez, [who are] wishing to disturb that service which might be done as which to your highnesses has been done and interfere with your royal crown, are set to bring them to justice, and were the said Diego Velázquez be coming, not only would the above mentioned delinquents remain without punishment but even that the rest of us who are here would suffer much damage to our persons and estates as is more fully . . .

your majesty in the signed instruction . . .

Thus I also require your graces in that which touches on the service of their highnesses and to the common good of all that the agents and judges be charged with and given authority explicitly for that . . .

and doing thus . . .

from which follows the benefit and service of their highnesses already stated and if necessary thus I ask as a notary.

FOLIO 3, RECTO

Likewise I say that in the instructions that your graces give to the representatives about the things that they are to request from his majesty there is a section in which all the people of this town and those coming into these parts, seeing that the lord Hernando Cortés has come to these parts in the service of their highnesses in order to conquer them and spent large sums of maravedis and left the company that he had made with Diego Velázquez from which he could have profited a great deal, and as a vassal and loyal servant of their highnesses he [Cortés] tried to settle this land so that their royal crown would be increased and with his industry and work all or the greater part of the land is already conquered and under service to their highnesses and because of this, as well as for many other things contained in the section especially for this purpose contained in the instruction, his majesty may be served to assign the office of conqueror and captain general and chief judge in these parts until the end of the pacification of this island and that he can distribute its Indians in perpetuity and having conquered and pacified it be given the governorship of it for the time that would be to the service of his highness, and so that this might be something of great service to his majesty and to the well-being of all it is suitable for lord Hernando Cortés[. . .

. . .]done the services that he has done as well as for all[

. . .]of his company in[. . .

. . .]treated with all love[. . .

. . .]as a good ca[pitan . . .

FOLIO 3, VERSO

So it seems because at the time that they came to these parts none of the people who left the city of Santiago with him came for any reason other than the great friendship and love and good relations that he had previously in his offices and as it seemed according to witnesses and these persons knowing that they were sending a report about this land they have instructed me to ask that his highness would be served to leave him in those offices and to not use any other person because if his highness appoints some other person or sends someone to these parts it would not be to settle here nor to want or have the will to remain. Therefore all have taken it as such, and in compliance with of all the companions citizens resident in this town who here sign their names I ask and request one, two, and three times and as many more as I can and should that likewise ask his majesty give the favor described here and according to the contained instruction strongly charging the representatives to take special care in this and that the first thing that they acquire from his majesty should be to confirm and do everything useful they send to his majesty and also send these requests in a public form so that their highnesses may be better informed and know how useful lord Hernando Cortés is in these parts for the service of his majesty and the benefit and well-being of all[. . . .]the comrades[. . .

Gonzalo de Alvarado

FOLIO 9, VERSO

And having presented and read to the lords judge and councilmen and as read as stated, Francisco Alvares Chico, agent, asked for that [record] from the scribe.

And then the lords said that, having seen that which was asked and requested by Francisco Alvares for himself and in name of the community and also that all the citizens residents and companions of this town as it seems from the request, said that they are ready to charge the lords Alonso Hernandez Puertocarrero and Francisco de Montejo to negotiate and procure what was asked and to that end entrusted and gave to them power of attorney because this is what is suitable to the service of their highnesses and good of all the community and that they ordered me the scribe to give this original request by Francisco Alvarez in public form so that their highnesses should be better informed of this, keeping an exact copy of it in my power, and they signed it with their names.

Alonso Hernandez Portocarrero (alcalde)
Francisco de Montejo (alcalde)
Pedro de Alvarado
Alonso Davila
Alonso de Grado
Christoval Dolid

And I Pedro Hernandez, clerk of their highnesses and . . . swear that the persons contained here . . . signed their . . .

Some persons who . . .

FOLIO 10, RECTO

Petition made by the citizens of this town. The account of which goes to be given to their Highnesses, and it goes closed and sealed with a seal from whom it is; passed before me, Pedro Hernández, clerk of the chamber of their Highnesses, public clerk of this said town.[1]

IN THE LAST TWO HUNDRED YEARS MANY SCHOLARS HAVE AT-
tempted to compile lists of the conquerors based on various accounts of the
conquest and on lists compiled after the fact, and through archival research,
as was outlined in chapter 3.[1] The following analysis of the composition of the
Cortés expedition has relied heavily on the works of Bernard Grunberg, Hugh
Thomas, Robert Himmerich y Valencia, and Peter Boyd-Bowman. Other scholars have also studied the composition of the expeditions which fought in other
regions of the Americas, including Panama, Colombia, Chile, and Peru. Consequently, one can begin to take a comparative look at the social and economic
diversity of the various companies.

Some of the earliest efforts to systematically analyze the bands of conquerors date from the mid-twentieth century. For Chile, Tomás Thayer Ojeda
and Carlos J. Larraín looked at the composition of the expedition which accompanied Valdivia.[2] The group was made up nearly completely of veterans
of the conquest of Peru, but not necessarily men who had participated in the
watershed moment in Cajamarca, when the Inca emperor, Atahualpa, was captured and ransomed for gold and silver. Unfortunately, unlike for Cajamarca,
and now Veracruz, there was no single document of the era which listed those
men, so Thayer Ojeda had to reconstruct the company on the basis of later
documentation.

As a precursor to the conquest of Peru, the exploration and settlement of
Panama was an important event. In a masterful work, Mario Góngora pieced
together the identities of the men who conquered and settled Panama in the
period 1509–1530, using a handful of primary documents listing participants
in various expeditions, persons who received grants of *encomiendas* in the region, and persons who received licenses to travel to the region from the Spanish
Crown.[3] Góngora's work was more rooted in the documentation of the period
than Thayer's but still looked at a fairly broad period of time—during which

several waves of settlers and conquerors arrived in Panama — rather than attempting a snapshot of a single group or moment.

James Lockhart focused his research on the men who received a portion of the booty at the capture of Atahualpa in Cajamarca.[4] His research was unique in that he was able to focus on a very specific cohort of men participating in a decisive moment in the conquest of Peru. Using the records of the allocation of booty, Lockhart then traced the biographies of the men via archival research in both Spain and Peru, producing a definitive study which serves as the gold standard for subsequent research.

Two individuals have studied the various expeditions into what is now Colombia: José Ignacio Avellaneda Navas and J. Michael Francis.[5] Again, in the absence of a single defining event which generated a list of conquerors, these scholars have produced an overview of the social and economic origins of the conquerors.

The identities of the men who served with Hernán Cortés in the conquest of Mexico have been largely unknown. Although there has been interest from the sixteenth century onward, it has always been difficult to determine which of the cohorts to study. The most famous comparison case has been the conquest of Peru under Francisco Pizarro. In that adventure one telling moment serves as a clear line of distinction: the capture of Atahualpa at Cajamarca. Those men who were in the company at that moment received a portion of the ransom paid for the emperor. Those who did not participate remained a class apart: conquerors but without the fabulous wealth the ransom provided. This also facilitated the identification of the individual participants, both from the records of the expedition and from subsequent histories, because they were clearly set apart from the rest of the larger expedition thanks to their not-insignificant wealth. The conquest of Mexico lacks this type of clearly defining moment. Although there were distributions of booty, the records are fragmentary and the amounts allocated were not so sufficient to set some men off from the others. What has been needed is a defining moment, and the records to support it.

In the conquest of Mexico, there are several such defining moments. As is seen in the synopsis of the conquest, the first of these was the establishment of the city of Veracruz. While scholars and others knew of this event, until now the full documentation has been lacking. Thanks to the Veracruz petition, we have not only the legal documents supporting the foundation of the city, but the signatures of most of the men present for that act.

Following the foundation of Veracruz, other crucial moments include the defeat of the forces of Pánfilo de Narváez, who had been sent to take over the expedition. Once the battle was over and the two companies were combined, there should have been a muster. Unfortunately the ravages of war and time have robbed posterity of that documentation.

After the Noche Triste, when the company regrouped in Tlaxcala, a second city was founded, Segura de la Frontera. In 1520 a letter was sent to the king describing the events of the conquest to that point, and it was signed by all the members of the enlarged company. That letter has survived, at least in the form of an official copy, and is the basis for much of the collective biography which has been written about the conquerors. Unfortunately, because it is an official copy, scholars need to rely on the ability of a scribe from the late sixteenth century to read signatures from the early part of that century. It is likely that several names were garbled in the process. Similarly, when that document was published in the nineteenth century, the editors also had difficulty deciphering the scribe's hand, and other names were garbled. Yet this document has been the basis of most research conducted on the conquerors of Mexico.

There were other moments in the conquest when lists of participants might have been drawn up and booty or other rewards distributed, especially at the time of the fall of Tenochtitlan. Quite simply, none of those documents have survived to the present or are known to exist. The Veracruz petition of 1519 and the Segura de la Frontera letter of 1520 thus are the cornerstones for understanding the composition of the Cortés company at two key moments in the conquest.

The Signatures

The names on the Veracruz petition tell us a great deal about the Cortés company, but they do not answer all questions, nor can one even be certain about what might seem obvious. What is clear is that about 318 signatures now appear. Because the document was damaged, there originally were perhaps as many as one hundred more signatures. Even among the 318 listed here, several are fragmentary and allow no hint as to who the signatory was. Many are extremely difficult to decipher. Many are such common names, such as Pedro López, that it is near to impossible to determine exactly who the person was.

There have been significant changes in Spanish orthography in the last five hundred years. For example, many names which today are written with an initial "J" were written with an "X" in the sixteenth century, including "Ximenez," now "Jiménez." Some names, such as "Xuarez," today might be written either as "Suárez" or as "Juárez." Because of the handwriting and the frequent use of abbreviations, it is difficult to tell if a given name is Juan, Francisco, or Pablo, since each consists of some sort of initial stroke followed by a superscript "o."

Lastly, although someone looking at the document might conclude that all 318 men were literate, both internal indications and the secondary sources lead to the conclusion that many of the men, perhaps upwards of a quarter, were illiterate and could not sign, or that, for unknown reasons, another person signed the document for them. In the end, nearly everything which can be written about the signatories is conjectural and subjective, arising as it does from interpretations of the documents.

About twenty of the signatures are damaged or simply illegible, for one reason or another. This includes signature 82, identified as Hernando Torres, a fairly well known member of the company, possibly, who signed the 1520 Frontera de la Segura letter and also received an *encomienda*. Another is signature 121, which seems to read "Francisco Donal," about whom there simply is no information. Signatures 264 and 265 provide us only with the first names of the conquerors, and thus not enough to draw any further conclusions.

Beyond this, approximately 140 signatures (45 percent), while legible, are extremely difficult to decipher, and many of these could be interpreted a number of ways. In the listing we have offered alternatives for thirty-five (11 percent) of the signatures. Even just among the first few there are a number of alternatives: either Pedro or Alonso Morales Negros (signature 1), either Alonso Ximénez de Herrera or Alonso Hernández de Herrera (signature 3), or Alonso Rodríguez or Alonso Rico (signature 4). In some cases only one of the alternative readings can be corroborated as having been a conqueror; in that instance we will assume the individual represented by the signature actually is the person known from other sources as the conqueror. For example, signature 275 could be Juan Darias or Juan Durán. No conquerors named Juan Darias, or Juan de Arias, are mentioned in the various sources. There was, however, a conqueror Juan Durán, and so we have assumed that the second reading is correct. Sometimes there are known conquerors for both of the alternative readings. In the example of signature 3, Alonso Ximénez de Herrera or Alonso Hernández de Herrera, there are known conquerors by variants of these names: Alonso Jiménez, Alonso de Herrera, and Alonso Hernández. In other instances we have deciphered surnames which are simply unknown. Examples of these are Juan Gómez Jayolo (signature 111), Martín Bajerol (signature 178), and Francisco Gutiérrez Coguyos (signature 194); Jayolo, Bajerol, and Coguyos are either unknown as surnames or extremely rare. For extremely rare surnames, it is actually easier to find the individual, simply because of that surname, as will be seen below.

While it might seem that all the signatories should have been able to sign their name, and thus demonstrate a minimal level of literacy, there are indications that this simply was not the case. Signatures in the sixteenth century consisted of two parts: the actual name, written out, and then flourishes, usually to each side of the name, called rubrics. Several conquerors signed the document with a mark or symbol. Since this mark is accompanied by a name written out in letters, it can be confused for a name and rubrics, although it seems highly probable that someone else actually wrote the name. Examples of conquerors who used a mark include Gonzalo Galindo/Galdós (signature 9; fig. 6.1), Alonso de Salamanca (signature 63; fig. 6.2), Diego Ramírez (signature 182; fig. 6.3), Gonzalo García (signature 209; fig. 6.4), Alonso Muñoz (signature 254; fig. 6.5), and Alvaro López (signature 278; fig. 6.6). Each of these examples is curious because there is a single symbol (a star for Galdós; a cross and shield for Salamanca; what looks like a jigsaw puzzle piece for Ramírez; cross-hatching for García; a key for Muñoz; and interlocking chevrons for López) and the name. The symbol is just that, a symbol, not one of a pair of rubrics.

In other instances there are pairs of crudely drawn symbols, of which the most common is cross-hatching with two or three lines each way. This is a design very similar to the symbol used by Gonzalo García (fig. 6.4). Examples of this appear for Hernando de Escalona (signature 66; fig. 6.7), Mendo Suárez (signature 169; fig. 6.8), and Lorenzo Suárez (signature 179; fig. 6.9). These examples of cross-hatching are very rectilinear, as opposed to the fluid strokes used in the rubrics of many conquerors. An example of the more fluid rubric, based on cross-hatching, is that of Fernando de Aldama (signature 269; fig. 6.10). These simple symbols and rectilinear rubrics seem to indicate that the author either was illiterate and signed with a symbol, or was barely literate and used a very crude rubric. In the case of Lorenzo Suárez, at least, other sources do indicate that he was illiterate.

Also of interest is the perception that whole groups of names were signed by a single person. The indicators of this are that the names themselves seem to be in a very similar hand while the rubric used in a whole range of cases is identical. The first set of examples appears on the first page of signatures (folio 4, recto), where there seem to be several signatures by the same hand: Bartolomé Múñoz (signature 24), Gonzalo de Bonilla (signature 25), Pedro López (signature 27), Juan Juárez/Alvarez (signature 28), Antón Quemado (signature 29), Juan de Camacho (signature 30), Martín de Vergara (signature 31), Juan Nizard (signature 39), Domingo Martín (signature 40), and possibly others. In this instance, Juan Juárez, if he is the same as the conqueror listed here, was known to be illiterate.

On subsequent pages similar concentrations of signatures also appear in what seems to be a single hand. In the middle of such a group on the third page of signatures (folio 5, recto), Alvaro Gallego (signature 88) is listed. Information from other sources indicates that after the conquest he was unable to sign his own name. Consequently one can assume that someone signed his name for him on the Veracruz petition.

FIGURE 6.1
*Signature 9: Gonzalo Galindo/Galdós,
with star.*

FIGURE 6.2
*Signature 63: Alonso de Salamanca,
with cross and shield (?).*

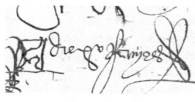

FIGURE 6.3
*Signature 182: Diego Ramírez,
with unidentifiable symbol.*

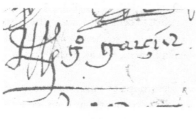

FIGURE 6.4
*Signature 209: Gonzalo García,
with cross-hatching.*

FIGURE 6.5
*Signature 254: Alonso Muñoz,
with symbol of a key.*

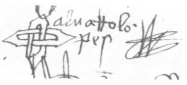

FIGURE 6.6
*Signature 278: Alvaro López,
with interlocking chevrons.*

FIGURE 6.7
*Signature of Hernando de Escalona,
with cross-hatching.*

FIGURE 6.8
*Signature of Mendo Suárez,
with cross-hatching.*

FIGURE 6.9
*Signature of Lorenzo Suárez,
with cross-hatching.*

FIGURE 6.10
*Signature of Fernando de Aldama,
with rubric resembling cross-hatching.*

One can draw two conclusions from the large number of similar hands. A few men signed for their comrades either because the comrades were illiterate (or did not know how to sign their names) — and there is evidence pointing to this in several cases — or because the comrades were not present to sign, or because their names were forged, against their will. There is some evidence that all of these options might have been in play.

While one expects to see the presence of several men with the name Pedro López, there is at least one man with an uncommon name who appears twice: Benito de Bejel or Bejer/Vejer (signatures 36 and 273; figs. 6.11 and 6.12). The signatures are quite distinct from each other; the spelling of the surname is even different. Although nothing in the records indicates that there were two men with this rather unusual name, two very different signatures appear on the document. He may have been illiterate. Some of his comrades remember him as "the lowest member of the company." Literacy and social status were closely linked in the period. On the other hand his occupation was musician, and this also probably contributed to his low social status.

FIGURE 6.11
Signature of Benito de Vexer.

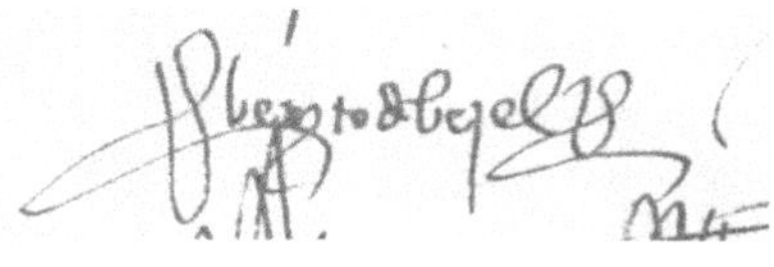

FIGURE 6.12
Signature of Benito de Bejel.

Another group of men who might not have signed the document them-selves is the two small companies who were off on various expeditions at the time the city of Veracruz was created, in particular those on the two ships under the command of Francisco de Montejo that had sailed north up the coast to look for a better port. Some scholars have assumed that the majority of these men were opposed to the idea of breaking with Velázquez and undertaking the conquest of Mexico. Several of the men known to have gone on these expedi-tions, however, do appear among the signatories, including Juan Alvarez (signa-ture 37), Juan de Limpias (signature 235), Antón de Alaminos (signature 243), Rodrigo Alvarez Chico (signature 246), and Pedro de Ircio (signature 301). All of these seem to be represented by unique signatures, and are not among the blocks of names in a single hand. Consequently one can conclude that the tra-ditional interpretation was incorrect, and that these men were in fact present at the creation of the city. The other possibility is that they added their names upon returning from the expedition. This might explain why of the five men identified, four appear in the last pages of the document.

Someone looking at the large sections of names in a single hand might esti-mate that slightly fewer than one hundred men did not sign the document themselves, either because they were illiterate, because they were absent, or be-cause they actually did not support Cortés and the majority of the leadership of the expedition. In each of these instances someone else would have signed the document for them. For the illiterates, it was an act of assistance to make them present and indicate their support of the events outlined in the Vera-cruz petition. For the absent, it similarly would have reflected their solidarity with the decision to break off from Velázquez and to chart a more indepen-dent course. Yet we know that there were those who disagreed with the action. If their names were placed on the document, they would have been unwillingly caught up in actions which they could not control and of which they did not approve. We cannot know for certain how many men might be included in each of these categories.

Mortality Rates

In 1520, following the flight from Tenochtitlan during the Noche Triste and after the company regrouped in Tlaxcala, they set about conquering small towns and villages in the regions surrounding the Valley of Mexico. The first of these was Tepeaca. To mark the beginning of this new phase of the conquest, the company founded another city, Segura de la Frontera. To report on this action, as had been done earlier at Veracruz, a letter was sent to the Crown that had been signed by the members of the company at that moment, some 545 men.[6]

The composition of the army at this point was different from when the Veracruz petition was signed. Many men had already perished as a result of encounters with hostile natives. The ranks of the company had swelled when Narváez was defeated and his men were incorporated into the company. Many, many men died in the flight from Tenochtitlan. Thus, by comparing the names included on the Veracruz petition with those on the Segura de la Frontera letter, one can get an idea of the shifts which occurred. Ninety-eight of the men who signed the Veracruz petition can be found among these recorded ranks of those who signed at Segura de la Frontera. In an additional fifteen cases, there is a possibility that the same man signed in both instances. The confusion stems from the repetition of common names, and from the vagaries of deciphering the sixteenth-century handwriting. Perhaps the best example concerns Hernando de Osma (signature 128). This exact name does not appear on the Segura de la Frontera letter, but a Hernando de Osuna is listed. In all likelihood this is the same man, and his signature has been interpreted or transcribed differently. Taken as a whole, then, just over a third of the men on the Veracruz petition can possibly be found on the Segura letter. On the surface, this would imply the mortality of nearly two-thirds of the company within the first fourteen months of the expedition.

There are, however, individuals who signed the Veracruz petition and are known to have survived the conquest, but who did not sign the Segura de la Frontera letter. The exact number is difficult to determine, given the fragmentary information we have for so many of the conquerors. But merely looking at those members of the company in Veracruz who went on to become *encomenderos* gives some indications as to the gaps in the Segura de la Frontera letter. At least twenty-three men who signed the 1519 petition and did not sign the 1520 letter survived the conquest long enough to receive an *encomienda*. A significant example of this is Francisco de Terrazas (signature 165). Terrazas was an aide to Cortés, his majordomo. He had served as captain of the guard which kept watch over Narváez after the latter's defeat. He received particularly rich towns in *encomienda*, Tulancingo and Igualtepec. His son, who was born in Spain before the conquest, became one of the leading poets of early Mexican society. The elder Terrazas did not die until 1549. We must assume that he simply was not present at Segura de la Frontera.

In addition, many more members of the company survived but did not, for one reason or another, receive an *encomienda*. One can see that the presence of the name of a conqueror on the Segura de la Frontera letter merely indicates that he was present and accounted for on that particular day. Many others were serving in the company and did not sign the letter. A perfect example of this is none other than Bernal Díaz del Castillo himself (signature 181). He signed the Veracruz petition but does not appear in the Segura de la Frontera letter; he survived the conquest and eventually settled in Guatemala, where he dictated his memoirs and died of old age.

As we have seen, many members of the company were injured in the flight from Tenochtitlan. These men — and one imagines others who cared for them — remained in Tlaxcala while the main body of the company attacked Tepeaca. This would seem to indicate that the extremely high mortality rate — two-thirds — predicted by a simple comparison of the two documents needs to be significantly revised downward.

Another way to adduce the overall mortality of the company is to look among the names on the Veracruz petition for listings of conquerors known to have survived the conquest. The biographies of the signatories of the Veracruz petition document only fifty-two as having died in the conquest. Finally, there are ninety-nine men whose names do not appear in any of the traditional sources dealing with the conquest. Consequently, one might imagine that they perished between the landing in Veracruz in 1519 and probably August 1520 — when the Segura de la Frontera letter was signed — but certainly before the end of the conquest.

Taking all this evidence together, we can say that approximately half of the men who signed the Veracruz petition in all likelihood died before the end of the conquest in 1521. This number might be even higher, because it does not take into account the fact that several men named Pedro García, for example, participated, a number of whom died before the fall of Tenochtitlan.

Information gleaned from a wide number of sources allows some observations to be made about ages of the men who signed the Veracruz petition. Of the 318 signatories, we have rough estimates of the birth and death dates for 121.[7] Of this group for whom data exist, the average age at the time of the Veracruz landing was 25.6 years, with the median being 24 and the mode being 19. The enterprise was obviously made up of men who were young and in their prime. As noted, the mortality rate during the conquest was tremendous, but the life expectancy of any conqueror who survived the conquest did not differ greatly from that of his contemporaries. The average age at death for the group of 121 men was 44.2 years old, with the median being 43 and the mode being 26. Here the mode reflects the huge numbers of men who perished during the conquest itself.

The oldest recorded survivor of the conquest was Francisco de Nájera (signature 143), who reportedly died at age 90. Close behind, in second place for longevity, was Bernal Díaz del Castillo (signature 181) himself, who died at approximately age 88. A total of 27 men lived into their sixties or beyond.

These data are quite similar to those found for other groups of conquerors. In his study of the conquerors of Peru, James Lockhart reports that the largest age group in the Pizarro company was the cohort of men aged 25–29, accounting for 41 of the 107 men about whom data were available.[8] Of the 326 conquerors from several expeditions into New Granada studied by José Ignacio Avellaneda Navas, the largest cohort was 25–30 years old, with 95 men, while the age group of 21–25 years included 84.[9] In an analysis of the New Granada expedition of Gonzalo Jiménez de Quesada, J. Michael Francis concluded that the 20–24 cohort was the largest, with 46 among the 121 conquerors he studied, although the 25–29 cohort included 28 men.[10] In terms of longevity of the conquerors, the case of Chile helps to provide a comparison.[11] Of the 110 members of the Valdivia company for whom age data were available, 1 man reached his one-hundredth birthday and another 6 died older than 80 years. The largest cohort was of those who died between their sixtieth and seventieth birthdays (23), although the distribution between 50 and 80 years is quite even, with 20 dying between 50 and 60, and another 19 dying between 70 and 80 years. Unfortunately, both Lockhart and Francis calculated the number of men who lived beyond the conquest not in terms of the men themselves but as a diminishing cohort, where 11 men lived twenty-eight years after Cajamarca and 2 lived fifty-eight years after the New Granada expedition studied by Francis.[12] Using this approach, of the 193 members of the Cortés company for whom we have approximate death dates, only two lived sixty years after the landing at Veracruz: Bernal Díaz del Castillo and Francisco de Nájera. Of 193, 56 died during the conquest itself, and another 42 died within a decade of the landing.

One other detail studied by scholars of the various conquests is the length of time the members of the expeditions had spent in the New World prior to the episode under study. In the case of the Cortés expedition, there is information about their arrival in the New World for 94 of the signatories. Three of the men arrived the same year as the landing at Veracruz, a near-impossibility. Another 9 had arrived the year before. The largest group had arrived within five years of the landing at Veracruz, accounting for 65 of the 94 men.

Identities

The greatest challenge in studying the men who signed the Veracruz petition is determining their exact identity. As noted above, fully one-third of the names do not match any known conqueror.

As we have said, part of the problem is the orthography. Many signatures are difficult to decipher. Moreover, spellings have changed; since most of the printed sources which include the information necessary to evaluate the biographies date from the nineteenth and early twentieth century, the problem is compounded. Scholars in those periods generally modernized spellings of names. Because of the difficulty of interpreting the signatures and the prevalence of common names, in approximately fifty-seven cases there are multiple individuals who could possibly own the signature. Combining this with the men whose names can be deciphered but regarding whom we have no solid information, fully half of the names on the document represent significant problems of identification.

Some of the most revelatory information in Lockhart's *The Men of Cajamarca* was the discussion of the origins of the conquerors, their social status, and other bits of personal information. For the members of the Cortés company, very little along these lines is certain. To begin with, we can only identify half of the men. Even of those men whom we can identify, very few are described in such way as to allow us to deduce their social status. We read that Bejel was a musician, and of low social status, and that Bernardino de Tapia was a member of the petty nobility.

Beyond this, although much ink has been spilled regarding the geographical origins of the conquerors, we frequently have to rely on the thinnest of evidence to make such a determination. Many men are associated with a hometown merely because Díaz del Castillo recalled several decades after the fact that they were from such and such a locale. In many instances we simply cannot know. In general, it would be a surprise if the members of the Cortés company in Veracruz did not largely come from Extremadura and Andalucía, since Cortés himself was from Extremadura, and many of the sailors in the expeditions to the New World came from the provinces of Huelva and Seville in Andalucía.

Geographical Origins

At the time of the conquest of Mexico what we know as Spain was in the process of being consolidated. In its most general sense, Spain consisted of the three major kingdoms of Castile, León, and Aragón. Castile and León had been unified for some time prior to the conquest, and were already well on the way to full integration. The northeastern mountainous regions were politically and socially quite different. Because a large percentage of the population spoke a foreign language and had different customs, this region is known as the Basque country, after the name of the local language. The Basque provinces of Guipuzcoa, Vizcaya, and Alava had been incorporated under the Castilian crown for over a century, although they retained their unique laws and language: Basque. Aragón was a more recent addition, thanks to the marriage of Isabel of Castile and Ferdinand of Aragón. Aragón consisted of several provinces, the most important of which was Catalunya, with its capital of Barcelona. This kingdom had its own legal traditions, and language: Catalá. Navarre was an outlying kingdom, frequently considered part of the Basque territory, which had been partially incorporated by the time of the conquest.[13]

In the sixteenth century what we know as Spain was hardly a unified territory. It was a patchwork of jurisdictions from towns and villages up to kingdoms, each of which had its own particular laws, customs, and even language and currency. In general the land was broken up into large communities. The ancient Christian strongholds of the north of the peninsula, regions known as Cantabria, Asturias, León, Castile, and New Castile, formed part of a large political entity which for convenience can be called Castile. The eastern kingdom of the peninsula was Aragón. The western region of Spain was known as Extremadura. The southern region was known as Andalucía. The leadership of the Cortés company was unquestionably dominated by men from the region of Extremadura, the home territory of Cortés himself. Interestingly enough, the Pizarro expedition to Peru was also dominated by Extremeños, since the Pizarro brothers were from Trujillo in Extremadura.

While the leadership of the expedition might have consisted of men from Extremadura, the same cannot be said for the expedition as a whole. Of the 318 men who signed the document, places of origin can be assigned to 122, just under 40 percent. The largest group was of the Castilians, who accounted for 50 members of the company. The second-largest contingent consisted of men from Andalucía, totaling 37 men. The Extremaduran group was the third-largest, with only 20 members. The Basques with 14, Aragonese with 3, and a single man from Navarre were the smallest. Quite clearly the expedition consisted largely of men from the central and western regions of Spain and very few from the eastern, with the exception of the Basque country. The one area which was completely absent in the origins of the signatories was the far northwest corner of Galicia.

This overall pattern coincides closely with data collected for all of the expeditions to Mexico — those of Hernández de Córdoba, Grijalva, and Cortés — analyzed by Grunberg.[14] It is also similar to what Lockhart found for the men of Cajamarca. Of the 168 men Lockhart studied, 55 came from the larger region of Castile, 36 from Extremadura, and 34 from Andalucía.[15] Clearly Extremeños played a more important role at Cajamarca and there were fewer Castilians, relatively speaking. There were more Andalucians in the Cortés company. The membership from Extremadura demonstrated the same pattern of many men coming from many villages, rather than from one or two towns. In the case of the Peruvian expedition the town of Trujillo provided an abnormally large contingent, but then again it was the home of Pizarro and his brothers.

Looking at the other parts of the Americas, we see that the regional composition of the conquering bands fell within the general ranges found at Veracruz and Cajamarca. In the conquest of New Granada, Andalucía provided more conquerors than any other region, with some 30 percent coming from that area. Old Castile was in second place, providing 16 percent, followed by New Castile and Extremadura, each with about 12 percent.[16] Nearby, Panama reflected the same general pattern, with 35 percent of the conquerors coming from Andalucía and 21 percent from Extremadura.[17] In Chile the regional composition of the Valdivia company was quite similar, with 26 of the 104 men for whom regional origins were known coming from Andalucía, followed by 17 from Extremadura, and 16 from New Castile.[18]

The following table summarizes these data. Since not all of the authors divided Spain into the same large provinces, it was necessary to find the best common divisions and so percentages may vary from those given in the prior paragraph. For example, in the table, the area designated Castile includes the regions of Old and New Castile, León, Asturias, Galicia, and the Canaries. Aragón includes Catalunya, País Valenciano, Murcia, and the Balearic Isles.

ANDALUCÍA, CASTILE, AND EXTREMADURA IN THE VERACRUZ PETITION

Some specific provinces and cities provided an extraordinary number of conquerors, as reflected in the Veracruz petition. The city of Seville itself accounted

	Veracruz	Mexico	Cajamarca	Chile	N. Granada	Panama
Andalucía	30.1	34.2	26.4	26.5	30.1	36.7
Aragón	2.4	3.7	1.5	3.1	4.9	1.3
Basque country	10.6	4.3	7.8	12.2	5.3	8.9
Castile	40.6	41.3	36.4	40.9	45.8	30.3
Extremadura	16.3	16.5	27.9	17.3	13.9	22.8

for ten men, if one includes the neighborhood of Triana with Seville. The province of Seville, including the city, provided eighteen conquerors. Also in Andalucía, the province of Huelva sent ten men to Mexico with Cortés, nearly all of them being sailors from the coastal villages of Palos, Moguer, and Huelva itself. While Castile provided the largest contingent, the group represented fifteen different provinces, ranging from the ancient kingdom of Asturias in the far north to the newly settled region of Ciudad Real in the south. The university city of Salamanca provided four men to the Cortés expedition, while the province as a whole saw eight men leave. The province of Valladolid had seven men, coming from five different towns. In Extremadura the province of Badajoz was the best represented, with twelve conquerors. No Extremeña city provided more than two men. Included in those providing two were Alcántara, Badajoz, Fregenal de la Sierra, and Medellín. At first glance one might think that the village of Garovillas also provided two conquerors, but in reality there are two different villages with similar names, one in Cáceres and the other in Badajoz: Garrovillas de Alconétar in Cáceres, home of Juan Méndez (signature 196), and Las Garrovillas, home of Rodrigo de Medellín (signature 205) in Badajoz.

BASQUES, NAVARRIANS, ARAGONESE, AND OTHERS IN THE VERACRUZ PETITION

Men from the Basque country, Navarre, and Aragón, although considered subjects of the Spanish Crown at the time of the conquest, might be looked upon as somewhat foreign, especially since each region had its own local language, culture, customs, and laws. Although it is difficult to determine the place of origin of many of the conquerors, the following men were in some instances considered as foreigners, or at least non-Castillians.

FROM OTHER TERRITORIES OF SPAIN

Signature 19	Ochoa de Veraza	Vizcaya
Signature 20	Juan Bono de Quepo	Vizcaya
Signature 31	Martín de Vergara	Guipuzcoa

Signature 61	Juan Catalán	Catalunya
Signature 77	Miguel Navarro	Navarre
Signature 83	Pedro Cornejo de Vitoria	Alava
Signature 103	Rodrigo de Lepuzcano	Guipuzcoa
Signature 117	Pedro Arias de Sopuerta	Vizcaya
Signature 167	Melchor de Alava	Aragón
Signature 176	Domingo Hernández	Aragón
Signature 213	Martín de Monjaraz	Vizcaya
Signature 222	Juan González de Heredia	Vizcaya
Signature 226	Francisco Martín	Vizcaya
Signature 245	Juanes de Fuenterrabia	Guipuzcoa
Signature 249	Juan Ramos de Lares	Vizcaya
Signature 250	Pedro Vizcaíno	Vizcaya
Signature 251	Cristóbal Rodríguez	Vizcaya
Signature 292	Juan Ochoa de Elejalde	Guipuzcoa

These men, while from territories under the Spanish Crown, were frequently looked upon as foreign or exotic. Another feature which set them apart—at least the men from Guipuzcoa and Vizcaya—was that they were considered noblemen (*hidalgos*) by virtue of their birth and origin in those two provinces. Several of these men had previous experience in European wars. Rodrigo de Lepuzcano/Guipuzcoano (signature 103) had served in Italy prior to emigrating to the Indies. He then fought in the conquest of Cuba with Diego Velázquez, later joining the Cortés company. After the fall of Tenochtitlan he fought in the conquests of Coatzacoalcos and New Galicia and finally settled on the west coast in Colima. Some of the older conquerors, already discussed, were also from these territories, such as Juan González de Heredia (signature 222), a Vizcayan who also had served earlier in Italy. Three Vizcayans all signed together, Juan Ramos de Lares, Pedro Vizcaíno, and Cristóbal Rodríguez (signatures 249–251). Ramos de Lares was illiterate. We assume from Vizcaíno's name that he was from Vizcaya. There were several men named Cristóbal Rodríguez, one of whom was a ship's carpenter from Vizcaya.

IT IS SOMEWHAT SURPRISING TO FIND CONQUERORS FROM OUTside of the territories of Spain. Nevertheless, one of the features of the expeditions and armies of the early modern period is that there was a certain degree of fluidity among their members. One day these individuals might fight under a Spanish flag, and another under the flag of a local duke or other leader. While not extensive, the number of foreigners in the Cortés company was significant.

Signature 11	Juan de Flandes (?)	Flanders
Signature 34	Feliche Napolitano	Naples
Signature 54	Juan de Magallanes	Portugal
Signature 161	Sebastián Rodríguez/Rodrigo	Portugal
Signature 173	Antón de Veintemilla	Genoa
Signature 179	Lorenzo Xuárez	Portugal
Signature 208	Juan Castaño	Portugal
Signature 256	Juan Ceciliano	Sicily

A plurality of these men came from Portugal. While Spain and Portugal were very independent nations at this time, there was a great deal of movement between the two. Certainly in the age of exploration there were Spanish seamen on Portuguese voyages and Portuguese seamen on Spanish voyages. Columbus himself sought support from both the Portuguese and Spanish Crowns. Many of the men from Portugal listed here had military experience elsewhere in Europe which had prepared them for the hazards and dangers of the conquest. Similarly, the other men come from Flanders and from various regions of Italy. At this time Spain had close ties with all of the areas. King Charles I of Spain — Charles V of the Holy Roman Empire — was himself from Flanders, and that territory was thus appended to the Spanish Crown. The kings of Aragón also had territorial claims on Sicily and Naples, known as the Kingdom of the Two Sicilies. Genoa was a major maritime power in the period and had close ties with Aragón. Columbus was, after all, from Genoa. Consequently even these foreigners had some real ties to what would come to be known as Spain.

As noted, we only have solid information about half of the men who signed the Veracruz petition, approximately 150. The foreigners, then, make up about 2 percent of the signatories. According to the available information, they fought as well as their Spanish colleagues. For example Juan de Magallanes (signature 54), a Portuguese perhaps related to the circumnavigator of the world, Ferdinand Magellan, is remembered by Díaz del Castillo as a good foot soldier. Although he seems to have deserted the Cortés expedition to join Narváez, once the two companies merged he fought with great zeal. He died with valor during the final battle for Tenochtitlan.

Within the document itself, names seem to appear in groupings representing cohorts or platoons. As seen above regarding the five men who were on the Montejo expedition at the time the city of Veracruz was founded, three of them signed quite closely to one another (signatures 235, 243, and 246). In checking the names against Díaz del Castillo we see a similar phenomenon occurring. Men who signed near one another were frequently described near one another in his recollections of the members of the company. Alonso de Ojeda (signature 89), Rodrigo de Castañeda (signature 91), and Francisco de Granada (signature 92) were also described on the same page in the printed edition of *Historia verdadera*.

There were approximately fourteen horses in the Cortés company at Veracruz. Their owners were regarded as important members of the company because of their wealth, manifested in the investment of a horse in the expedition. Three of these men signed in very close proximity to one another. Francisco Donal/Donaire (signature 121), Cristóbal Ortiz (signature 122), and Bernardino de Tapia (signature 125) all owned horses. In the case of Donal/Donaire there is some uncertainty about his exact identity because of the uncommon surname. In the case of Ortiz, an equally valid reading of the signature might be Antonio Xuarez, who is unknown. Yet it should come as no surprise that the cavalrymen would sign as a group. The horsemen will be studied in greater depth below.

Further on are three men described as mature, *viejo*, who signed in proximity to one another. Andrés de Paredes (signature 170), Santos Hernández (signature 172), and Lorenzo Xuárez (signature 179) were all mature men at the time the city was founded. Most of the members of the company seem to have been quite youthful, largely in their twenties. Paredes died during the conquest. Hernández lived until about 1558, was married, and had at least two children, a son and a daughter. Xuárez was Portuguese, from Evora. He had long experience in the Indies, having first sailed out with governor don Nicolás de Ovando in 1502. After the conquest he married a woman from the Spanish petty nobility, but the marriage was a troubled one, and he eventually killed her. To avoid civil justice and to do penance for this act he joined the Franciscan order. It seems that these men at least had their age in common, making them slightly more than acquaintances when it came to signing the petition.

There were several sets of relatives in the company, and logically they tended to sign near to one another. The brothers Juan and Pedro de Carmona (signatures 15 and 16) signed next to one another. Martín, Andrés, and Gregorio de Monjaraz (signatures 213, 230, and 233) signed near one another. Juan Rico de Alanís and Juan Ruiz de Alanís (signatures 100 and 101) signed next to one another. They might have been kinsmen, but were mostly likely from the same town, the village of Alanís in Andalucía, and thus probably friends of one another. Very close to them is the signature of Pedro de Alanís (signature 105). Again, he might be a kinsman or merely from the same village. Slightly above these one finds Diego Hernández (signature 98). Although this conqueror has been tentatively identified as Diego Hernández Borrego, from the village of Saelices de los Gallegos, in the province of Salamanca, it is possible that he was Diego Hernández de Alanís, yet another kinsman or native of Alanís.

Other kinsmen also tended to sign in close proximity to one another. Juan Martínez Narices (signature 144) signed right above his wealthier and better-known kinsman Martín López (signature 146). Further down the page, Miguel de Navarra (signature 151) signed just before his possible kinsman, Alonso de Navarra (signature 153). Neither of these men appears in any of the standard sources describing the conquest of Mexico, so it is purely conjectural to assume their kinship, but the proximity of the signatures to one another and the shared surname or place of origin are highly suggestive. On the last page two men with the surname Godoy signed near to one another: Diego de Godoy (signature 302), one of the public scribes of the expedition, and Beltrán de Godoy (signature 306), otherwise unknown, but because he appears so close to Diego one might assume that they were related.

Not all kinsmen signed the petition close to their relatives. The brothers Martín and Pedro de Ircio/Dircio (signatures 43 and 301) signed in very distinct sections of the document. The two men of the Alaminos family, Gonzalo (signature 155) and Antón (signature 243), also signed in very different places. The signatures of four kinsmen are scattered around the document. Francisco de Terrazas (signature 165), Rodrigo Alvarez (signature 246), Francisco Alvarez? (signature 260), Juan Alvarez (signature 28 or 37), and Francisco Alvarez Chico (signature H) all appear in very distinct sections of the petition. We do not know what the exact relationship was between the Alvarez brothers and Terrazas, but there is one mention that Francisco Alvarez and Francisco de Terrazas were kinsmen. Terrazas, as noted, was an important member of the company who received a very rich *encomienda* after the conquest. Alvarez Chico was one of the captains of the company and elected as an agent of the town of Veracruz. The three Alvarez brothers had a fairly long history in the New World, having sailed there in 1511. Their brother Hernando died in Santo Domingo. Francisco was a businessman and was one of the few conquerors to leave Mexico following the conquest, returning to settle on the island of Hispaniola. Rodrigo held several positions of power and authority, serving, for instance, as one of the guards of Moteuczoma and, later, as overseer of the royal treasury. He died at the hands of natives during the exploration and conquest of Colima. Juan is the least well known of the brothers.

There were undoubtedly other kinship groups present in the Cortés company. For example, the two men with the slightly uncommon surname Nájera (signatures 118 and 143) might well be related. In addition Díaz del Castillo indicates that Francisco González Nájera arrived with a son, Pedro, and two nephews surnamed Ramírez (possibly signature 236).

Surprisingly few of the members of the company were related to Cortés himself. Only three men stand out, and in two cases the relationship is tenuous. Diego Pizarro was generally held to be a relative of Cortés. He served as a captain of one of the detachments during the conquest, including during the confrontation with Narváez, when Díaz del Castillo was a member of his corps. The other example is Vasco de Via, or Villa (signature 287). Again on the basis of a comment by Díaz del Castillo, Villa's wife might have been a relative of Cortés's wife. Considering the large number of Pizarro relatives in the conquest of Peru, it is remarkable that so few of the relatives of Cortés were engaged in the conquest of Mexico.

At the same time, several men whose signatures are scattered throughout the document can be identified as members of Cortés's personal staff.

Signature 40	Domingo Martín	footman
Signature 42	Maestre Diego	cook and physician
Signature 56	Juan Blanco	steward
Signature 66	Hernando de Escalona	page (possibly in Cortés's retinue)
Signature 69	Pedro Gallego	equerry, page
Signature 96	Juan de Medina	servant
Signature 120	Cindo del Portillo	guard
Signature 195	Alonso de Monroy	page or steward
Signature 236	Juan Ramírez	equerry, page
Signature 266	Juan Bautista Maestre	physician
Signature 303	Simón de Cuenca	steward

While some men seem to have signed in cohorts, these men are listed throughout the document. They ranged in age from mature men, such as Maestre Diego and Juan Bautista Maestre, to young boys, such as Hernando de Escalona, Pedro Gallego, and Juan Ramírez. These latter seem to have been some of the youngest members of the company. Díaz del Castillo was very upset when two of the pages, Pedro Gallego and Francisco Martín Vendabal (not a signatory), were captured and sacrificed by the Mexica. He criticized Cortés roundly for having failed to better protect the boys.

The two physicians were extremely active during the conquest. They were aided by other men of the company, who used various cures to try to heal their wounded fellows. Alonso de Monroy seems to have been a bit older. He had sailed to the Indies in 1514, settling on Hispaniola. His father was a high-ranking officer in the military-religious Order of Santiago in Spain, being the *comendador* of Santisteban. Monroy had the nickname of "Salamanca," since he either was from that city or perhaps had attended the university there. He survived the Noche Triste because of his speed and nimbleness. Unfortunately, later on in the conquest he was captured and executed in sacrifice by the natives.

Occupations

The vast majority of the occupations mentioned in biographies of the conquerors have to do with crucial activities of the expedition. There were numerous men who had served as ship's masters and pilots. There were carpenters, blacksmiths, and crossbowmen, and even a locksmith. Other occupations which were needed both in military and civilian life included scribes, notaries, and musicians. After the conquest the men generally occupied themselves in mining, taking part in business affairs in general, and managing rural estates, while some practiced their occupations as carpenters or blacksmiths.

PILOTS AND MASTERS

A total of fourteen men either identified themselves as pilots or ship's masters, or are so called in available biographical information.

Signature 4	Alonso Rodríguez/Rico
Signature 9	Gonzalo Galindo/Galdós
Signature 20	Juan Bono de Quepo
Signature 27	Pedro López
Signature 30	Juan de Camacho/Tamayo
Signature 37	Juan Alvarez
Signature 104	Alonso Alvarez
Signature 107	Diego Bermúdez
Signature 117	Pedro Arias de Sopuerta
Signature 155	Gonzalo de Alaminos
Signature 243	Antón de Alaminos
Signature 255	Francisco Quintero
Signature 263	Luis de Cárdenas
Signature 266	Juan Bautista

The most famous by far of the pilots was Antón de Alaminos (signature 243), who was the principal pilot for the expedition. He also charted the course which took the representatives from Veracruz back to Spain, with that unfortunate stop in Cuba along the way. In all likelihood Alaminos was the first pilot to recognize and use the Gulf Stream as a quick and sure route from the Americas to Europe. As noted, his kinsman Gonzalo de Alaminos (signature 155) might have also been a pilot. Another man from a prominent sailing family was Diego Bermúdez (signature 107). In his signature he noted that he was a pilot. He had sailed on Columbus's first voyage to the New World in 1492. His brother, Juan Bermúdez, was very famous for having discovered the island which would bear his name, Bermuda. Unfortunately, Diego died during the conquest of Mexico.

Several of the identifications of pilots and ship's masters in the expedition are conjectural. For example, Pedro López is an extremely common name, and one of the men with this name was a pilot. The Juan Alvarez who signed the petition may or may not be the same Juan Alvarez who was a ship's pilot. Juan Bautista identifies himself as a *maestre*, which could imply that he was a master at any number of occupations.

Several of these men gained a certain renown during the conquest and its aftermath. Juan Bono de Quepo (signature 20), originally from Vizcaya, served as a pilot on Columbus's last voyage to the New World. Bono served as a ship's master and pilot in several important expeditions, including that of Ponce de León to Florida. He probably made more than one voyage to Mexico, perhaps with Hernández de Córdoba. He might well have been one of the seamen who accompanied Alaminos and the representatives of the city of Veracruz when they returned to Spain. It is also possible that he disembarked on the island of Cuba. This would explain why some eyewitnesses placed Bono in the Narváez company, since he might well have returned to Mexico as a pilot for that expedition, too. Immediately following the conquest he abandoned Mexico, sailing first to Cuba and then to Spain. He secured various royal grants and returned to Mexico with important royal documents for Cortés. After that, Bono returned to Cuba, where he settled permanently, eventually becoming the lieutenant governor of the island.

Juan Alvarez (signature 37) identified himself as a ship's master. Díaz del Castillo tells us that he had the nickname of the "little one-armed fellow" (*el manquillo*). He was originally from the seaport town of Palos in southern Andalucía. He served as a pilot for the Hernández de Córdoba expedition, and then with Cortés. He was one of the pilots of the expedition to Pánuco, which occurred while the events described in this petition were taking place. After the conquest, because of a falling out with Cortés, he left Mexico and went back to his career as a pilot. Alvarez was not the only pilot to have a falling out with the leader of the expedition. Luis de Cárdenas (signature 263) became an outspoken critic of Cortés, earning himself the nickname of "the talker" (*el hablador*). Originally from the Triana neighborhood of Seville, Cárdenas sailed to the New World in search of riches. Early on he became disillusioned about the way the booty was distributed, with 40 percent going to Cortés and the king, major shares going to the captains, and all the others having to share the remainder. At the first opportunity Cárdenas returned to Cuba and continued to complain. Eventually Cortés awarded him a lump-sum payment, but Cárdenas took his petitions to the court in Spain and was awarded an annual pension of one thousand pesos, to be paid in Mexico. At that point he returned to Mexico and settled in Mexico City, and even received an *encomienda*.

CARPENTERS

In the days of wooden sailing ships, carpenters were essential members of any crew. Once the expedition landed and set out overland, carpenters were also important members of the company because of their skills. In the case of the Cortés company carpenters were extremely valuable, given that the final assault on Tenochtitlan occurred in a combined land and naval attack. Carpenters were required to fabricate the brigantines used in the naval assault and in the construction of portable bridges and other war machines needed for the land assault. Among the men signing the Veracruz petition were about a dozen men who served as carpenters.

Signature 65	Alonso Pérez
Signature 94	Cristóbal de Jaén
Signature 98	Diego Hernández [*one of many*]
Signature 136	Francisco López
Signature 140	Juan Larios
Signature 144	Juan Martínez Narices
Signature 146	Martín López
Signature 157	Pedro Hernández [*one of many*]
Signature 182	Diego Ramírez
Signature 217	Martín Pérez
Signature 251	Cristóbal Rodríguez
Signature 258	Juan Díaz, *carpintero*
Signature 278	Alvaro López

Perhaps the most famous of all the carpenters was a man who in fact had set out for the Indies as a merchant, Martín López (signature 146). Leaving his home in Seville in 1516, he was carrying far more supplies than he might possibly need himself, obviously with an eye to selling them in the Indies. He became wealthy in this manner, and by the time the Cortés expedition set out he routinely traveled with three servants to assist him. All three of these men were carpenters: Miguel and Pedro de Mufla and Juan Martínez Narices (signature 144). The Mufla brothers (also known as Mafra, Nufla, or Nuflo) participated in the conquest of Mexico, but do not seem to have signed the Veracruz petition. Pedro de Mufla was killed by the natives in the final battle for Mexico.[19] Although López does not seem to have been a carpenter, Cortés ordered him to supervise the construction of two sets of brigantines, one set to explore the Mexican coast and the other to be used in the final assault. Cortés did this in recognition of López's skills as a manager, not as a carpenter. The brigantines used in the assault were built first at Tlaxcala, from lumber harvested on nearby mountains, notably the peak now known as Malinche. They were then dismantled and carried over the high peaks surrounding the Valley of Mexico, and then reassembled in Texcoco. The Crown recognized his singular contributions to the conquest by awarding him a noble coat of arms in 1550.

Because of their trade, many other carpenters of the expedition participated in the construction of the brigantines used against the Aztecs. For example, Diego Hernández (signature 98) was a sawyer and is credited for sawing the boards used in the construction of the brigantines. He was known to be a very strong man, capable of hurling a stone as if it were shot from a cannon.

What is notable about this group of men is that they all have fairly common surnames (other than Larios and Jaén). In Spanish society of the time folks who sported the simplest of surnames, those ending in "-ez," were normally from the lower social groups. Carpenters, men who worked with their hands with wood, would have been considered part of the lowest working classes, slightly higher than field hands but certainly lower than shopkeepers or people who worked with more precious materials, such as silversmiths and jewelers.

Two of the men listed as carpenters undertook one of the most arduous adventures of the conquest. The company at one point came close to running out of gunpowder and needed to make more. The manufacture of gunpowder required three main ingredients: saltpeter, charcoal, and sulfur. The charcoal and saltpeter were readily available, the latter being found in the evaporation fields of the lakes which ringed the city of Tenochtitlan. Cortés assumed that the volcanoes which dotted the central Mexican landscape would be sources of sulfur, and so he sent out several men, ordering them to climb the volcano called Popocatepetl (Smoking Mountain), descend to the caldera, and search for the element. Of this group, Juan Larios (signature 140) and Alvaro López (signature 278) were carpenters.

Alvaro López had a particularly colorful life. Originally from Guadalupe in the province of Cáceres, he might have been illiterate, since his signature is em-

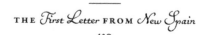

bellished with two interlocked chevrons, perhaps his mark (see fig. 6.6). In the conquest he stood out for a few reasons. After Cortés had landed on the island of Cozumel, off the east coast of Yucatan, López constructed a small chapel for the veneration of the Virgin Mary. He also crafted the cross which was erected on the Grijalva River. He helped in the construction of all of the ships used once the expedition had landed in Mexico. He later settled in the city of Puebla, where he was considered one of the founders. He served on the town council as a judge and later received a permanent appointment as councilman.

Two of the carpenters went on to have very interesting careers following the conquest. Diego Ramírez (signature 182) had arrived in the Indies in 1502. In the conquest he helped to build the stockade which protected the city of Veracruz. Along with all the other carpenters, he worked on the brigantines used in the siege of Tenochtitlan. After the conquest he settled in Mexico City and became a businessman, active in the purchase and sale of both land and slaves, although he was illiterate. Martín Pérez was remembered as a good carpenter who worked on the brigantines. He settled in Mexico City, but was part-owner or manager of the most famous inn of the period, the one at Perote on the Veracruz-to-Mexico royal road. This inn was located at the point where the road climbed from the tropical lowlands to the temperate zone. It was a very important way station on the route.

BLACKSMITHS

After carpenters, the next-most essential men for both sailing ships and military expeditions were blacksmiths. These men were in charge of the repair of all the important metal equipment both at sea and on land. Because they worked with their hands they too lacked high social status. Nevertheless, they were essential for the success of the expedition.

While Díaz del Castillo could only remember three,[20] five men who signed the Veracruz petition can be tentatively identified as blacksmiths. They include Francisco Donal/Donaire (signature 121), Hernán Martín Herrero (signature 129), one of the men named Pedro Hernández (signature 157), Hernando Alonso (signature 174), and one of the men named Francisco Hernández (signature 145). One highly specialized type of blacksmith was the locksmith, of which the Cortés company included at least one: either of the two men named Pablo de Guzmán (signature 289). In addition to that skill, Guzmán also built several crossbows (*ballestas*) and repaired the numerous ones used by the company.

Of the blacksmiths, the best known was Hernán Martín. His second surname might simply be the indication of his occupation, since *herrero* means blacksmith. Martín was probably from Palos, on the south Andalucian coast near Huelva. He played a very important role in the conquest, since it was the blacksmiths who were in charge of removing the iron fittings from the ships when they were scuttled in Veracruz. While wooden timbers for new ships could always be fabricated from local wood, iron was very hard to come by and so everything made of iron was saved. He was second in command to Martín López in the building of the assault brigantines. After the conquest he settled in Mexico City and continued to work as a blacksmith, later expanding his practice to include other metals, including lead, silver, and gold.

WEAPONS MEN

Certain occupations were of particular utility only in time of war. Those men who were good with a crossbow, a harquebus, or artillery occupied an important place in the company. Traditional sources report that upon their arrival in Yucatan, several weeks before the signing of the Veracruz petition, there were thirty-two crossbowmen in the company. There were thirteen harquebusiers, and only fourteen pieces of artillery, four falconets, and ten brass cannon, not otherwise described.[21] Among the signatories of the Veracruz petition about whom we have biographical information, some seventeen served as crossbowmen (*ballestero*).

Signature 3	Alonso Hernández
Signature 22	Diego López de Guadalupe
Signature 27	
and signature 253	Pedro López [*one of several*]
Signature 48	Martín Vázquez
Signature 71	Juan López [*one of several*]
Signature 72	Diego de Peñalosa
Signature 77	
and signature 151	Miguel Navarro/de Navarra [*one of several*]
Signature 105	Pedro de Alanís
Signature 161	Sebastián Rodrigo/Rodríguez
Signature 166	Martín Díaz Peñalosa
Signature 173	Antón de Veintemilla
Signature 179	Lorenzo Xuárez
Signature 180	Cristóbal Díaz
Signature 198	Juan Sánchez Galindo
Signature 208	Juan Castaño
Signature 219	Miguel de Losa
Signature 250	Pedro Vizcaíno

This group of men differs slightly from the carpenters and blacksmiths. Their surnames are generally more complex, indicating slightly higher social status. At least four were undoubtedly considered foreigners. Antón de Veintemilla (signature 173) was from the Genoa area of Italy. He arrived in Cuba in 1518 and then joined the Cortés company. He probably had experience serving in one of the European armies of the era before sailing to the New World. After the conquest of Tenochtitlan he continued to serve in later expeditions, including one to Michoacan and Guatemala, where he eventually settled. Lorenzo Xuárez (signature 179), mentioned earlier as a man who arrived in the Indies already mature, was a Portuguese from the city of Évora. Juan Castaño (signature 208) was probably from Portugal. He appears several times in accounts of the conquest. During the Noche Triste he incorrectly announced the death of Cortés to members of the rear guard. In the factional disputes following the conquest, he remained loyal to Cortés and when enemies of the conqueror gained power, he was stripped of his *encomienda*. One of the other foreigners was Sebastián Rodrigo/Rodríguez (signature 161). There were two conquerors by this name. One of them was from Oliveira, Portugal, and served as a crossbowman both in the conquest of Mexico and in the later expedition to Honduras. Following the conquest he settled in Mexico City in 1533, but the following year moved to Puebla. In Puebla he eventually became a town councilman. He owned land in and around Atlixco, which was a very productive agricultural area southwest of Puebla developed shortly after the conquest. Rodríguez actively bought and sold land in and around Puebla. He also received two villages in *encomienda*, Chocaman and Tozongo. Another two men among the crossbowmen were non-Castilians: Miguel Navarro/de Navarra (signatures 77 and 151) and Pedro Vizcaíno (signature 250).

Taken as a whole, then, the places of origin of the crossbowmen are at odds with what we would expect for the company as a whole. Of the seventeen men identified as crossbowmen, four unquestionably come from outside of the territory considered Spanish and another two come from outside the kingdoms of Castile and Aragón. In short, as few as a quarter of the crossbowmen were foreigners, depending on the definition of "foreign," and as many as a third. This might reflect the fact that warfare was common in Europe at the time and that men who were skilled with the crossbow were highly sought-after. Similarly, skill with a crossbow might enable a man to more easily succeed in the rough-and-tumble world of the expeditions of discovery and conquest.

Men with experience with guns (harquebuses) and artillery were far less common. Only four men are mentioned as having these skills: Juan Catalán (signature 61), Juan González de Heredia (signature 222), Francisco de Horozco (signature 240), Juan Ceciliano (signature 256). The pattern established among the crossbowmen is repeated with the artillerymen. Two of the four were from outside of the Castilian core regions. Catalán, one assumes, was from the province of Catalunya in Aragón, while González Heredia was a Biscayan. Juan Ceciliano, as his name indicates, was from Sicily. For his part, Orozco had seen service in various Italian campaigns and was a war-hardened veteran prior to his arrival in the New World. Somewhere in his adventures he had picked up syphilis, or some other disease characterized by red and swollen lymph nodes (*bubas*). He sailed to the Indies in about 1513, eventually settling in Cuba. He joined the Cortés expedition and, because of his military experience, was made the captain of the artillery brigade. This was a very small unit, given that the company had only a few pieces. He was wounded during the Noche Triste, and stayed in Segura de la Frontera during the final siege of Tenochtitlan. During that episode, the artillery pieces were mounted to the brigantines so that they could function as floating gun platforms in the attack on the city. He was later one of the founders of the city of Oaxaca. Another important artilleryman was Gonzalo de Alvarado (signature A), the brother of Pedro de Alvarado. Gonzalo served as the captain of the artillery company on several occasions.

LOOKING AT THE MEMBERS OF THE PIZARRO EXPEDITION IN terms of the occupations and activities just studied, a very different picture emerges. Of the 168 members of that company, only two were men of the sea. Only two were gunners, and only two were carpenters.[22] It is evident that in creating his expedition to Peru Pizarro was extremely careful to have many different occupational specialties represented, but each with at most two practitioners. At the same time it is quite possible that among the 120 or so men of Cajamarca who were not listed as having a known or presumed occupation, many might have in fact been carpenters or smiths or pursued other occupations.

The expedition studied in the conquest of Panama more closely resembles the Cortés company. Of the eighty-four members for whom data are available, just over half (forty-four) had military or naval experience. About a third were farmers or artisans, while about 10 percent had some sort of profession or were from middle-ranking urban occupations (such as scribes, pharmacists, or physicians).[23]

HORSEMEN

Along with crossbows and guns, horses were some of the most important tools of warfare in the sixteenth century in Europe and unquestionably in Mexico, where the animal was simply unknown to the natives. The horsemen were among the socially most prominent members of the company; in the sixteenth century a gentleman (*caballero*) was defined by his ownership of a horse (*caballo*). Díaz del Castillo and others report that there were some sixteen horses in the expedition at the time it first landed in Yucatan.[24] That number seems to have diminished to fourteen by the time the expedition landed at Veracruz. Fourteen signatories of the Veracruz petition are identified as horsemen. This contrasts strongly with the experience of the Pizarro expedition. In the roll formed at Cajamarca, 62 of the 168 men of the company were listed as horsemen.[25]

Signature 18	Gonzalo Domínguez
Signature 48	Martín Vázquez
Signature 92	Francisco de Granada
Signature 93	Juan de Palacios
Signature 121	Francisco Donal/Donaire
Signature 122	Cristóbal Ortiz
Signature 125	Bernardino de Tapia
Signature 172	Santos Hernández
Signature 179	Lorenzo Xuárez
Signature 206	Bartolomé García
Signature 211	Hernán López Dávila
Signature 215	Pedro de Solís
Signature 247	Francisco Flores
Signature 267	Gonzalo de Sandoval

A glance at the list of horsemen indicates that they tended to cluster, perhaps keeping company with one another. Granada and Palacios signed together. Donaire, Ortiz, and Tapia all signed together. Hernández and Suárez signed near one another, as did López Dávila and Solís. It is also interesting that two of the men — Vázquez (signature 48) and Xuárez (signature 179) — listed as crossbowmen also appear among the horsemen, in spite of the different social status of these two groups. It is possible that not only were they crossbowmen but they owned the crossbow, a valuable implement of war. Similarly, not only were they horsemen, but they owned their horses.

It is possible that not all of these men actually owned horses, or even provided them for the company. But they were known for their skills as horsemen. In fact the group can be divided among those who either were reported as providing horses or who claimed to have provided them, and those merely known for their skills of horsemanship. Domínguez (signature 18) owned a very fast, good horse. Unfortunately, Domínguez was killed near Chimalhuacan Chalco when his horse misstepped during battle, fell, and crushed the conqueror. The horse provided by Donaire (signature 121) was called Motilla and described as a dark chestnut and a good runner. He was so famous that even the king of Spain had heard of him, according to Díaz del Castillo. Ortiz and García (signatures 122 and 206) were part-owners of what was generally considered to have been the best horse in the company. Cortés purchased it from them. Both Ortiz and García died in the conquest. Tapia (signature 125) was always recognized as one of the horsemen of the conquest, although Díaz del Castillo does not mention his horse. Pedro de Solís (signature 215) had an unfortunate accident: as the company returned to Tenochtitlan, after defeating Narváez, Solís was thrown by his horse into the water. This was taken as a bad omen by other members of the company. Solís was later sent by Cortés to the island of Jamaica to acquire more horses for the company.

Gonzalo de Sandoval (signature 267) was a well-known horseman whose physique derived from his many years in the saddle: he is described as not too tall, well proportioned, with a broad and high chest, a bit bow-legged, and a good horseman. His horse too was called Motilla, and was described as a chestnut with a white star on its forehead and a white left hoof. It is possible that Sandoval purchased Motilla from Donaire, since both horses called Motilla were dark chestnut in color.

Martín Vázquez (signature 48) is also frequently described as one of the horsemen of the conquest, and he also served as a crossbowman. Juan de Palacios (signature 93) was a horseman in the later expedition to Honduras. In that action his horse simply died, having expended all of its energy and burned up all of its body fat. Díaz del Castillo writes that Santos Hernández (signature 172) was a horseman who survived many of the principal battles and died a natural death. Several sources indicate that Hernán López Dávila (signature 211) was a horseman who provided his own horse for the company. He was considered one of the principal members of the company and took on many offices of trust and confidence both during the conquest and afterward.

Three men claim to have provided a horse in the conquest, but are not otherwise described as horsemen. Francisco de Granada (signature 92) asserted that he had lost a horse during the conquest and sought remuneration from the Crown. Lorenzo Xuárez (signature 179), seen before, also provided testimony to support his contention of having provided not just a horse but his own crossbow in the conquest. Francisco Flores (signature 247) was considered a member of the petty nobility by Díaz del Castillo. In Flores's petitions to the Crown, he claimed to be the last horseman to have left Tenochtitlan during the flight in the Noche Triste, and asserted that he was wounded in that action.

Nobility

Nobility was an important social distinction in early modern Spain. Nobles enjoyed privileges unknown to commoners: an exemption from many forms of taxation and an exemption from being imprisoned for debt were among the most important.

There were three levels to the Spanish nobility. "Nobility" in Spanish is *hidalguía*, derived from the word for nobleman, which is *hidalgo*. In turn, the word *hidalgo* is itself a contraction of the phrase *hijo de algo*, or "child of someone," indicating the person is of a known lineage. The highest level of nobility consisted of those persons who enjoyed the noble titles of "duke," "marquis," or "count." There were no titled nobles who participated in the Cortés expedition. The next level of nobility included those persons who were related to titled nobles but did not themselves possess a noble title, and other individuals who had been ennobled by the Crown. These individuals were distinguished through the consistent use of the honorific title "don" or "doña," in the case of a woman. There were no representatives of this noble group among the signatories of the Veracruz documents. The last group was made up of persons who enjoyed nobility, had been recognized as such by the Crown and royal courts, but could not use the honorific. This group is generally referred to as the petty nobility. There were several members of the petty nobility in the Cortés company, including Hernando Cortés himself.

Thirteen men can be identified as having some claim to nobility, although as will be seen some claims were very thin and most were circumstantial. The nobles would then represent only 4 percent of the total signatories. If we consider only those men about whom we have fairly solid information, essentially half the company, the percentage of nobles would then increase to about 8 percent.

Signature A	Gonzalo de Alvarado
Signature B	Alonso Hernández Portocarrero
Signature D	Pedro de Alvarado
Signature E	Alonso de Avila
Signature F	Alonso de Grado
Signature G	Cristóbal de Olid
Signature 83	Pedro Cornejo de Vitoria
Signature 146	Martín López
Signature 163	Pedro de Guzmán
Signature 195	Alonso de Monroy
Signature 228	Juan de Cárdenas
Signature 247	Francisco Flores
Signature 292	Juan Ochoa de Elejalde

In respect to the men in this group, nobility is ascribed because of their relationship to individuals of nobility. For example, both of the Alvarado brothers (signatures A and D) are sons of an officer in the military-religious Order of Santiago. In order to enter an order one needed to demonstrate the purity of one's lineage, and be generally recognized as noble. The orders had gained large tracts of land in the Iberian Peninsula during the Reconquest. In order to administer these estates, the orders named members to supervise them. These supervisors received the title of *comendador* and were usually among the leading members of the order. The Alvarado brothers' father was a *comendador*, and consequently one might assume that they would also be petty nobles. Similarly, Hernández Portocarrero's (signature B) father was a *comendador* and his mother a descendant of the counts of Medellín. He clearly had a claim to nobility. Avila (signature E) also came from a family in which the father was a *comendador*, in this case of the Order of Calatrava. Juan de Cárdenas (signature 228) also was descended from a *comendador*: the *comendador* mayor don Alonso de Cárdenas, of Santiago, according to Díaz del Castillo.

Three members of the company were generally reputed to be from the petty nobility. These were Martín López (signature 146), Pedro de Guzmán (signature 163), and Cristóbal de Olid (signature G). López was from a well-known and respected Seville family, the Osorios. Guzmán was held to be from the noble family of Guzmán from Toledo, and quite possibly a kinsman of the later judge and governor Nuño de Guzmán. Olid was born in Baeza, of an old Navarese family, and was considered by some to be of the petty nobility. Pedro Cornejo de Vitoria (signature 83) might have been a member of the petty nobility. Díaz del Castillo mentions a member of the company by the surname of Cortejo who was an *hidalgo*.

According to Spanish practice in the fifteenth and sixteenth centuries, any person born in the Basque provinces was considered a noble in the realms of Castile, because of their long and respected lineages. Juan Ochoa de Elejalde (signature 292), from the Basque country, was widely considered to be a noble person as a result of this heritage. As noted earlier, there were thirteen other members of the company from the Basque provinces who would have qualified for membership in the petty nobility. The case of Francisco Flores (signature 247) is more problematic. At one point Díaz del Castillo refers to him as a "noble person." Unfortunately, rather than being descriptive of his noble status, it probably merely refers to his generous character.

These numbers and percentages are roughly similar to what Grunberg found in his study of all conquerors of Mexico, in which he concluded that perhaps as many as 10 percent might be noble.[26] In his study of the Pizarro expedition, James Lockhart found a much higher percentage of nobles. Of the 168 men of Cajamarca, 38 were noble and another 6 were borderline cases.[27] This represents a significant difference in the social composition of the two expeditions. The men who participated in the conquest of Panama resembled the men of Veracruz far more closely than did the men of Cajamarca. In the Panamanian example, only 8 of the 84 members of the company could be ascribed to the nobility, even in a broad definition of the estate.[28]

After the Conquest

Those members of the company who survived the conquest then sought to establish themselves either in the newly conquered lands or back in Spain. Many of the men participated in one or more of the conquest expeditions which followed the fall of Tenochtitlan. Yet once those expeditions had concluded they tended to settle in one of the newly formed cities of the territory.

Information exists regarding the residency of about 102 of the men who signed the Veracruz petition. Considering that approximately half of the men did not survive, that is a relatively high number. Of those men, the overwhelming majority (63 individuals) settled in Mexico City at some point following the conquest. It was the third Spanish city established in what would soon be known as New Spain, after Veracruz and Segura de la Frontera-Tepeaca. Because Tenochtitlan was the old Aztec capital and still had over a million inhabitants within the larger valley, it quickly became the seat of power for the Spanish. Not all of the conquerors settled first in Mexico City, but at some point nearly two-thirds did reside there. Thirty-one of the men lived in more than one place following the conquest, approximately a third of the total.

Not all conquerors stayed in Mexico or even New Spain. One, Juan Bono de Quepo (signature 20), returned to Cuba. Spain was the destination for seven of the men, while Guatemala and Central America received ten of the conquerors, including Bernal Díaz del Castillo. Two went on to Peru: Pedro de Guzmán (signature 163) and Francisco Quintero (signature 254). In fact, Quintero holds the record for the most documented moves. After fighting in the conquests of Mexico, Pánuco, and Guatemala, he first settled in Mexico City, becoming a *vecino* in 1527. He then moved to Puebla after about five years. Nonetheless, by 1537 he was back in Mexico City. He then sailed to Peru around 1548.

Of the men who returned to Spain, two were pilots, who continued to engage in their trade: Antón de Alaminos (signature 243) and Luis de Cárdenas (signature 263). Several others returned to Spain to press various claims at court and simply did not return to Mexico for one reason or another. The return to Spain was fraught with difficulty and by no means always a pleasant experience. The most tragic of these cases was that of Gonzalo de Sandoval (signature 267). A well-known horseman and one of the captains of the expedition, following the conquest he returned to Spain with Cortés and another captain, Andrés de Tapia (not a signatory). Upon landing in Spain the three men split up, each to visit his own family and then, one assumes, to rejoin one another at court. Unfortunately Sandoval had become ill during the sea voyage to Spain. The group landed at Palos de la Frontera and Sandoval was lodged with a local rope maker, to allow him to recover from his illness. Within a matter of days the rope maker had absconded with several bars of gold Sandoval had brought back from the Indies. Soon after the conqueror died from his illness.[29]

Several conquerors manifested a certain wanderlust in the decades following the conquest. Bartolomé Sánchez began mining immediately after the conquest. In 1529 he formally became a *vecino* of Mexico City. But at some point he moved to Oaxaca, where he eventually was elected as a city councilman. In 1547 he began to petition the Crown for various privileges in recompense for his service in the conquest. One of these requests was granted in 1562, when the Crown recognized him with a coat of arms. Sánchez had also requested a seat on the Puebla city council, arguing that living in Oaxaca was deleterious to his health. By 1548 he had moved to Puebla, but does not seem to have gained the city council seat there he desired.

ENCOMIENDAS

The issue of how the members of the company were to be remunerated for their service plagued the expedition. The general expectation was that participants would receive profits from the expedition in direct proportion to their investment in it. It was a company, in which the members invested their efforts, talents, and materiel. In this manner men who provided a horse, crossbow, or gun might receive a greater portion than would a simple foot soldier. There was dissatisfaction over the practice of subtracting, before any portions were allotted, 20 percent of the total for the Crown, as the royal fifth. Cortés, as commander, received another fifth of the proceeds. Thus everyone else had to compete for the remaining 60 percent, with some receiving enhanced portions as noted. After the Noche Triste, when much of the booty was lost in the scramble to flee the city, the distributions became smaller and smaller, while the company grew larger with the addition of Narváez's men and other expeditions who joined along the way. The amount of booty was simply insufficient to cover the expenses of the expedition.

To resolve this dilemma, Cortés resorted to a practice which had begun in the Antilles but was not entirely supported by the Crown. This was the bestowing of the *encomienda*, whereby the tribute payments and labor obligations of a specific native population were diverted to a specific conqueror by way of pension. In fact one of the specific requests made by the members of the company in the petition to the monarchs analyzed here was to grant this specific power to Cortés: "that he can distribute its Indians perpetually." Under the Aztecs the natives also provided labor service to the state. As a result, they were required to provide labor to the Spaniards who received their tribute. In the same way that booty was distributed, when the districts of Mexico were divided up among the conquerors, approximately 20 percent were assigned to the king, as his fifth, while Cortés claimed another fifth for himself.

The institution of *encomienda* was at the center of the political maneuvering and factional disputes which overtook New Spain following the conquest. Not everyone who felt that they deserved a grant received one. While there was some partisan bickering in Mexico in opposition to Cortés, his presence quieted opposition significantly, but in 1524, when he led an expedition to Honduras, his absence from Mexico allowed his detractors and opponents to take advantage of the situation. Cortés had placed the reins of government in the hands of the royal treasurer, Alonso de Estrada, a man he trusted. Yet the factions became even more unruly and Estrada at last capitulated to Cortés's opponents, especially when word reached Mexico that the conqueror had been killed in Honduras. Estrada and those opposed to Cortés proceeded to revoke the *encomienda* grants to many of the conquerors, and then to give them to their own supporters. When Cortés returned from Honduras, very much alive, he then reversed the process, but on a selective basis. He also rescinded grants which he himself had made to those men who eventually became his enemies.

Cortés left New Spain in 1528 to seek a royal appointment as governor, a noble title, and other preferment from the Crown in return for his conquest of Mexico. In his place the Crown had sent out a group of judges to become the high royal tribunal (*audiencia*) for the territory. Unfortunately the judges were more concerned with gaining wealth for themselves. The leader of the court, Nuño de Guzmán, was an ally of various officials who opposed Cortés. As a result the court stripped many Cortés supporters of their *encomiendas* and in turn granted them to their own followers. Within two years, a new set of judges was appointed and many of the grants made by the first court were rescinded. Consequently, taken as a whole, the nine years between the fall of Tenochtitlan and 1530 saw a great deal of flux in the possession of *encomienda* grants.

A significant number of the surviving conquerors received *encomiendas*, but not every one of them. Of the 150 signatories or so who survived the conquest, 61 received grants of *encomienda*, about 40 percent. One assumes that these individuals played more important roles in the conquest than their colleagues who did not receive such recompense. Yet because of the troubled history following the conquest, the reality of the situation was that receiving and successfully keeping an *encomienda* was more like winning the lottery: much depended on chance.

THE *Members* OF THE *Company*

An example of a conqueror who lost and then gained an *encomienda* is Rodrigo de Castañeda (signature 91). Castañeda was a very colorful member of the company. He was one of the few conquerors who earnestly tried to learn the dominant native language, Nahuatl. He also dressed in a flamboyant manner, frequently wearing a hat decorated with a feather cockade. He was no shrinking violet, but was also a fierce warrior in the field. As a result of his fine dress and fierce demeanor the native allies from Tlaxcala gave him the nickname of "Xicotencatl," the name of one of their historic leaders who was known for his finery but also for prowess in war. During the conquest Castañeda became a close ally and captain under Pedro de Alvarado. When Cortés and Alvarado later had a falling out, this colored Castañeda's relationship with Cortés. Nevertheless, Cortés did grant Castañeda an *encomienda* in the first set of grants to be issued. In the time of turmoil, Castañeda lost his grant, and began to support himself as an interpreter for the royal court. He was also appointed to serve as a local magistrate in several districts. In 1527 the Crown awarded him a coat of arms for his exemplary service in the conquest. Finally, sometime after 1530 the Second Audiencia awarded him an *encomienda*, the village of Puctla, far to the east and south of Mexico City, in further recognition of his service.

Martín Vázquez (signature 48) was already fairly wealthy when he arrived in the Indies early in the sixteenth century. Originally from the village of Martín Muñoz in Segovia, although some folks thought that he was from Olmedo, Vázquez participated in the conquest and settlement of Panama (Tierra Firme) under Pedrarias Dávila. He then went to Cuba, where he married a woman who was rumored to be a native and had three children with her. He eventually joined the expedition of Hernández de Córdoba to Mexico. Later, he provided his own horse and crossbow in the Cortés expedition. During the conquest he reportedly was one of the men chosen to guard Moteuczoma during the ruler's captivity. He testified that he had been wounded several times in battle. After the conquest, he settled in Mexico, and received the villages of Xilocingo, Chicuautla, and Mixtepec in *encomienda*. These were taken from him during the rule of the First Audiencia. A few years later he was granted the village of Tlaxiaco in recompense. He was an active businessman and gold prospector after the conquest. Some people complained that he ran an illegal gambling establishment out of his home in Mexico.

In order to better divide the villages among the conquerors, it was sometimes necessary to assign half of a village to one man and the other half to another. It was also not uncommon for relatives to share a grant. The village of Atlatlauca, to the south and east of Mexico, in north central Oaxaca, was split between the Crown and a conqueror. Juan de Mancilla (signature 274) received that half-village along with Tetela del Río, north and west of Mexico City.[30]

He was wounded during the Noche Triste. He was chosen to serve as captain of one of the brigantines used during the siege of Tenochtitlan and claimed to have captured the king of Texcoco, Cacamatzin. He later participated in expeditions of Sandoval and Alvarado to the south. He settled in Mexico City in 1525 and became an outspoken critic of Cortés, even accused of painting slanderous statements on the conqueror's home at night. When the confrontation heated up, Mancilla sought refuge in the Franciscan monastery. He served for a while as city councilman in Mexico, but renounced his seat in favor of another conqueror, Francisco de Terrazas (signature 165). Mancilla then sold his rights in the *encomienda* of half of Atlatlauca and Tetela and returned to Spain.

The Monjaraz brothers, Andrés and Gregorio (signatures 230 and 233), shared the *encomienda* of Coatlan in recognition of their service in the conquest. They had joined the Cortés company along with their uncle, also called Andrés. The younger Andrés had a story much like that of Vázquez. He was a strong supporter of Cortés who later joined the Alvarado expedition to Guatemala, serving as a captain in that company. Upon his return to Mexico he became one of the men opposed to Cortés. He settled in Tlaxcala for a time, but eventually moved to Mexico City. He invested in various mining endeavors. By 1528 he was being identified as one of Cortés's main enemies. During the time of turmoil he and his brother lost their *encomienda*. Nevertheless, later they were granted the villages of Jaso and Teremendo in the province of Michoacan, to the west of Mexico City.

In general, large, well-populated villages closer to the main Spanish cities of Puebla or Mexico were greatly preferred over small, isolated villages, because the *encomendero*, the man who held the grant, was responsible for receiving the tribute and was expected to live somewhere near the granted villages. Yet some men who received prime grants still preferred to abandon them and return to Spain. Cristóbal Corral (signature 307) received the large village of Cuauhtitlan, located just a few leagues to the northwest of Mexico City. Corral had served as the standard-bearer, *alférez*, for the company. This was a highly prestigious office in the expedition. At one point, he was wounded in battle and fell while trying to keep the banner aloft. As natives moved in to kill him, he fought them off with his dagger. Corral was eventually rescued by his fellows. He became one of the city councilmen in Segura de la Frontera. In spite of receiving a very lucrative village in *encomienda* he decided to return to Spain.

The requirement that *encomenderos* live near the villages of their grants played itself out among the conquerors as they began to settle in Spanish towns and cities. Juan Pedro (Rodríguez) de Villafuerte (signature 304) was a close supporter of Cortés and had served in various leadership roles during the conquest. He helped in the supervision of the construction of the brigantines and was appointed captain of the fleet by Cortés. Unfortunately, on the first day out he almost lost his ship, and so was replaced in command by Martín López. After Tenochtitlan fell, Cortés placed Villafuerte in charge of the garrison there while the main body of the army completed the pacification of the other cities in the valley. At the command of Cortés, Villafuerte established the shrine to Nuestra Señora de los Remedios, Cortés's patron and the image emblazoned on the banner they carried into battle. Villafuerte also participated in the conquests of the west, in Michoacan and Zacatula. He married the granddaughter of Cacamatzin, last king of Texcoco. When his first wife died, Villafuerte married Juana de Zúñiga, a kinswoman of Cortés's first wife. Villafuerte settled in Zacatula in about 1525. Cortés granted him several villages on the south coast, located within the general district he had helped to conquer and where he had taken up residence.

Another important participant in the conquest who received several small villages in a more out-of-the-way region was Francisco de Lugo (signature 272). Díaz del Castillo mentions him numerous times in his account of the conquest. Lugo was the illegitimate son of the lord of several towns near Medina del Campo. Lugo was one of the few conquerors who brought along a war dog, something which greatly terrorized the natives. He was part of the company that attacked Narváez and later served as one of the captains of the foreguard on the Noche Triste. He was a captain in expeditions to Coatzacoalcos with Sandoval and Michoacan with Olid. He received a handful of small villages in the Coatzacoalcos region as his *encomienda*. Lugo then sailed to Spain, where he served as an agent at court for many other conquerors. Upon his return, he became a citizen (*vecino*) of Veracruz. What these grants to Villafuerte and Vázquez have in common is that the men received villages in regions in which they had provided leadership in the particular conquest: of the west for Villafuerte, and Coatzacoalcos for Lugo.

Most of the men who signed the Veracruz petition, who served throughout the conquest, and who remained in New Spain did not receive *encomiendas*. Cortés's footman, Domingo Martín (signature 40) had significant experience in the conquest. Originally from Brozas, in Cáceres, he had sailed with Grijalva, and then joined Cortés's household. During the conquest he also served as a minor commander under Bernaldino Vázquez de Tapia (signature 125). After the conquest, Martín became a *vecino* of Mexico City. He married a Spanish woman who lived next door to him. He did not receive an *encomienda*. As a result he was appointed to serve as a local magistrate in districts which were assigned to the Crown. Rules prohibited *encomenderos* from serving as local magistrates. Eventually Martín also received a pension from the king, an annual stipend paid by the royal treasury in Mexico. Unfortunately these were notoriously difficult to collect, since the value of the grants authorized greatly exceeded the resources available.

One of the highest forms of recognition a conqueror could receive was a noble coat of arms from the Crown. This was an important manifestation of nobility. It signaled the singular acts of the recipient and paved the way for seeking higher honors, including titles of nobility. Eight men who signed the Veracruz petition received coats of arms.

Signature C	Francisco de Montejo
Signature D	Pedro de Alvarado
Signature 47	Francisco Maldonado
Signature 88	Alvaro Gallego
Signature 91	Rodrigo de Castañeda
Signature 92	Francisco de Granada
Signature 146	Martín López
Signature 207	Bartolomé Sánchez
Signature 292	Juan Ochoa de Elejalde

Alvarado and Montejo are perhaps the most famous of this group, because each went on to lead a successful conquest of his own. After the fall of Tenochtitlan, Alvarado headed the expedition to Guatemala, for which he received his coat of arms. Similarly, Montejo eventually led the conquest of Yucatan. In recognition of his service both in the conquest of Mexico and in Yucatan, the Crown awarded Montejo a coat of arms, which was then carved into the façade of his palace in Mérida (see fig. 6.13).

Francisco Maldonado was another one of the more colorful members of the expedition. Díaz del Castillo reports that he had the nickname "the wide," perhaps because of an ample figure. His father, Alvaro Maldonado, also fought in the conquest and had the nickname of "the wild beast." Francisco served as a captain in a later expedition to the region of the Zapotecs. He was rewarded for his service in the conquest with an *encomienda*: the villages of Chachiutla, Chicoma, Aguatepec, Mistla, and Tecomastlahuaca, in the region of Oaxaca. He was awarded a coat of arms in 1538 in recognition of his service in the conquest (fig. 6.14).

Surprisingly, the signatures of three of the men who received noble crests appear essentially side by side on the Veracruz petition (folio 5, recto). Gallego, Castañeda, and Granada signed with one another and all eventually received coats of arms. Gallego received his heraldic device in 1529 for exceptional bravery in taking the main temple in Tenochtitlan (fig. 6.15). Castañeda, discussed above, called Xicotencatl by the natives, was credited for singular bravery throughout the conquest, receiving his coat of arms in 1527 (fig. 6.16). Gra-

FIGURE 6.13
*Coat of arms of Francisco de Montejo, façade of the Montejo house,
Mérida, Yucatan. Photo by John F. Schwaller.*

FIGURE 6.14
*Coat of arms of Francisco Maldonado.
Drawn by Danielle Weires.*

FIGURE 6.15
Coat of arms of Alvaro Gallego.
Drawn by Danielle Weires.

FIGURE 6.16
Coat of arms of Rodrigo de Castañeda.
Drawn by Danielle Weires.

nada distinguished himself in battle, provided a horse to the company, and was shot in the face with an arrow during the Noche Triste. The Crown awarded his decoration in 1532 (fig. 6.17).

As we saw earlier, López was responsible for the naval siege which brought an end to the conquest (fig. 6.18). Bartolomé Sánchez received his coat of arms in 1562, after a career in New Spain living in Oaxaca and Puebla and working as a miner (fig. 6.19).

Juan Ochoa de Elejalde (fig. 6.20), a prominent member of the company, came from Guipuzcoa and thus was considered noble, *hidalgo*. Arriving in Santo Domingo in 1508, he fought in conquests on Puerto Rico and Cuba before joining the Cortés company. During the conquest he served as the judicial officer appointed by Cortés, a type of sheriff. He was charged with reading all of the documents captured when Narváez was defeated. He also served as the person to whom the estates of men who died in the conquest were entrusted until they could be delivered to the proper heirs, the *tenedor de bienes de difuntos*. He served as a royal scribe on the expedition to Tehuantepec. After the conquest he returned to Cuba and was a witness to the testament of Diego Velázquez. He returned to Mexico and received a large *encomienda*. After settling

FIGURE 6.17
Coat of arms of Francisco de Granada.
Drawn by Danielle Weires.

FIGURE 6.18
Coat of arms of Martín López.
Drawn by Danielle Weires.

FIGURE 6.19
Coat of arms of Bartolomé Sánchez.
Drawn by Danielle Weires.

FIGURE 6.20
Coat of arms of Juan Ochoa de Elejalde.
With permission of the Gilcrease Museum, Tulsa, OK.

in Mexico City in about 1524 he took on additional responsibilities, including serving as an agent before the royal court and before the Holy Office of the Inquisition. He eventually moved to Puebla and acquired land in the region. He served in a series of offices for the city council, ending with an appointment as city councilman. In 1546 he was granted a coat of arms in recognition for his singular services to the Crown.[31]

A close comparison of the individuals whose signatures appear on the Veracruz petition with other primary documents of the conquest and studies carried out over the ensuing years indicates that many people who in all likelihood were present in Veracruz on June 20, 1519, did not sign the petition.

By far the leading person absent from the document is Hernán Cortés himself. One must remember that the petition is from the town council of Veracruz. Strictly speaking, Cortés was not a member of the council. The council members selected him to serve as governor for the province. The petition was written with an eye to securing royal recognition of the town, validating the selection of Cortés as governor, and quashing any claims Velázquez might have over the area. Cortés was not an active agent in these deliberations. The town selected him and empowered him. Consequently, for the purposes of the petition, there really was no reason for Cortés to sign. This was especially true in light of the fact that the conquerors, and Cortés, were pursuing a fiction that the company sought recognition independent of their leader, and that the members of the company were not directly parties to the spat between Cortés and Velázquez.

An important feature of the New Conquest History focuses on restoring ignored participants to the story of the conquest. Two groups in particular are absent from the Veracruz petition: women and natives. It is clear that several Spanish women accompanied the Cortés company: accompanying spouses, as domestic servants, or merely as unsung members of the expedition. Yet no women are represented on the Veracruz petition. Perhaps the central reason for this was that they were not considered to be members of the company. Although they were part of the expedition, their investment in the company was not considered, at the time, to be on a par with that of the men, who were expected to bear the brunt of the fighting, should it come to that. One woman whose husband signed the petition was Isabel Rodríguez. Her husband was Sebastián Rodríguez (signature 161). Among other services she rendered to the expedition, she acted as a nurse in caring for the wounded. Other sources suggest that she was a servant in the household of Diego Colón in Santo Domingo prior to the Cortés expedition. She had several marriages, the last of which was to Rodríguez.[32]

The next group of persons obviously absent is the native auxiliaries who assisted the company. Admittedly, at the time of the Veracruz petition the Spanish had acquired very few native allies, but there were some. The most important at this point in the conquest were native women in general and even more specifically doña Marina, also known as La Malinche. Her absence from the signatures is no surprise, given that at this time she was not literate in Spanish, and had been a member of the expedition for only a few weeks. Her role would prove decisive but, like the other women, she was not considered a member of the company (that is, an investor) to the degree that Spanish men had invested themselves. While there were other native women who accompanied the expedition at this point, most remain anonymous to the historical record. There simply is little documentation regarding either native men or native women who served with the company. Clearly the natives were not considered members of the company but rather more like spoils of war.

The last group of "missing persons" includes individuals generally accepted as having been present for the events at Veracruz, but whose names do not appear on the list of signatories. On the surface their absence can be easily explained by the fact that the document is damaged and as many as one-third of the names might have been lost. Several scholars have estimated that the company could have included as many as six hundred persons, although five hundred seems to be more generally accepted. This would mean either that as many as two hundred signatures were lost, or that many members did not sign the petition.

One can identify some forty men who do not appear on the Veracruz petition but can be determined through a variety of sources to have been present. They fall into several general groups: men who were personal servants of Cortés; men who served in positions of authority, such as ship captain or captains of brigades in the company; and individuals closely allied to or associated with Diego Velázquez, the governor of Cuba against whom the company was acting. Members of the group of Cortés's servants include Diego de Coria, his page; a man named Guzmán (either Esteban, Juan, or Cristóbal, depending on the source) who was a steward; Cristóbal Martín Millán de Gamboa, his groom; Juan Ortega/Orteguilla, a page; Rodrigo Rangel, another steward; and Antonio de Villaroel/Villareal, his standard-bearer. Several of these individuals went on to play important roles in the conquest, and in the life of the colony after the fall of Tenochtitlan.

Diego de Coria served as a page to Cortés during the conquest. He remembered that after the departure of the fleet from Cuba, Cortés spent eight days writing letters, probably to garner support for the expedition. He was one of the men who stayed in Tenochtitlan while Cortés returned to the coast to confront Narváez. After the conquest he settled in Mexico City, where he served a variety of posts, including a stint as tithe collector for the Church. On several instances he served as a witness in testimony taken for other conquerors. He served in several later conquests, most notably in Jalisco in the 1540s. For his service, he was rewarded with an *encomienda* in Oaxaca, which was taken away from him when Cortés fell out of favor. He complained of great poverty in the 1550s, having married twice and needing to support four sons and two daughters. Finally, the second viceroy, don Luis de Velasco, awarded him a post as local magistrate.[33] The wealth of information about him places him in Vera-cruz at the time of the petition.

Another member of Cortés's household whose name does not appear on the Veracruz petition is Antonio de Villaroel/Villareal, his *alférez*, or standard-bearer. He held this title thanks to an appointment by Diego Velázquez, who had made him standard-bearer for the expedition. He later indicated that he also provided some of the horses used in the campaign. He served as the field marshal for the conquest of the western part of New Spain under the leadership of Nuño de Guzmán, in a campaign known for its brutality. Villaroel received several villages in *encomienda* in recognition of his service, including Guauchi-nango and Cuernavaca. Unfortunately he lost the latter to Cortés when he got embroiled in a conflict with the captain. Villaroel became an implacable foe of Cortés. Eventually Cortés was granted the noble title of Marqués del Valle, which included Cuernavaca as part of his seigniorial state. In spite of having lost the town in *encomienda*, Villaroel kept at least one sugar mill in the region, although he failed to turn it into a money-making proposition. Villaroel served as a witness for several of his comrades in arms when they sought preferment from the Crown. He was active in the government of Mexico City, first as sher-iff and then holding one of the city council seats. In 1525 he traveled to Spain as an agent of the city council, and also sought recognition from the Crown for his own exploits in the conquest. In so doing he changed his name from Villaroel to Serrano de Cardona and received an appointment as a city council member. He died in 1545.[34] Villaroel was involved in several lawsuits, either as defendant or as accuser. The available documentation indicates that Villaroel would have been in Veracruz to sign the petition.

The second group of men present but not appearing includes some of the ship captains and military commanders, such as Juan Bautista, Juan Gutiérrez de Escalante, Francisco de Mesa, Francisco Morla, Diego de Ordaz, Francisco Orozco, Andrés de Tapia, and Juan Velázquez de León. At the same time, there were other ship and company captains who did sign, such as Juan Rodríguez de Villafuerte, seen earlier. Of this group of men absent from the petition, both Diego de Ordaz and Andrés de Tapia were perhaps the most important and famous within the expedition.

Diego de Ordaz arrived in the New World in about 1510 and participated in expeditions to Panama before becoming a conqueror of Cuba. He served Diego Velázquez as his chamberlain. When Velázquez began organizing the Cortés expedition, he appointed Ordaz one of the ship captains under Cortés, in order to have a large number of allies in positions of power. When events began to unfold at Veracruz, Cortés arrested Ordaz and charged him with treason for having supported Velázquez. Nonetheless, Cortés relented and had him freed. In letters written after the conquest, Ordaz commented that Cortés had as much of a conscience as a dog.[35] Díaz del Castillo remembers Ordaz as having been around forty years old, of good height, a good man with a sword, not a horseman, with a full face and a thin dark beard. He spoke with a little bit of a stutter, which plagued him in pronouncing some words.[36] After the events at Veracruz, Ordaz became a strong supporter and ally of Cortés. He was one of the men who climbed the Popocatepetl volcano in order to get a better view of Tenochtitlan. When he finally received a coat of arms from the Crown for his service in the conquest, it was adorned with a picture of the volcano. Although he survived the Noche Triste, he was badly wounded, losing a finger and being injured in three places. Diego Velázquez confiscated his *encomiendas* and other possessions back in Cuba for his treason. Cortés then sent Ordaz to Spain to continue to lobby the Crown for recognition of the expedition. He received several important perquisites from the Crown, including his coat of arms, membership in the military-religious Order of Santiago, and positions on the city council of Tepeaca. He also received several towns in *encomienda* in New Spain. Upon his return to New Spain, Ordaz served for a period in 1525 as the royal magistrate for Mexico City, and then in 1528 he became one of the city council members, a post he held until 1530. In that year he received a royal grant to carry out the conquest of Marañón, in northeastern South America. He died on the return voyage from his unsuccessful conquest attempt.[37] His absence from the list of signatories at Veracruz can well be ascribed to his having been imprisoned by Cortés at just that time.

Andrés de Tapia was another important figure in the conquest, and one of the leading captains of the Cortés expedition. He was a relative latecomer to the expedition. He had served in the household of Diego Colón in Seville and only arrived in Cuba in 1518, possibly to be a member of Velázquez's household, to whom he was related by marriage, although he also later reported that he had known Cortés's family back in Medellín in Spain. Velázquez assigned him to the expedition. Tapia arrived in Santiago after Cortés had set sail, but caught up a little later. He gave an eyewitness account of his adventures in the conquest in a *relación* written in 1539.[38] In his account, Tapia described the Veracruz petition and went on to note that "It was signed by almost all the marqués' [Cortés's] company . . ."[39] Tapia's signature, however, is itself absent from the document.

Tapia remembered the events at Cholula, where the Spanish fought off an attempt to stop their progress. He also described encounters with Moteuczoma and the palace where he lived. Tapia claimed to have participated in the destruction of a native temple, throwing down the idols. This became a singular event in his participation in the conquest. Tapia was one of the leaders of the expedition against Narváez. Reportedly he disguised himself as a native in order to infiltrate the opponents' camp. Following the rout of Narváez, Cortés sent Tapia immediately back to Tenochtitlan with the news. He survived the subsequent Noche Triste and documented the loss of treasure in the flight from Tenochtitlan, mentioning that they considered using gold and silver in their cannons for lack of cannonballs. He was present at the fall of Tenochtitlan, and accompanied Cortés on several later expeditions, also describing the death by torture of the last Aztec emperor, Cuauhtémoc. Tapia received the large city of Cholula in *encomienda*, but Cortés took it away and granted him instead a collection of villages in the Pánuco region.

Following the conquest, Tapia became a sheriff in Mexico City, and later one of the city council members. He returned to Spain in 1528, along with Cortés, but immediately came back to New Spain. The Crown appointed him accountant and justice for the royal treasury in Mexico. He was a frequent witness in the testimony given by his comrades in arms after the conquest. He was one of the most widely respected of the conquerors, although he did not become as fabulously wealthy as some. He died in about 1560.[40] The absence of Tapia from among the signatories of the Veracruz petition is a mystery, unless his was one of the signatures lost when the document was damaged.

Those conquerors whose names do not appear on the Veracruz petition and were closely tied to Velázquez include Francisco Cervantes, Juan Escudero, Francisco de Morla, Pedro Morón, Diego de Ordaz (discussed above), and Gonzalo de Umbría. Both Morla and Ordaz were commanders in the company and close allies of Velázquez. Several of these men, including Ordaz, were implicated in the attempted revolt in the spring of 1519, which prompted the creation of the villa of Veracruz. For example, Juan Escudero was hanged for his participation in the conspiracy, having attempted to commandeer a brigantine to return to Cuba. Escudero was a close ally of Velázquez who had been a sheriff back in Cuba. In 1515 he had even arrested Cortés in the course of his duties.[41] Francisco de Morla was a steward in the Velázquez household and became one of the ship captains of the Cortés expedition. He too was arrested along with other Velázquez supporters in Veracruz, but gained his freedom and later became a staunch supporter of Cortés. Morla was a horseman, with a gray mount. Some have posited that the reputed vision of Saint James riding into battle to aid the Spaniards was in fact Morla on his gray. Morla died during one of the battles in the conquest, although sources disagree on which.[42] Given that many of the Velázquez supporters were imprisoned during the creation of the town of Veracruz, it is understandable that they either could not or would not sign the petition to the Crown.

The remaining men known to have participated are a mixed group. Some, like Gerónimo de Aguilar, joined the expedition under unique circumstances, having been rescued from Maya Indians, and going on to serve as a translator for the expedition.[43] Juan Jaramillo was an important member of the company, and married doña Marina sometime after the conquest. Jaramillo served in the expedition in a variety of ways, including as head of the rear guard on the way into Tenochtitlan. In testimony outlining his services, he described the manner in which Moteuczoma was held captive. Jaramillo went with Cortés in the encounter against Narváez, and then later participated in the rear-guard action during the Noche Triste. Following the conquest he remained in New Spain, receiving the wealthy province of Jilotepec in *encomienda*. Jaramillo served both as a municipal judge and as a city councilman in Mexico City. He joined Cortés on the Honduras expedition. Upon their return, Jaramillo married doña Marina, with whom he had a daughter. After the death of doña Marina, he married doña Beatriz de Andrade, the daughter of one of his comrades in arms from the conquest, the *comendador* Leonel de Cervantes.[44] There is no clear explanation for his absence from among the signatories.

Juan Garrido, who was an African, joined the expedition after a long series of adventures.[45] Pedro Garao Valenciano was known as the cardsharp of the group. He had the dubious honor of having made the first deck of cards in New Spain, which he crafted from the skins taken from a native drum.[46] Finally, several sets of relatives are missing: Jorge and Gómez de Alvarado, brothers of the captain Pedro and Gonzalo de Alvarado; Rodrigo Alvarez Chico's brother, Juan; and Antonio Pinto and his nephew Nuño Pinto. It is not at all clear why some of these family members' signatures appear and others do not.

Looking broadly at the men known to be present for the creation of Veracruz but whose signatures are absent from the document, we can draw a few tentative conclusions. Several of the men probably were not, strictly speaking, members of the company. For example, Gerónimo de Aguilar was rescued by the company long after it had departed Cuba. The ship captains, while important, had not signed on for a land expedition and probably believed that they would be sailing back to Cuba. The supporters of Diego Velázquez either refused to sign, for fear of angering their patron, or were unable to sign because they were under arrest at that moment, precisely for having opposed the founding of the town and the concomitant rejection of Velázquez. Yet these considerations do not explain why many men who we know were present at the time the document was signed fail to appear. The remaining explanation would be that they in fact signed, but their signatures were lost when the document was damaged.

As has been noted several times, the paucity of information regarding so many of the signatories must cause one to be especially cautious about grand conclusions. Many of the identifications of the men have been made on the basis of very thin evidence. Nonetheless, one can attempt to better understand the group of men who served with Cortés at this crucial moment in the conquest of Mexico.

The composition of the Cortés company did not differ significantly from other expeditions. It fairly closely mirrors what Grunberg discovered in his general survey. It does not differ dramatically from the findings of James Lockhart in his analysis of the men of Cajamarca, or of similar studies for Panama, New Granada, and Chile. Nevertheless, there are differences. In the Cortés company many more men are identified as having an occupation, from sailors and pilots, to carpenters and harquebusiers. The Cortés and Pizarro companies reflected the same regional origins of their members, who were overwhelmingly from Castile, Extremadura, and Andalucía, with only small contingents from the eastern kingdoms and provinces of the Iberian Peninsula, plus a smattering of true foreigners. Proportionally more men from Extremadura accompanied Pizarro than in the other expeditions. The percentage of nobles in the Pizarro company also is nearly twice as high as the Cortés company. Perhaps reflecting this, there were far more horsemen in the Pizarro company than the Cortés company.

Scholarship on Panama, New Granada, and Chile tends to reinforce the general picture of the conquering groups. The regional origins of the men at Veracruz were far more like those of the cohort which accompanied Valdivia to Chile than any other company of conquerors. A few more of Cortés's men came from Andalucía, and a few less from the Basque region, than their Chilean counterparts. All of the conquering bands consisted largely of young men. The age cohort between 20 and 29 at the time of their expedition reflected the plurality of all conquistadores. The Mexican expedition seemed to be one of the most costly in terms of lives. Only half of the men who signed the Veracruz petition lived to see the fall of Tenochtitlan. In Peru more men died in fighting among the bands of conquerors than did fighting in the conquest.[47] The conquerors of New Granada exceeded even the impressive longevity achieved by the men of Cajamarca. In New Granada fully half of the men lived nearly thirty years after the initiation of hostilities.[48]

This analysis of the makeup of the Cortés company has shed additional light on the nature of the expeditions which played an important role in the imposition of Spanish culture on wide swaths of Latin America. Without a defining moment and the appropriate documentation to illuminate that moment, it has been very difficult to know precisely what the composition of the expedition organized by Cortés looked like. The addition of the Veracruz petition to the corpus of documents has helped to shed more light on the nature of the expedition and the impact of the conquest on the Spaniards themselves.

CHAPTER 7
Biographies OF THE Signatories OF THE Veracruz Petition

Abbreviations

Alvarez   Victor M. Alvarez, *Diccionario de conquistadores*, 2 vols. (Mexico: INAH, 1975).

BB   Peter Boyd-Bowman, *Indice geobiográfico de cuarenta mil pobladores españoles de América en el siglo XVI, 1: 1493–1519* (Bogota: Instituto Caro y Cuervo, 1964).

Cortés   Hernán Cortés, *Cartas y documentos* (Mexico: Porrúa, 1963).

DdelC   Bernal Díaz del Castillo, *Historia verdadera de la conquista de la Nueva España*, 2 vols., 7th ed. (Mexico: Porrúa, 1977).

Dor   Baltasar Dorantes de Carranza, *Sumaria relación de las cosas de la Nueva España* (Mexico: Porrúa, 1987). Includes "Conquistadores de México" by Manuel Orozco y Berra, 279–419. The signatories to the 1520 Segura de la Frontera letter are included on 337–351; a list of these is reproduced in our appendix.

G   Bernard Grunberg, *Dictionnaire des conquistadores de Mexico* (Paris: L'Harmattan, 2001).

Himmerich   Robert Himmerich y Valencia, *The Encomenderos of New Spain, 1521–1555* (Austin: University of Texas Press, 1991).

HT   Hugh Thomas, *Who's Who of the Conquistadors* (London: Cassell, 2000).

Icaza   Francisco de Icaza, *Diccionario de conquistadores de la Nueva España*, 2 vols. (Madrid: Imprenta "El adelantado de Segovia," 1923).

Thomas   Hugh Thomas, *Conquest: Montezuma, Cortés, and the Fall of Old Mexico* (New York: Simon and Schuster, 1993).

Villar   Ignacio de Villar Villamil, *Cedulario heráldico de conquistadores de Nueva España* (Mexico: Museo Nacional, 1933).

JOHN F. SCHWALLER

A. *Gonzalo de Alvarado*. Gonzalo was one of the four Alvarado brothers who served in the conquest of Mexico, the most famous of which was Pedro (see signature D). The brothers were originally from Badajoz. Gonzalo arrived in the New World in 1510, landing in Santo Domingo. He had moved on to Cuba by 1517, settling in the town of Trinidad. He was elected one of the town councilmen (*regidor*) of Veracruz. He might have signed the 1520 Segura de la Frontera letter, since there is an incomplete name which might well be his. He served as a company captain, generally of the artillery, on various occasions during the conquest. He served as Cortés's representative in Veracruz in 1521, but later turned against the conqueror. He joined his brother's expedition to Guatemala, where he became the sheriff for the city (*alguacil mayor*). Nonetheless, he also became a *vecino* of Mexico City and served as *regidor* there in 1527. By the next year he was back in Santiago, Guatemala, and became *regidor*. He received several towns in *encomienda*, including Teposcolula, and several towns in the province of Tututepec. While serving as *alguacil*, he gained a reputation for cruelty. He eventually died in Oaxaca in about 1541 (HT, 5; G: item 41).

FOLIO 9, VERSO

B. *Alonso Hernández Portocarrero*. Hernández Portocarrero was elected one of the judges of Veracruz when the town was founded. He was one of the few members of the nobility (*hidalgo*) in the company. He was born in Medellín, of a noble family. His father was one of the officers of the military-religious Order of Santiago. His mother was related to the counts of Medellín. In 1515 he received a grant from the king to land and an *encomienda* in Cuba. He left Spain in 1516 and settled in the town of Espíritu Santo. In spite of his noble status, according to Díaz del Castillo, he neither owned a horse nor had the resources to buy one, and so Cortés provided him with one (DdelC, 1:87). He was the captain of one of the ships in the Cortés expedition, and a leader throughout. When Cortés was given the Indian woman known as doña Marina, he in turn granted her to Hernández Portocarrero. When the expedition entered the regions in which Nahuatl was spoken she became a crucial asset to the company. At the time Hernández Portocarrero sailed to Spain, doña Marina passed back to Cortés's direct supervision. Hernández Portocarrero was elected one of the two municipal judges of Veracruz and then one of the two agents of Veracruz who would carry the treasure and documents back to Spain. Díaz del Castillo indicates that once in Spain, Hernández Portocarrero had a confrontation with the bishop of Burgos, don Juan Rodríguez de Fonseca. Bishop Rodríguez was the effective governor of Castille in the absence of the king, as the president of the Council of Castille. The bishop opposed having the agents proceed on to Flanders to meet directly with King Charles. To prevent the trip, Rodríguez had Hernández arrested for supposedly having taken a married woman to Cuba from Spain. Hernández Portocarrero seems to have died in Spain (DdelC, 2:339; HT, 68–70).

C. *Francisco de Montejo*. Montejo was born in Salamanca, but lived for several years in Seville before sailing to the New World in 1514, when he accompanied Pedrarias Dávila (Pedro de Arias Dávila) to Panama. From there he settled in Cuba, where he held large tracts of land. He sailed with Grijalva as captain of one of his ships. He was known to be more of a supporter of Velázquez than of Cortés. After landing at Veracruz, Montejo was sent as the captain of a small fleet to explore the coast to the north. He discovered a better place to settle, near the native village of Quiahuiztlan. Montejo was the other judge elected for the town of Veracruz, and he was also elected as one of the agents of the town who took the letters, petition, and treasure to court, with Hernández Portocarrero (see signature B). Montejo served as the agent for the expedition in the Spanish court. In 1524, after the fall of Tenochtitlan, he returned to Mexico. He was assigned the villages of Azcapotzalco, Matlactlan, and Chila in *encomienda*. He then became the agent of the Mexico City council, and returned to Spain. There he secured royal permission to launch a new expedition, leading the conquest of Yucatan with the title of *adelantado*. Díaz del Castillo describes him as he looked at the outset of the Mexican expedition: he was of medium build, with a lively face, a friend of celebrations, a businessman, and a good horseman. He was about thirty-five years old when he arrived in Mexico; he was liberal and had already spent more than he had in income. He died in Spain (HT, 91–93; DdelC, 2:351–352).[1]

D. *Pedro de Alvarado*. Pedro de Alvarado was second in command of the expedition, after Cortés. He played a key role through the conquest and went on to lead the conquest of Guatemala. As noted, Alvarado was one of four brothers from Badajoz who joined the Cortés company (see signature A). Their father was an officer in the military-religious Order of Santiago, and thus the family would have been considered members of the petty nobility, *hidalgo*. Díaz del Castillo lists him first among the various captains after Cortés. He describes him as having a certain air about him in military matters. At the time of the expedition, Díaz del Castillo estimates, Alvarado was about thirty-four. He had a good build, very well proportioned. He had a very jovial face and appearance. We know from other sources that he was quite tall, perhaps even as much as six feet, and had bright red hair. All of this made the natives of Mexico call him *Tonatiuh*, which means "the sun." He was a good horseman, and very much given to frank and open conversations. He enjoyed dressing in gold and jewels, wearing a gold chain and jewels around his neck, along with a diamond ring.

Díaz del Castillo participated in the conquest of Mexico and Guatemala with Alvarado and can thus be considered to be less than objective in his views of him (DdelC, 2:333, 351). Pedro de Alvarado arrived in the New World in about 1510, and by the eve of the Cortés expedition had settled in Cuba. He served as captain of one of the ships in the Grijalva expedition. Alvarado seems to have provided one of the ships to the company, having sailed independently to Yucatan and Cozumel, where he joined up with the rest of the expedition. At the creation of Veracruz he was elected as one of the town councilmen, *regidores*. He led one of the first expeditions inland, looking for gold and food to trade. When Cortés left Tenochtitlan to confront Narváez, Alvarado remained in the city as captain. He ordered the massacre of the Aztec nobility that resulted in the Spaniards eventually being expelled from the city. One of the colorful stories of the Noche Triste features Alvarado. In the flight from the city he was placed in the rear guard. By the time he reached the first set of bridges which pierced the causeway from Tenochtitlan to the western shore of the lake, it had been removed or destroyed by the natives. According to the legend, Alvarado ran and took the gap in a single leap. This particular location in Mexico City today is known as "Alvarado's Bridge" (Puente de Alvarado). In testimony after the conquest, Alvarado discounted the story and merely said that he had taken the horse of another conquistador in order to get over the gap. He was in charge of the testimony gathered at Segura de la Frontera. He was captain of the horse company in the final siege of Tenochtitlan. He received several towns in *encomienda* after the conquest, but sought greater glory. He led the conquest of Guatemala, as *adelantado* and governor. He became a knight of the military-religious Order of Santiago. He took a large expedition to Peru to assist in the conquest in 1534, returning to Mexico in 1536. He eventually died during the Mixtón War in western Mexico, in 1541 (HT, 6–12; G: item 44).

E. *Alonso Dávila* (de Avila). Dávila was another of the captains of the expedition. He too came from the Spanish petty nobility. He was a native of Ciudad Real or La Puebla de Montalbán in Avila. His father was an officer in the military-religious Order of Calatrava. Dávila sailed to the New World in 1512 in the company of his brother Gil González Dávila, as a minor treasury official. He became one of the captains of one of the ships in the Cortés company. When the treasure was first inventoried at Veracruz, Dávila was made treasurer or accountant. He was also named as one of the town councilmen (*regidor*). After Montejo's departure he became a municipal justice. Díaz del Castillo describes him as hardworking, but also as someone who dealt in rumors. Because of this Cortés feared that he might create dissension in the company and so sent him to Hispaniola to serve as the company's agent before the royal governors on the island, and also to secure additional supplies for the expedition, along with Francisco Alvarez Chico (see signature H). After the conquest he joined the company in Mexico and was granted an *encomienda*, the rich villages of Cuauhtitlan, Huehuetoca, Zumpango, and Coyotepec. He was entrusted with the gold and treasure for the king. While sailing to Spain he was captured by French pirates under the command of Jean Florin. After two years of captivity he was released. He returned to Mexico and joined the Montejo expedition to Yucatan, again as a treasury official. He died in about 1534 (DdelC, 2:334–335; HT, 17–19).

F. *Alonso de Grado.* Alonso del Grado is one of the more famous members of the company. He was a member of the petty nobility, perhaps from Alcántara near Cáceres. He probably sailed to the Indies before 1515. He was an *encomendero* on the island of Hispaniola before joining the Cortés expedition (G: item 413). He was elected one of the town councilmen (*regidores*) of the town of Veracruz, and became one of the treasury officials, the *veedor*. As the expedition moved inland, Grado pressed to return to the relative safety of Veracruz. Once the expedition entered Tenochtitlan, he was finally sent to Veracruz as a chief constable, *alguacil mayor,* by Cortés. He caused some problems in Veracruz, seeking to enrich himself, exploiting the natives, and forcing them to provide him with food, jewels, and native servers. He was arrested by Gonzalo de Sandoval and sent in chains to Cortés in Mexico, probably for having been more loyal to Velázquez than to Cortés. Cortés imprisoned him. Grado was subjected to public humiliation in the stocks. But ultimately Cortés had him released and withdrew all charges. Later Grado resumed his duties as a treasury official, as *contador,* accountant. He was obviously a close adviser to Cortés because he was one of the co-signers of the third letter to the monarchs, May 15, 1522 (Cortés, 202). He was known more as a businessman than as a valiant fighter (DdelC, 1:298–300). He led a force into the Isthmus of Tehuantepec and Coatzacoalcos. He frequently accompanied another captain, Luis Marin, in expeditions, as did Díaz del Castillo. Grado married doña Isabel, one of the daughters of Moteuczoma, in 1526, but unfortunately he died a year later (DdelC, 2:96, 133, 146, 336). Later in the conquest he had suggested the possibility of rebelling from royal control. Nevertheless, he was chosen by Cortés to accompany the payment of royal taxes back to Spain, in 1522–1523 (G: item 413; HT, 62–64). After the conquest he was appointed as an inspector of the Indians. By virtue of his marriage to doña Isabel, he received the town of Chiautla in *encomienda.* He and doña Isabel had no children, and upon his death the *encomienda* was reassigned. He did have one natural child, a daughter (Himmerich: item 176).[2] He might be related to Alvaro del Grado (signature 135).

G. *Cristóbal Dolid* (de Olid). Olid was also one of the commanders of the expedition, frequently leading a small company of men into battle. A native of Baeza, Olid was also a member of the petty nobility. He arrived in Cuba in about 1518. He was one of the captains of the ships which brought the company and owned one of the horses. He quickly became one of Cortés's closest advisors, and served as field marshal (*maestre de campo*) for much of the conquest. Díaz del Castillo describes him in a very colorful way, comparing him to Hector, the fearless Trojan champion, in hand-to-hand combat. He also writes that Olid was about thirty-six years old at the start of the conquest. He was a good-sized man, of somewhat fair hair and complexion. His lower lip was always cracked. His speech was full and somewhat unnerving, although he was a good conversationalist. He had been a young man in the household of Diego Velázquez and had learned the local native language of Cuba. He was nevertheless a strong supporter of Cortés and not of his former patron. Díaz del Castillo considered him to be more of a follower than a leader, however (DdelC, 2:130, 333). He became lieutenant governor and judge for Veracruz. He commanded one of the groups in the confrontation against Narváez. He continued as a captain throughout the conquest. After the fall of Tenochtitlan he led an expedition west, into Michoacan. He was also the commander of an expedition into Honduras, where he led a rebellion against Cortés. A punitive expedition was sent after him. Olid was captured and hanged (HT, 101; G, 726).

H. *Francisco Alvarez Chico.* Sources disagree on Alvarez Chico's hometown. Some say it was Villanueva del Fresno and others say he was from Fregenal, both of which are in the province of Badajoz in Extremadura. There is agreement that he left for the New World from Oliva in the Condado de Niebla, in southwestern Spain. He was a cousin of another conquistador, Francisco de Terrazas (see signature 165). Díaz del Castillo believed that Alvarez Chico, and his brother, Juan Alvarez Chico (either signature 28 or 37), also a conquistador, came from Fregenal. He also notes that Alvarez Chico was one of several merchants in the expedition who died in Santo Domingo (DdelC, 2:336). It seems that Alvarez Chico and another brother, Fernando, arrived in the Indies in about 1516. Fernando died in Puerto Rico, killed by Indians. Francisco possibly led an expedition to search for pearls in Cubagua in 1516. He might have also had another brother, Rodrigo Alvarez Chico (see signature 246), who was also a member of the company. Francisco was elected one of the municipal judges and one of two agents of the town of Veracruz sent to the Spanish court. At one point he was sent to Jamaica and Hispaniola to purchase more horses and supplies for the company. It is not at all certain when he died; we have only Díaz del Castillo's note that he passed away in Santo Domingo (HT, 15; G: item 49).

I. *Pedro Hernández, escribano.* Hernández was one of the royal scribes in the expedition and served as the scribe before whom the petition and letter were presented. His is, however, a very common name. (See signature 157.) Díaz del Castillo indicates that he was Cortés's personal secretary before being selected to serve the town of Veracruz. He was a native of Seville and died at the hands of the natives during the conquest (DdelC, 2:343). Grunberg and Thomas give him a second surname, calling him Hernández Navarette. They indicate that he came from Béjar in Salamanca, near the frontier with Extremadura. In his function as a notary he received Moteuczoma's declaration of fealty to the king of Spain; was sent with Rodrigo Alvarez Chico (see signature 246) to interview Narváez before the battle between the two companies; and, following the Noche Triste, inventoried the gold and treasure which remained with the company. In contradiction to Díaz del Castillo, Grunberg holds that he survived the conquest and settled in Mexico with his wife, Ana de Rebolledo. He received the town of Acayuca in *encomienda*, which passed to his son upon his death (G: item 475; Himmerich: item 136). By 1527 he had settled in Mexico City, where he signed several contracts and was involved in lawsuits. In 1528 he was chosen to be an assistant sheriff of the city. He died before 1547 (Alvarez: item 510). Thomas indicates that a brother, Juan Pérez de Herrera, shared the *encomienda* of Epatlan and so probably was a conquistador. Their father, García Hernández, was a member of the Narváez expedition (HT, 67–68). Unfortunately these other men were probably related to the Pedro Hernández who was a member of the Narváez expedition and not of the secretary to Cortés (Himmerich: item 199).

The Members of the Company

1. *Pedro [Alonso?] Morales Negros*. While various sources indicate that there were several members of the company with the surname Morales, none is listed as being "Pedro." Díaz del Castillo mentions one man named Morales, who became an *alcalde ordinario* in Veracruz. Díaz del Castillo writes that he was already old at the time of the conquest, suffered from a limp in one leg, and served in the retinue of the *comendador* Solís, perhaps Francisco de Solís (DdelC, 2:345). Grunberg lists a Francisco Moralesnetros who, he believes, died during the conquest, around 1521 (G: item 671). (See also signature 95.)

2. *Antonio Saldaña*. Antonio Saldaña was among the members of the company who signed the 1520 Segura de la Frontera letter. Díaz del Castillo mentions a Saldaña as having participated in the expedition, but notes that a man of this name died in Tabasco along with two others, whose names he could not recall (DdelC, 2:349). This information tells us that it is unlikely that Saldaña lived to see the fall of Tenochtitlan (G: item 942).

3. *Alonso Ximénez de Herrera; or Alonso Hernández de Herrera*. While the given name and the second surname of this member seem clear, the first surname is open to question. Grunberg lists an Alonso Jiménez de Herrera and

notes that he probably died during the conquest (G: item 509). Díaz del Castillo mentions an Alonso de Herrera, native of Jerez, who was a member of the company. This Alonso de Herrera, Díaz del Castillo relates, was sent in later times as captain of an expedition to pacify the Zapotec villages. At the same time another captain was assigned this mission, with a larger force. When the two groups met, there was a melee and Herrera killed the other captain with a knife (DdelC, 2:270, 273–274). (See also signature 83.) Boyd Bowman includes several men named Alonso de Herrera as early emigrants to the Indies, including the one detailed above. In addition he lists another who participated in the Cortés expedition, went to Nicaragua and Honduras in 1529, and served in Cumaná in 1532 (BB: items 1165 and 4451). Díaz del Castillo also includes an Alonso Hernández within the company. He mentions that this individual narrowly escaped capture by the natives while looting houses for clothing. Díaz del Castillo later notes that Alonso Hernández was the nephew of another member, Alonso Hernández Paulo (Palos?). The younger Alonso was a good shot with the crossbow and later died at the hands of the natives (DdelC, 1:487; 2:342). Only Díaz del Castillo mentions company members with the surname Jiménez. He notes that two brothers of this name accompanied Cortés; they were natives of a small village in Extremadura. One of them died at the hands of the natives, and the other of old age (DdelC, 2:340).

4. *Alonso Rodríguez, piloto; Alonso Rico, piloto.* Although this member of the company signed his name with the occupation of pilot, no one having either of the possible names was known as a pilot. Díaz del Castillo mentions Alonso Rodríguez several times, usually to note that he owned several rich silver mines on the island of Cuba. On another occasion he mentions that Rodríguez was killed by the natives while climbing a hill, Los Peñoles, near Chimalhuacan Chalco (DdelC, 1:86 and 474, 2:350). Four men named Alonso Rodríguez signed the Veracruz petition (see signatures 90, 138, and 187). Only one well-known conqueror had the surname Rico: Juan Rico de Alanís.

5. *Miguel de Palma.* Only one source mentions Miguel de Palma. Many years after the conquest, Francisco de Chavez requested recognition for his service to the Crown. In his petition he noted that he was married to a daughter of Miguel de la Palma, and that Palma was one of the early conquerors of the land. The daughter had earlier been married to Antón Caizedo (Caicedo), also a conqueror. Her name was Marina Montes de Oca (Icaza: item 433; Himmerich: item 67). Pedro de Palma appears frequently in the historic record, but it is unknown if he was related to Miguel, although Grunberg indicates that this was an alias for Miguel. Pedro de Palma was held to be a member of the original Cortés company. Pedro survived the conquest, and joined a later expedition to Honduras with Cristóbal de Olid, during which Olid attempted to declare his independence. Palma was among those captured and executed in 1524 for his

involvement in the rebellion. He married Elvira López and had two daughters, as alluded to above. Pedro received several villages in *encomienda*, including Matacoya, Gualtepec, and Gaiatana (G: item 758).

6. *Rodrigo Cervantes*. This is one of the more difficult signatures to decipher. None of the existing sources lists any conqueror with similar names. There were several Cervantes who served, including a Francisco Cervantes nominally part of the initial expedition.

7. *Diego Suárez*. Hugh Thomas indicates that Suárez was part of the retinue of the conqueror Pedro de Ircio (signature 301) and a native of Seville (HT, 124). He is listed as a signatory of the 1520 Segura de la Frontera letter. Díaz del Castillo tells of several men with the surname Suárez or Juárez; none had the given name Diego. Grunberg notes that Diego Suárez participated in the conquest of Mexico and in later expeditions in New Spain. In 1525 he received land for a house in Mexico, thus becoming a *vecino*. He gave testimony in several suits after the conquest, and by 1545 was living in Puebla with an Indian wife and a son named after him (G: item 1022).

8. *Sancho de Bretes; Gonzalo de Bretes*. The sources are generally silent regarding this conqueror. He does appear on the list of conquerors who signed the 1520 Segura de la Frontera letter as Gonzalo de Bretes (name was transcribed as "Valte": Dor, 350.) Thomas believes that he died in 1521 (HT, 294).

9. *Gonzalo Galindo; Gonzalo Galdos*. (See fig. 6.1.) Díaz del Castillo mentions a pilot named Galdín who returned to Cuba in 1520 (DdelC, 2:347). There was a later conqueror, Juan Sánchez Galindo, who by his own account came in the second wave (Icaza: item 141; Himmerich: item 142). Grunberg lists an Alonso (?) Galdunos as a member of the company who had died by 1521 (G: item 326).

10. *Gonzalo de Arcos*. Arcos signed the 1520 Segura de la Frontera letter. Several scholars have placed Arcos among the reinforcements who arrived later in the conquest (HT, 150). One might imagine that he was originally from the village of Arcos de la Frontera, in Andalucía. Grunberg lists this conqueror as Arcos Cervera. He notes that in 1528 he was the town crier for Mexico City (G: item 64).

11. *Juan de Sandes [Fandes?]*. There are no known conquerors with the name Sandes or Sande. While the surname looks as though it might be "Fandes," which would be extremely uncommon in sixteenth-century Spain, a more logical reading would be "Flandes," yet there is no visible "l." Some sources indicate that Juan de Flandes, also known as Juan Flamenco, arrived with the Narváez expedition. He is listed as one of the signatories of the 1520 Segura de la Frontera letter. Later Flamenco settled in Coatzacoalcos, where he reputedly held an *encomienda*, which passed to his son Pedro Flamenco (Icaza: item 235; BB: item 5126).

Biographies OF THE *Signatories*

12. *Cristóbal Vanegas.* The surname Vanegas or Venegas was rare in the early years of the New World. Grunberg includes one conqueror named Vanegas, who died early in the conquest (G: item 1093). A Juan de Valladolid Vanegas signed the 1520 Segura de la Frontera letter.

13. *Juan Jiménez.* Two men with this name signed the Veracruz petition (see also signature 203). This conqueror also signed the 1520 Segura de la Frontera letter. Díaz del Castillo writes of two brothers with the surname Jiménez who came originally from a village outside of Trujillo, Herguijuela. They sailed to the Indies in 1516 (BB: item 1005; DdelC, 2:340). One of these died at the hands of the natives, and the other of old age. Other sources indicate that a Juan Jiménez died during the Noche Triste (HT, 203). His brother was called either Gonzalo Jiménez or Gonzalo Hernández. Grunberg writes that Juan Jiménez survived the Noche Triste and the conquest of Mexico, only to die during the expedition to Cimatlan (G: item 506). Boyd Bowman lists yet a third brother, Miguel (BB: item 1006). Both Miguel and Gonzalo signed the 1520 Segura de la Frontera letter.

14. *Fernando Xuarez* [Juarez]. There is just one reference to this conquistador: that he signed the 1520 Segura de la Frontera letter (HT, 245). Nader's transcription of the letter has rendered the name as Mendo, not Fernando.

15. *Pedro de Carmona.* (See the following.)

16. *Juan de Carmona.* Several sources, including Díaz del Castillo, tell of two brothers from Carmona who died of old age (DdelC, 2:340). Of the two brothers, Juan appears more in records of the era. Rather than being from Carmona, he was originally from Jerez de la Frontera; he sailed to the New World in about 1513. Juan participated in the conquest of Mexico with Cortés, signing the 1520 Segura de la Frontera letter, and later in the conquest of Guatemala with Pedro de Alvarado, becoming a resident of Santiago de Guatemala at least until 1541 (BB: item 1155; Icaza: item 201; G: item 189). The 1520 Segura de la Frontera letter lists his brother as being "Esteban."

17. *Ochoa de Arcia; Ochoa de Arcos/Arce?* A conqueror named Ochoa de Asno signed the 1520 Segura de la Frontera letter, possibly the same man. (See also signature 19.) There are few indications as to who this conqueror might be. Hugh Thomas suggests that Cortés's personal servant or page was simply named Ochoa (HT, 99). Díaz del Castillo writes of a Basque named Ochoa who became a rich settler in Oaxaca. He notes that Ochoa was also the first *alguacil* of Veracruz (DdelC, 1:139; 2:347). Four conquerors or early settlers used the surname of Arcos. No one with the surname Arcia appears in the literature.

18. *Gonzalo Domínguez.* Domínguez was well known as an accomplished horseman and a native of Extremadura. He signed the 1520 Segura de la Frontera letter. Díaz del Castillo first mentions him among the members of the

company who brought a horse, in his case a very fast and good dark chestnut. Thereafter Díaz lists him among the horsemen. He was badly wounded during the flight from Tenochtitlan on the Noche Triste, but kept his horse. Because of his horsemanship and other leadership qualities, Domínguez became one of the captains of the company. Domínguez died during a battle near Chimalhuacan Chalco and Tlalmanalco, when his horse took a misstep and fell. His passing caused great sorrow among the company. Elsewhere, Díaz del Castillo comments that Domínguez died after being captured by the natives. Consequently, while the details of his death are cloudy, it seems clear that he did die during the conquest (DdelC, 1:92, 113, 393, 400, 410, and 465; 2:330 and 336; G: item 270; HT, 54).

19. *Ochoa de Veraza.* (See also signature 17.) Hugh Thomas lists Veraza among the members of the Narváez expedition (HT, 252). Boyd Bowman includes a settler in Cuba by a similar name (Ochoa de Verazu or Azúa), who was originally from the Basque country (BB: item 5318). That identification was based on research by Orozco y Berra, who also places him among the members of the Narváez expedition, but lists his name as Verazu de Ochoa (Dor, 326). Because of the similar given name, Ochoa, this conqueror and Ochoa de Arcia (signature 17) might be conflated in the literature.

20. *Juan Bono de Quepo.* The second surname of this conqueror appears in several different variants: Queipo, Quepo, Quexo. Nevertheless, he left a significant trail in the documentation. Most interesting, several scholars have placed him not among the initial Cortés expedition, but in the Narváez company. Clearly that is an error. Originally from Vizcaya, Bono had as much experience in the New World as any other member of the company, since he was reputedly a pilot on Columbus's last voyage to the New World in 1502. After that he took part in several other expeditions, even serving as ship's master on Ponce de León's voyage to Florida, among others. He became a settler and *encomendero* on Puerto Rico. He ran mines and held many Indian slaves (HT, 170–171). The confusion regarding Bono's time of arrival arises from the probability that he made at least two voyages to Mexico. His signature on this document likely indicates that he arrived with the rest of the company. He also signed the 1520 Segura de la Frontera letter. Cortés and Díaz del Castillo agree that he was part of the Narváez expedition. Díaz del Castillo lists him among the closest advisors to Narváez, captain of one of the ships under his command and then captain of one of the companies on land. In the battle between the forces of Narváez and those of Cortés, Bono was taken prisoner. He and other followers of Narváez served under Cortés through the Noche Triste. Eventually they requested permission from Cortés to return to Cuba, which was granted. In early 1522 he returned to Mexico from Spain with news and royal documents while the company was in the province of Pánuco (Cortés, 207;

DdelC, 1:343, 360, 365, 372, 428, 430; 2:100; G: item 141). Bono might have been a conspirator against Cortés. Cristóbal de Tapia had come out ostensibly to investigate the finances of Cortés, but probably to overthrow him. Bono carried with him blank royal documents, possibly intended to assist Tapia, but did not know that Tapia had left Mexico a few weeks earlier, having been unable to stir up sufficient opposition to Cortés (Thomas, 554). Consequently it seems likely that Bono de Quepo was a member of the group that left Veracruz after our document was signed as part of the expedition back to court. We know of course that the ship stopped in Cuba, allowing Velázquez to learn of Cortés's actions and prompting him to send the Narvéz expedition. Bono de Quepo thus emerges as a key figure for understanding the dynamics of the conquest. Following the conquest, he returned to Cuba, where he continued as an *encomendero*. He also served as the lieutenant governor of Havana (G: item 141).

21. *Francisco de Ledesma.* The original sources list a Juan de Ledesma as a conqueror, but not a Francisco. Of the scholars of the conquest, only Thomas lists a Francisco Ledesma, originally from Ledesma in Salamanca, whom he places in the original Cortés company, noting that he later went on to become a *procurador* for Mexico (HT, 74). Two members of the company at the time of the fall of Tenochtitlan were named Juan de Ledesma. One of these supposedly arrived among the Garay reinforcements. That Juan was from Ocaña, in Toledo province. According to his testimony twenty years later, he had fought with Cortés in Mexico and Alvarado in Guatemala (Icaza: item 170; BB: item 4303; G: item 520). The other Juan de Ledesma arrived with Narváez, and was a native of Sazelle, near Salamanca (BB: item 2747; HT, 204). Boyd Bowman lists yet another Juan de Lesdema as being a conqueror, this one a native of Seville and a veteran of one of the early voyages to northern South America under Nicuesa (BB: item 3639).

22. *Diego López de Guadalupe.* Some scholars have confused this conqueror with Alvaro López (see signature 278) because Alvaro was from the village of Guadalupe in the province of Cáceres. According to most accounts, Diego López arrived at the time of the siege of Tenochtitlan, well after the period of this Veracruz petition. He was a crossbowman who became a tailor after the conquest and never married. He was one of the first settlers and a *vecino* of Puebla (HT, 301; G: item 540). The name of this conqueror indicates that he might have originally been from Guadalupe in Extremadura.

23. *Gaspar de Tarifa.* Two or three Tarifa brothers (Francisco, Gaspar, and Hernando) served in the conquest. They were from the town of Tarifa, in Andalucía, the southernmost town on the Iberian Peninsula. Gaspar signed the 1520 Segura de la Frontera letter. According to Díaz del Castillo, one brother became a *vecino* of Oaxaca and married a woman named Muñiz (Catalina

Muñoz). The other was called "White Hands" (*manos blancas*) because he simply was not suited for soldiering or hard work, but only talked about the old days ("no era para la guerra ni para cosas de trabajo, sino hablar de cosas pasadas," DdelC, 2:348). Thomas identifies Gaspar as "White Hands" (HT, 130). Dorantes de Carranza lists four of Gaspar's grandchildren (Dor, 174). Gaspar was a *vecino* of Mexico City and held a small *encomienda*, Chicomexochitl. He had legal trouble, having been falsely accused of misdeeds by some native chiefs. In testimony he was described as knowing the native language well, probably Nahuatl. He held land in Mexico City and was an active witness for other conquerors. Later, by 1531, he probably moved to Oaxaca, where he became a *vecino* (G: item 1036; Himmerich: item 452).

24. *Bartolomé Múñoz*. None of the standard references lists a Bartolomé Múñoz as a member of the company. Nevertheless, there are several other persons with the surname Múñoz, including Diego, Gregorio, Hernán, and Juan (2). Three (Fernán, Gregorio, and Juan) signed the 1520 Segura de la Frontera letter. An early settler named Bartolomé Múñoz lived in Puebla, having come to New Spain with three brothers, originally from Villagarcía (Icaza: item 967).

25. *Gonzalo de Bonilla*. There are no references to a Gonzalo de Bonilla. This might be the Gonzalo de Virola who signed the 1520 Segura de la Frontera letter.

26. *Juan Ruiz*. Several men named Juan Ruiz participated in the conquest. (See also signature 101.) This particular one might be known also as Juan Ruiz de Viana (rather than Ruiz Sedeño or Ruiz de Mansilla) (HT, 117). Díaz del Castillo recalls two men named Juan Ruiz: Ruiz de Alanís (see signature 101) and Ruiz de la Parra (DdelC, 2:339–340). Ruiz de Viana was a signatory to the 1520 Segura de la Frontera letter. Juan Ruiz, from the town of Lepe in Huelva, was in Cuba in 1519, was a conqueror in Mexico in 1520, and was hanged in Mexico in 1524 (BB: item 1812).

27. *Pedro López*. The name Pedro López was extremely common. If one includes all the possible conquerors with compound surnames, there are as many as seven. Díaz del Castillo mentions four men simply called Pedro López: one was a physician; another, a pilot; the last two, crossbowmen (*ballesteros*). This one was probably one of the crossbowmen, since the physician and the pilot might well have identified themselves as such in their signatures. One of the crossbowmen arrived with Narváez and died of old age. The other left New Spain with Alonso de Ávila for Hispaniola and stayed there (DdelC, 2:347). Díaz del Castillo also recalls that López the crossbowman was assigned to guard Moteuczoma. López grew weary of his duty and complained that he was sick to death of guarding "that dog of a prisoner." Cortés, upon hearing of it, had him flogged for disrespect of the royal prisoner (DdelC, 1:302). Grunberg lists only Pedro López de Alcántara and Pedro López Marroquín (G: items 549 and 554).

28. *Juan Juárez; Juan Alvarez.* Only one person potentially could be Juan Juárez, an illiterate from Seville, also known as Juan Suárez (HT, 245). There are as many as five men who could have been Juan Alvarez: two persons known simply as Juan Alvarez, Juan Alvarez Chico, Juan Alvarez, *el manquillo* ("the little one-armed fellow"), and Juan Alvarez Rubazo. One Juan Alvarez became a witness hostile to Cortés in the aftermath of the conquest. His testimony indicates that he had been close to the events of the war and had seen the various objects given to Cortés by the Aztec emperor. He was attached to Alvarado during the massacre in the temple (HT, 12–14). Two men named Juan Alvarez signed the 1520 Segura de la Frontera letter. (See signature 37 below.)

29. *Antón Quemado.* Only one source confirms the presence of a conqueror with a similar name, listed as Antonio de Quemada, as a signatory of the 1520 Segura de la Frontera letter. Grunberg assumes that he died in the conquest (G: item 828).

30. *Juan de Camacho; Juan de Tamayo.* Water damage has made this signature quite difficult to decipher. Díaz del Castillo lists a conqueror with the surname Camacho. A native of Triana, Camacho was a pilot for Cortés and on the earlier Hernández de Córdoba expedition. He piloted the vessel on which Díaz del Castillo sailed. The last mention of him is in the narrative of the landing on the island of Cozumel (DdelC, 1:95). Grunberg indicates that his given name was Diego (G: item 172). The surname Tamayo does appear, but with the given names Bartolomé and Rodrigo. Bartolomé Tamayo is listed as a signatory of the 1520 Segura de la Frontera letter. Grunberg notes that Bartolomé came with the Narváez expedition (G: item 1029).

31. *Martín de Vergara.* A signatory of the 1520 Segura de la Frontera letter, Vergara was probably from the village of Vergara in Guipuzcoa (BB: items 12662g–h). A Juan de Vergara, perhaps a relative, also signed. The notary who accompanied Narváez was also surnamed Vergara (DdelC, 1:338). Grunberg lists three men with this surname: Alonso, Diego, and Juan (G: items 1128–1130).

32. *Pedro de Maya.* This conqueror signed the 1520 Segura de la Frontera letter. He participated in the conquest of Mexico and later went on to Guatemala. By 1525 he had settled in Mexico and become a *vecino*. He was active in local business dealings. A bit later, by 1531, he had become a *vecino* of Oaxaca. Pedro de Maya was recognized as a first conqueror, and he was assigned the *encomienda* of Nochistlan, in the region of Oaxaca. In 1542 the Indians of his *encomienda* complained to the viceroy about the mistreatment they received from Maya. After a royal investigation, Maya was fined and lost the fruits of the grant, which had escheated to the Crown by 1545. He seems to have died of natural causes in that year (G: item 626; Himmerich: item 265). Some sources indicate that he might have also been known as Pero Antonio Maya, a native

of Cuéllar in Segovia province (BB: item 2875). Antonio de Maya was a member of the Grijalva expedition, prior to that of Cortés. His son testified that he had accompanied Narváez in his return to Mexico. The testimony also indicates that Antonio Maya died during the final assault on Tenochtitlan (Icaza: item 273; Dor, 194). Consequently, there might have been two conquerors, Pedro de Maya, part of the Cortés expedition; and Antonio de Maya, a member of the Grijalva and Narváez companies. This surname was also sometimes written as Amaya (see signature 80).

33. *Beltrán (Belgrán?) Rodríguez.* Numerous persons with the surname Rodríguez participated in the conquest of Mexico. None seems to have carried the name Beltrán, or anything similar.

34. *Feliche Napolitano.* Also known as Felipe. It is reasonable to assume that he was from Naples. He signed the 1520 Segura de la Frontera letter. Some sources indicate that he arrived with Narváez (Dor, 345). Solid evidence demonstrates that he survived the conquest, taking up residence in Texcoco and appearing as a party in some lawsuits. Grunberg, however, held that he died in the conquest (HT, 216; G: item 700).

35. *Juan de Meco.* Water damage makes this signature very difficult to read.

36. *Benito de Vexer.* The name of this conqueror appears twice among the signatories of this letter, yet the two signatures are quite different (see also signature 273; figs. 6.11 and 6.12). Vexer also signed the 1520 Segura de la Frontera letter. He appears under the various spellings of Bejer, Vejer, or Bejel. Benito was a veteran of the Italian campaigns, where he'd served as a drummer. He was also a musician in the Cortés company and was also known as "Benito the Tambourine Player" (*el tamborino*). He died of natural causes. He was married to a woman with the surname Gómez (DdelC, 1:358; 2:66, 345). He probably was also a member of the earlier Grijalva expedition: when the Cortés company landed in Yucatan the natives asked for him to play, remembering his previous visit. One of his fellow conquerors remembered him as "the most humble member of the whole army" (HT, 20–21). He settled in Mexico City, where he continued to be a musician and ran a dance school. He received part of the town of Axacuba in *encomienda*, which he lost when it was confiscated by the Second Audiencia. He probably died before 1528 (G: item 1111; Himmerich: item 478). Benito was probably from the village of Véjer de la Frontera in the province of Cádiz (BB: item 1244a).

37. *Juan Alvarez, maestro.* (See signature 28 above.) In all likelihood, this is *El manquillo* ("the little one-armed fellow"). *El manquillo* was well known during the conquest. Díaz del Castillo writes that he was originally from Huelva (others say Palos), and was a ship's pilot. As a result of his training he served as a pilot for both the Hernández de Córdoba and the Grijalva expeditions. As well, he was one of a handful of pilots who served in the Cortés expedition

(DdelC, 1:44, 60, 105, 131; 2:347; BB: item 1889). Since he identified himself as "maestro" it suggests that he was a ship's master, in keeping with his training as a pilot. Alvarez sailed to the Indies in about 1514. In the period in which the Veracruz petition was written, Alvarez was sailing up the coast with Montejo in search of a better port (HT, 15). After the fall of Tenochtlan, Alvarez became a member of the Garay faction, and fearing that Cortés might punish them for disloyalty, he fled Mexico. He was the pilot of a ship which arrived in Mexico in 1537 (G: item 47).

38. *Diego de Orrios; Diego de Lorros; Diego de Porras.* The signature is quite distinct, but might be interpreted in any number of ways. Neither Orrios nor Lorros appears in the sources. Two men named Diego de Porras signed the 1520 Segura de la Frontera letter. One of these, originally from Seville, arrived in the Indies in 1513 and most likely died during the conquest (G: item 815). The other of these men named Diego de Porras arrived with the Narváez expedition, after having earlier served with Hernández de Córdoba. Following the conquest he settled in Oaxaca, where he became a city councilman, *regidor*. He received a coat of arms for his service in the conquest (Villar: item 121). On several occasions he represented other conquerors and settlers before the royal officials. He held several estates in the Oaxaca region. He was granted the village of Achachalintlan and others in *encomienda*. He died sometime around 1549 (HT, 226–227; G: item 816). Boyd Bowman conflates the two men into one (BB: item 3887).

39. *Juan Nizard.* No known conqueror has a similar name. The closest would be Juan Lizana. (See also signature 97.)

40. *Domingo Martín.* Martín was a well-known member of the company, coming originally from the village of Brozas in the region of Cáceres. He participated in the Grijalva expedition before joining Cortés. He was a member of the company at the fall of Tenochtitlan. He was a footman, *mozo de espuelas*, for Cortés. He also served Bernardino Vázquez de Tapia (see signature 125). After the conquest he settled in Mexico, becoming a *vecino* of the city. He married the sister of Diego Rodríguez, his neighbor. He served as local magistrate for various jurisdictions between 1539 and 1550. He served as a witness for other conquerors as they sought recompense from the Crown. Although he was not granted an *encomienda*, he did eventually receive a pension from the Crown (Icaza: item 37; Alvarez: item 643; G: item 597). A Domingo Martínez signed the 1520 Segura de la Frontera letter.

41. *Diego Ruiz de Yllescas; Diego Perez de Yllanes.* A water stain makes this signature difficult to read. This conqueror might be Diego Ruiz de Yesares or Diego Ruiz de Yllanes. Grunberg believed that Ruiz de Illanes died early in the conquest, after signing the 1520 Segura de la Frontera letter (G: item 923). This conqueror also might have simply been Diego Ruiz. Diego Ruiz hailed from

Moguer, near Huelva. He fought throughout the conquest and eventually settled in Zacatula (Icaza: item 48; HT, 117). Thomas refers to one conqueror named Diego Yllan (HT, 141). There do not seem to have been any conquerors named Diego Pérez.

42. *Maestre Diego*. This conqueror has been identified as Cortés's cook. A long-time resident of the Indies, having arrived as early as 1498, he became a member of the Cortés household. In addition to his services as a cook, he acted as a physician (BB: item 4465; HT, 54).

43. *Martín de Idiáquez; Martín Dircio [de Ircio]*. No conquerors are known to have the surname Idiáquez. Martín de Ircio, or Dircio, was a well-known conqueror. He and his brother, Pedro (see signature 301), served in the conquest and were rewarded with large and wealthy *encomiendas*. Both signed the 1520 Segura de la Frontera letter. Some sources indicate that Pedro served with the initial Cortés company while Martín arrived with Narváez, a point seemingly confirmed in testimony he gave regarding his services (Icaza: item 48; HT, 202; G: item 492). Martín de Ircio received one of the largest *encomiendas* in New Spain, encompassing the villages of Oapa, Huitziltepec, and Mochitlan, in south central Mexico. He married the half-sister of Viceroy Antonio de Mendoza, doña María de Mendoza. Their daughter, doña María de Ircio, married the son of the second viceroy, don Luis de Velasco. The younger don Luis also became viceroy (Alvarez: item 304).

44. *Alonso*. A tear in the original prohibits us from knowing the surname(s) of this conqueror. First surname might begin with the letter G.

45. *Juan Cervantes*. The most famous Juan de Cervantes arrived in the last phases of the conquest to join his relative, the *comendador* Leonel de Cervantes, a conqueror with Cortés (HT, 320). This Juan Cervantes might be the individual about whom Díaz del Castillo writes, calling him *el loco* ("the crazy one") or *el chocarrero* ("the slob"); Grunberg identifies the referent of these epithets as Francisco de Cervantes (G: item 223). Before the company departed from Cuba, this Cervantes poked fun at the governor, Diego Velázquez, and his appointment of Cortés to head the expedition. Throughout the adventure, Díaz del Castillo reports, that Cervantes continued with his antics on numerous occasions. When the Narváez expedition arrived, Cervantes was one of a handful of Cortés's men who changed camps. He was badly wounded in the ensuing battle, but survived, finally dying at the hands of the Indians (DdelC, 1:82, 320, 335, 341, 374; 2:348).

46. *Juan de*. Only a fragment remains, and it does not provide the surname(s) of this conqueror.

47. *Francisco Maldonado*. Maldonado was one of the better-known conquistadores who left an impact on the documentary record. He was from Salamanca. Maldonado served in the company along with his father, Álvaro, who is not included among the names on this document. Each had a colorful nickname. Díaz del Castillo writes that Francisco was called *el ancho* ("the wide"); his father was *el fiero* ("the wild beast") (DdelC, 1:431). Francisco had already participated in some expeditions before joining the Cortés company, possibly with Grijalva. Díaz del Castillo qualifies him as "a prominent person who had been a captain on other expeditions" (DdelC, 2:336). Francisco was a signatory of the 1520 Segura de la Frontera letter. He served with distinction in the conquest, acting as a captain, appointed by Cortés, in the pacification of the Zapotec region of Oaxaca. He was rewarded with an *encomienda* and eventually with a coat of arms. In 1524 he received land in Mexico City and became a *vecino* there. He served as a *regidor* of the city and was active in business and real estate. He gave testimony for other conquerors seeking royal grants. The Inquisition investigated him in 1536 on charges of blasphemy. He was found guilty and fined and made to do penance. He appealed his conviction to the archbishop of Seville. Maldonado became a landowner near Atlatlauca, in the valley south of Mexico, and received permission to use native labor in the construction of his house there. By about 1542 he was living in Oaxaca, where he became a *vecino*. He also served as local magistrate in several districts. He held the villages of Chachiutla, Chicoma, Aguatepec, Mistla, and Tecomastlahuaca, in the region of Oaxaca, in *encomienda*. The Crown granted him a coat of arms in 1538 in recognition of his services (Villar: item 62). (See fig. 6.14.) He married Isabel de Rojas, the widow of a fellow conqueror, Juan Velázquez. That union had no children, although Maldonado claimed a natural son back in Salamanca and a daughter living in Oaxaca. Upon Maldonado's death in about 1545 the *encomienda* passed to his wife, who proceeded to marry don Tristán de Luna y Arellano, a wealthy and well-connected settler (G: item 577; Himmerich: item 247).

48. *Martín Vázquez*. Vázquez is another well-known member of the company. Díaz del Castillo describes him as a native of Olmedo, a rich and prominent man who resided in Mexico City, and who died a natural death (DdelC, 2:348). In testimony given decades after the conquest, Vázquez claimed that he in fact came from the village of Martín Muñoz in the region of Segovia. He said that he had traveled to the New World in the early years of settlement and had participated in the expedition of Pedrarias Dávila to Panama. He first sailed to Mexico in the company of Hernández de Córdoba, and later joined the Cortés company. He participated in many of the important battles, was present at

the fall of Tenochtitlan, and also served in several later expeditions. He was a horseman and a crossbowman in the conquest. He married while in Cuba, and had three sons and a daughter. For his service he received the village of Tlaxiaco in *encomienda* (Icaza: item 180). In fact, Vázquez initially received Xilocingo, Chicuautla, and Mixtepec in *encomienda*. These were taken from him during the period following Cortés's departure for Spain. Later he was compensated for their loss with the grant of Tlaxiaco. Some sources indicate that his wife was a native woman from Cuba. The *encomienda* remained in the family until the end of the sixteenth century, when it escheated to the Crown (Himmerich: item 477). In other testimony, Vázquez claimed to have been one of the guards of Moteuczoma. He also testified to having received numerous wounds during the various battles. Others reported that his house in Mexico City became a center for cards and gambling (HT, 135–136). He had settled in Mexico by 1525 and became a *vecino* there. He was active in the local economy, buying and selling some items of gold and precious stones. He prospected for gold and owned slaves (G: item 1102).

49. *Francisco Bonal.* A native of Salamanca who, sources indicate, had arrived in Cuba by 1518 and joined Cortés (BB: item 2660). He was one of the men sent by Cortés to spy on the Narváez camp prior to the attack. He signed the 1520 Segura de la Frontera letter. He fought in two of the later expeditions, to Tuxtepec and the Zapotec region. He served as an *alcalde* in Veracruz, after the conquest, being a *vecino* of the town. He was denounced to the Inquisition for blasphemy, but not convicted. He became a resident and local magistrate in Medellín, near Veracruz, also serving as a local treasury official there. In 1534 he became a *vecino* of Puebla without actually living in the city. He received the villages of Guatusco and Iztayuca in *encomienda*. He was married to a Spaniard, Ana de León. By 1535 these villages had escheated to the Crown (Himmerich: item 54).

50. *Alonso del Alberca.* Boyd Bowman lists Alberca as a native of Don Benito in the province of Badajoz. He received a license to pass to the Indies in 1516 (BB: item 343). This might be the conquistador identified by Díaz del Castillo as Alberán (in other editions as Alberza), who died at the hands of the natives, although Díaz del Castillo believed that he was from Villanueva de la Serena, also in Badajoz (DdelC, 2:350). The two villages lie within 3 kilometers of one another. Boyd Bowman has a second entry with the name Alberza from Villanueva, on the basis of the Díaz del Castillo information (BB: item 594). Grunberg repeats the information from Díaz del Castillo (G: item 21).

51. *Pedro Martín Parra.* Thomas lists a conqueror by a similar name, Pedro Martín de Porras, but includes him among the Narváez expedition (HT, 210). Grunberg lists an Alonso Martín Jara, who, he indicates, arrived with Narváez (G: item 615).

---

52. *Pedro García.* A conqueror of this name signed the 1520 Segura de la Frontera letter. Thomas has a Pedro García Casado (HT, 297). Grunberg includes a Pedro García who, he suggests, died in the siege of Tenochtitlan (G: item 358). Boyd Bowman lists five men of this name as emigrating to the Indies before 1519.

53. *Alonso Romero.* Alonso Romero is one of the better-known members of the expedition. He was a signatory to the 1520 Segura de la Frontera letter. Originally from the province of Soria, in Spain, he had arrived in the Antilles by 1512. He became a *vecino* of a town on Hispaniola. Most pertinent to our study, Romero was elected as one of the *regidores* of La Villa Rica de la Vera Cruz, according to Díaz del Castillo, although that information is not included in the document (DdelC, 1:139). Díaz del Castillo goes on to note that Romero became a rich man following the conquest and died of natural causes (DdelC, 2:345). After the conquest he remained in Veracruz as a *vecino*. He received the town of Tlacotalpa in *encomienda*. Tlacotalpa was located within the Veracruz district to the southeast of the Spanish city. He also shared the *encomienda* of Tampacayal and Topla, located in the Valles de Oxitipa district to the northwest of Veracruz, with Cristóbal de Ortega. Romero lost his portion to Ortega. Moreover, Romero and his wife, Isabel Velez, had no children. Upon Romero's death the *encomienda* of Tlacotalpa passed to his wife, and then upon her death in 1541 it escheated to the Crown (Himmerich: item 388; G: item 908). There is contradictory evidence that Velez then married an early settler, Juan Sánchez de Olea. Sánchez de Olea argued that because Romero died so shortly after the conquest the inheritance provisions of the *encomienda* grant were not properly recognized (Icaza: item 1217).

54. *Juan de Magallanes.* Díaz del Castillo remembers Magallanes, a Portuguese, as a very nimble soldier ("bien suelto peón") (DdelC, 2:344). He was one of the members of the Cortés expedition to join Narváez when the latter came to challenge Cortés on behalf of Velázquez. Nevertheless, he rejoined Cortés and continued to fight in the company. He died when captured by the natives during the siege of Tenochtitlan, although others report that he died in the arms of Isabel Rodríguez (BB: item 5268; G: item 574). Thomas supposed that Magallanes was a relative of the circumnavigator (HT, 81).

55. *Alonso García.* There were three different men named Alonso García who participated in various stages of the conquest and settlement of New Spain (signatures 147 and 309). This one might well be the Alonso García who was killed when the forces of Narváez battled Cortés and his followers at Cempoalla. He was also known as *el carretero* ("the teamster") (DdelC, 1:374). One Alonso García signed the 1520 Segura de la Frontera letter.

56. *Fernán Blanco; Juan Blanco.* There are in fact two individuals mentioned in the literature. Fernán, or Fernando (Hernando), Blanco was one of the sig-

natories of the 1520 Segura de la Frontera letter. He probably came from Cumbres de San Bartolomé in Huelva, arriving in the New World in about 1516 (BB: item 1718). Juan Blanco is mentioned in one of the testimonies left by the conquerors. He was identified as Cortés's own steward (*dispensero*) (HT, 21).

57. *Alonso Fernández*. Fernández signed the 1520 Segura de la Frontera letter. Several men with the name Alonso Fernández immigrated to the New World, but all of them used a compound surname, such as Fernández Caballero or Fernández de Ecija. The absence of such a phrase here implies that this Alonso Fernández did not normally use a compound surname. Grunberg lists two conquerors of this name, both of whom died in the conquest (G: items 447–448).

58. *Juan Melgarejo*. Melgarejo signed the 1520 Segura de la Frontera letter. Other than his having a relatively unique surname, nothing is known of this conqueror. Grunberg assumes that he died by 1521 in the conquest (G: item 635).

59. *Diego González*. González was a native of La Parra, in Badajoz (BB: item 518). He served with Cortés through the fall of Tenochtitlan and beyond. He married a native woman from Cuba, who died shortly after the birth of their son. He married a second time in New Spain (Icaza: item 44). He settled in Puebla in 1543 and became a *vecino*. In subsequent years he received grants of land both in the city and in the surrounding territory. He might have also passed some time in the Taxco mining district. He received the town of Guazalingo, north of Puebla and south of Huexotla, in *encomienda*, which was later taken from him, and the grant passed to another around 1540 (Himmerich: item 170; G: item 401). He drew up a will in 1537, but does not seem to have died at that point. Between the conquest and his death he was a merchant (Alvarez: item 423).

60. *Ginés Nortes*. Nortes was one of the officers within the company. Early in the expedition he provided and captained one of its smaller ships. Later, during the siege of Tenochtitlan, he was captain of one of the brigantines. In the immediate wake of the fall of Tenochtitlan, Nortes remained loyal to Cortés even when others began to question his leadership and royal officials came from Spain to investigate his supposed treason against Diego Velázquez. He settled in Mexico City, where he held some property. Nortes eventually died in Yucatan, having been captured by warring natives (DdelC, 1:96, 101, 499; 2:238, 246, 342; G: item 710). Two men named Alonso Nortes signed the 1520 Segura de la Frontera letter.

61. *Juan Catalán*. Catalán had training as a gunner, and was assigned to clean and check the cannons for the expedition prior to their departure from Cuba. During the conquest he treated some of the wounded using the sign of the cross and with charms in the final battles during the siege (DdelC, 1:91; 2:19). His surname indicates that he was from Catalunya. After the conquest

he became a *vecino* of Mexico City. He received the town of Tlahuelilpa in *encomienda* along with part of Atitalaquia, in the Tula district (both north of Mexico City), until his death in about 1547. He shared these with a foreigner, Juan Ceciliano (see signature 256). With his death, the grants passed first to his widow, Ana de Segura, and then to his daughter, Juana de Acevedo. Ana had been married first to Diego Remón and was a maid in the household of a first settler, Juan de Cervantes (Alvarez: item 231; G: item 217; Himmerich: item 87).

62. *Melchor de Contreras.* No sources mention a conqueror of this name. An Alonso de Contreras signed the 1520 Segura de la Frontera letter and took an active role in the conquest; Alonso does not appear in the Veracruz petition.

63. *Alonso de Salamanca.* (See fig. 6.2.) An Alonso de Salamanca was a resident of Concepción on the island of Hispaniola in 1514 and then in Cuba in 1519, which would put him in the right place to be a member of the expedition (BB: item 2714). Two men by the name of Alonso de Salamanca signed the 1520 Segura de la Frontera letter. Grunberg includes him among the conquerors who died early in the conquest (G: item 932).

64. *Francisco de Medina.* There were at least two men of this name in the company. One of them participated in Gonzalo de Sandoval's expedition to Tuxtepec. This might also be one of the captains in Cortés's expedition to Coatzacoalcos. Díaz del Castillo reports that the captain was originally from Aracena in the district of Huelva (DdelC, 2:96, 194, 199, 236, 336). Unfortunately, he was killed while carrying messages to Cortés. López de Gómara writes that he died in a particularly cruel way: his body was pierced with burning splinters while he was forced to walk around a large hole[3] (HT, 88; G: item 629). The other Francisco de Medina, a good soldier, was from Medina del Campo and later became a Franciscan friar (DdelC, 2:345). He settled in the northern town of Santisteban, where he was active for a few years. By 1528 he was a *vecino* of Mexico City, and shortly thereafter he entered the Franciscan order (G: item 628).

65. *Alonso Pérez.* The only Alonso Pérez commonly found in lists of the conquerors was a university graduate, with the title of *bachiller*. Curiously, however, the signature on the Veracruz petition seems to be by exactly the same hand as that of Francisco de Medina, which is right beside it. Most notably, the rubrics — the curlicues before and after the actual signature — are identical. This implies that one or the other was illiterate and had his friend sign for him. It is possible that Pérez signed for Medina. Both came from the province of Huelva: Pérez was from Trigueros and Medina from Aracena, which were some 80 kilometers from one another. It is odd but not unheard of that Pérez would not include his title as part of his signature. On the 1520 Segura de la Frontera letter there were at least three persons with the name Alonso Pérez,

one of whom used the title *bachiller* (and who signed twice). As a result one must conclude that the Veracruz petition signer is not the *bachiller* Alonso Pérez. Grunberg assumed that they were three different men. In addition to the *bachiller*, one Alonso Pérez was a carpenter who sailed with Cortés but deserted upon the arrival of Narváez, only to be enlisted again with Cortés. The other Alonso Pérez left no details and probably died early in the conquest (G: items 780–782). Boyd Bowman lists a total of ten men of this name in his guide to early settlers, along with another eight with compound surnames such as Alonso Pérez Bocanegra (BB, 211). Alonso Pérez de Zamora also appears as a conqueror (Alvarez: item 822). It is possible that sources have conflated information about the different Alonso Pérezes into one biography (Alvarez item 821, for instance, might well include information about more than one person). Possibly this Alonso Pérez came from Béjar in Salamanca, traveled to Cuba in 1518, and participated in the conquest of Mexico (BB: item 2562).

66. *Hernando de Escalona.* (See fig. 6.7.) Díaz del Castillo mentions one member of the company with this surname, simply called "Escalona, *el mozo*" ("Escalona, the boy"). He died during the conquest (DdelC, 2:345). Boyd Bowman held that "the boy" was in fact Hernando de Escalona (BB: item 4266). Grunberg indicates that this Escalona was the one who deserted Cortés to join with Narváez, and who was badly wounded in the ensuing battle (DdelC, 1:335, 374; G: item 286). A Lucas de Escalona signed the 1520 Segura de la Frontera letter.

67. *Marcos Ramírez [Reyes?].* None of the traditional sources includes this conqueror. Only a Diego Ramírez signed the 1520 Segura de la Frontera letter. Grunberg mentions a Martín de los Reyes, who was a pilot for Narváez (G: item 856).

68. *Cristóbal Suárez.* None of the traditional sources mentions this conqueror. The abbreviation of the surname in the manuscript makes full identification difficult. There was a Cristóbal Suárez who sailed to the Indies in 1514 (BB: item 4218).

69. *Pedro Gallego.* There were two conquerors with this name. One was a footman, *mozo de espuelas.* He was captured by the Mexica and sacrificed. Díaz del Castillo criticizes Cortés for having failed to prevent the attack, which resulted in the death of two boys, the other being Francisco Martín de Vendabal (DdelC, 1:490, 2:339; G: item 338). The other Gallego was one of the better-known members of the company. Díaz del Castillo describes him as witty and a good talker. He settled down and ran an inn on the Veracruz-to-Mexico road (DdelC, 2:345). Grunberg held that he also went by the name of Lucas Gallego. He arrived in the Indies in about 1508 and served on expeditions of Ponce de León to Puerto Rico, acting as an interpreter. This Gallego supposedly arrived in New Spain with Narváez. It was he, according to Grunberg, who owned the

inn on the Veracruz-to-Mexico road. This Gallego received the village of Cua-cuacintla in *encomienda*. He married Catalina Rodríguez, the daughter of an-other conqueror, Francisco Rodríguez Magarino (G: item 337). There was also an early settler of this name who eventually became the third husband of doña Isabel Moctezuma and who received half of the village of Izcuinquitlapilco in *encomienda* (Himmerich: item 149; Thomas [HT, 59] conflated the conqueror with an early settler of the same name).

70. *Diego de Utrera*. None of the traditional sources mentions this con-queror. There was a conqueror identified as Diego de Olvera from Utera who appears in some lists (BB: item 4186), although Thomas makes him a native of Olvera in the district of Cádiz (HT, 219). That conqueror reportedly came with the Narváez expedition and thus would not have been a member of the company in Veracruz. He received the villages of Tecaxique, Chicaguaso, Aca-tlan, Cintla, and Xalapa in *encomienda* (Himmerich: item 317; G: item 730).

71. *Juan López*. As with other common names, there were several individuals with variants of this name; Díaz del Castillo, for instance, recalls Juan López de Aguirre, Juan López de Recalde, and Juan López de Ximena, but no simple Juan López. Among the signatories of the 1520 Segura de la Frontera letter there is a Juan López from Seville and another, a crossbowman from Zaragoza. The Juan López from Zaragoza also appears as Juan López Zaragozano. Yet another Juan López, from the village of Ronda in Andalucía, came with Nar-váez (HT, 206).

72. *Diego de Peñalosa*. There was one Peñalosa, a crossbowman, who was a companion of Sebastián Rodríguez (DdelC, 2:348). Thomas indicates that Diego Peñalosa was one of the men who climbed the volcano Popocateptl in search of sulfur in order to make more gunpowder (HT, 106). Grunberg writes that he was first a settler in Santo Domingo on the island of Hispaniola. After the fall of Tenochtitlan he went on to the conquest of Michoacan, and then by 1524 had established himself as a *vecino* of Mexico City. He died of natural causes sometime around 1528. He held the village of Ucila in *encomienda*, but upon his death it was reassigned (G: item 773).

73. *Juan de Trujillo*. Three men with this surname appear in Díaz del Cas-tillo (see also signature 290), but none seem to have been named Juan. Alonso, Andrés, and Pedro de Trujillo signed the 1520 Segura de la Frontera letter. One was a sailor who accompanied the expedition inland and served as one of the guards for Moteuczoma. He was notable for his lack of manners and poor up-bringing. He seriously offended the native lord. In particular, one night while guarding the native ruler, Trujillo said some scandalous things and stared di-rectly at the king, something prohibited by Mexica custom. Moteuczoma called on him the next day and gave him a large nugget of gold, asking him to stop staring. When Trujillo continued, thinking that he might get another

bribe, Moteuczoma complained to the captain of the guards, Juan Velázquez, who dismissed Trujillo from the guard (DdelC, 1:301–302). One of the other men named Trujillo was in fact a native of Trujillo in Extremadura and was known as being very hardworking; another was from Moguer, or Huelva, perhaps the sailor seen above, and was also known as a hard worker; the third was from León. All three died at the hands of the natives (DdelC, 2:339). None of the sources mentions a conqueror Juan de Trujillo. One Juan de Trujillo, from Plasencia in the province of Cáceres, sailed to Puerto Rico in 1511 (BB: item 1037). Another man going by this name, from Estepa in the province of Seville, immigrated to the Indies in 1511 (BB: item 3077).

74. *Hernando Dávila; Hernando de Avila.* None of the traditional sources mentions this conqueror. Díaz del Castillo writes that three members of the company had this surname. One was Gaspar de Avila; another was a member of the company led by Andrés de Tapia; and Díaz could not remember the details of the third man (DdelC, 2:344). Boyd Bowman lists two men with this name. One, from Avila, traveled to the Indies in 1515; the other, from Seville, was in Cuba in 1517–1518, immediately before Cortés set sail with his expedition (BB: items 121, 3248).

75. *Gutierre de ??? [Badajoz?].* The paper is torn, and thus the surname is a conjecture. Two men named Gutierre signed the 1520 Segura de la Frontera letter: Gutierre de Badajoz and Gutierre de Samont. The more famous of these is Gutierre de Badajoz, a letter combination which could fit with the partial signature on the document. Unfortunately the extant documentation indicates that this individual arrived in New Spain with Narváez, and thus could not have been present to sign the Veracruz petition (Icaza: item 64). Gutierre de Samont, also known as Samos, participated only in the early phase of the conquest and by mid-1521 had returned to the island of Hispaniola (G: item 948).

76. *Diego Pizarro.* Díaz del Castillo refers to Pizarro as a relative of Cortés who served at various times as a captain in the company (DdelC, 2:343). One of his first assignments was to take a small group of soldiers from Mexico City north to Tuxtepec to determine if there were mines in the area. The expedition included four soldiers with mining experience and took some forty days. He returned with only one companion but with over a thousand pesos' worth of gold dust. Two local lords from that territory also accompanied Pizarro. They offered friendship to Cortés and the Spaniards. The remaining miners rejoined the company after it was expelled from Tenochtitlan on the Noche Triste (DdelC, 1:317–320, 500). In the battle with Narváez, Pizarro was a captain of a small company of sixty men, mostly younger, including Díaz del Castillo. Their charge was to silence Narváez's artillery pieces. Then a similar company under the command of Gonzalo de Sandoval was to rush the native temple upon which Narváez had placed his command center, and capture him

if possible. Cortés promised three thousand pesos to the first man to capture Narváez. As a result, once Pizarro and his men completed their assignment, they too attacked the temple, seeking to capture Narváez (DdelC, 1:368–371). Pizarro was eventually captured and died at the hands of the natives (G: item 806; HT, 109).

77. *Miguel Navarro; Miguel de Navarra.* (See also signature 151.) It can be assumed that Miguel came from the kingdom of Navarre. Díaz del Castillo recalls a man named Navarro who had served in the company of Gonzalo de Sandoval within the larger expedition. After the conquest he settled in Veracruz and died there (DdelC, 2:345). There was a Juan Navarro among the signatories of the 1520 Segura de la Frontera letter. That conqueror survived, settled in Puebla, and was granted several villages in *encomienda*. According to testimony in the 1540s, he was a relative of the count of Belchite and a native of Xulbe (sic) in Aragón. He served with Cortés as a crossbowman. He died in the 1540s (Icaza: item 18). Grunberg includes an Antonio de Navarra, who, he stated, arrived with Narváez (G: item 702).

78. *Alonso Mi[. . .* The signature is too damaged to allow even a partial identification.

79. *Alonso de Vitoria.* The signature is badly damaged. Thomas includes him among the probable members of the company (HT, 141). Vitoria was originally from Madrid and sailed to the Indies in 1517. Following the conquest he settled in Oaxaca, although he may have also lived in Mexico City (Alvarez: item 1138). Grunberg includes an alias, Alonso Zimbrón de Vitoria. He writes that Vitoria arrived in a relief expedition of Pedro González de Nájera, and they participated in the conquest of Mexico. He remained in Mexico and in 1525 signed a contract with Juan de Salamanca to recover some money he was owed. By 1528 he was a *vecino* of Mexico City, married to a Spanish woman and eventually the father of a daughter and three sons. He served as a witness for other conquerors in their efforts to gain pensions from the Crown. He held the *encomienda* of Xalapa and Zenzontepec, which were taken away from him by the Second Audiencia (G: item 1154; Himmerich: item 505).

80. *Diego Anaya.* Díaz del Castillo mentions a good soldier by the name of Amaya who survived the conquest, settled in Oaxaca, and died there (DdelC, 2:340). Grunberg states that this was Pedro de Amaya, also known as Pedro de Maya (see signature 32). Díaz del Castillo also wrote about a member of the Narváez company who had the surname Anaya. He was one of four men sent to Veracruz by Narváez to meet with Gonzalo de Sandoval and explain the legal basis for his opposition to Cortés. Anaya was said to be a kinsman of Diego Velázquez. A little later, Anaya and a priest by the name of Guevara returned to Narváez and explained that Cortés was quite reasonable and urged

him to call off the attack. Narváez banished them from his sight. As a result, somewhat later, Anaya was among those followers of Narváez who repudiated him and declared their allegiance to Cortés, likely lured by promises of bounties for their decision (DdelC, 1:33, 342, 361). Thomas lists a Pedro de Anaya as possibly having been with the Cortés expedition (HT, 293). Grunberg includes Antonio de Amaya and Pedro de Amaya. Antonio died during the conquest (G: items 625–626).

81. *Pedro González.* It is possible that this conqueror had a second surname. Under any circumstances, this is also a very common name for the period. Díaz del Castillo mentions several men named Pedro González and with a second surname: Pedro González de Trujillo, Pedro González Nájera, and Pedro González Sabiote. To complicate matters even further, there was a Pedro González Nájera in both the Cortés company and the Narváez company. One of them was known as *el mozo* ("the younger").

82. *Hernando [de] Torres.* Torres signed the 1520 Segura de la Frontera letter. He was a native of Jaén in Andalucía. He sailed to the Indies in 1513 and arrived in Cuba in about 1518 (BB: item 2139). After the conquest he received land in Mexico City and became a *vecino.* He supported himself by being a miner in company with an early settler, Martín Jiménez, a *vecino* of Colima. Torres initially received the village of Tepecuaquilco in *encomienda.* He received an additional grant of some fifty small villages in the 1520s. He married Juana de Loaysa, who had a very valuable dowry, worth some 2,500 pesos. They had a daughter, doña Bernardina de Torres. Hernando de Torres died around 1548. The *encomienda* remained in the family throughout the sixteenth century (Himmerich: item 462). According to Grunberg, however, this conqueror arrived with Narváez and thus could not have signed the Veracruz petition. Grunberg states that Torres moved to Puebla in about 1537 and became a *vecino* there. He later served as a *regidor* of the city. He also provided testimony for other conquerors seeking royal grants. He died sometime in late 1541 (G: item 1049).

83. *Pedro Cornejo de Vitoria.* A Pedro de Vitoria immigrated to the Indies in 1513, and might possibly be this conqueror (BB: item 32). Díaz del Castillo writes of one soldier by the name of Cortejo, who was a member of the petty nobility in Spain. Cortejo was a companion of Alonso de Herrera (possibly signature 3). Herrera had wounded one of their companions, named Figueroa, and then fled. Cortejo was arrested and threatened with having his hand cut off (DdelC, 2:274–275). A Diego Gómez Cornejo signed the 1520 Segura de la

Frontera letter, as did a Pedro Vizcaíno (although Vitoria is in the province of Alava, another of the Basque provinces). Grunberg lists a Pedro de Villoria as a conqueror (G: item 1153).

84. *Juan de Ballesteros.* Ballesteros signed the 1520 Segura de la Frontera letter. In all likelihood he died during the conquest, since nothing further is known about him. Grunberg posits that he was killed during the final siege of Tenochtitlan (G: item 105).

85. *Juan de Escobar.* Díaz del Castillo mentions two members named Escobar. One was a *bachiller* who served as a pharmacist to the company. Although a solid soldier, the other man with the surname Escobar conducted himself badly, was temperamental, and raped a woman. For that crime he was hanged (DdelC, 2:348). Thomas concludes that Juan de Escobar was the bad conqueror (HT, 55). Grunberg identifies Pedro (Martín) de Escobar as the villainous one (G: item 289). He does not list a Juan de Escobar.

86. *Pedro Ruiz.* This is a common name. There were a few conquerors with the basic name, but often they had additional surnames. This conqueror might have been Pedro Ruiz de Guadalcanal. He arrived in Cuba in about 1518 and joined the Cortés expedition. After the conquest he became a resident of Zacatula. He received several villages in *encomienda*. He had five daughters and possibly one son by the same name, although the *encomienda* was inherited by his eldest daughter (Himmerich: item 401; G: item 920).

87. *Martín Izquierdo.* Díaz del Castillo mentions Martín Izquierdo and notes that he was a native of Castromocho, in the province of Palencia, in Spain. After the conquest he became a *vecino* in San Miguel in the province of Guatemala (DdelC, 2:344). He probably arrived in the Indies in 1513 and was in Cuba by 1518 (BB: items 2439 and 2440; G: item 494).

88. *Alvaro Gallego.* Gallego became a *vecino* of Mexico City and married a sister of some fellow named Zamora (DdelC, 2:347). In 1514 he was a settler in Hispaniola and received four estates on that island. He must have moved to Cuba in about 1518. Several sources indicate that he was a tailor with Narváez, although Grunberg has him as a member of the Díez de Aux expedition. He was one of the men credited with having gained access to the main temple in Tenochtitlan, with his shield in one hand and sword in the other. As he charged up the pyramid, pushing aside the defenders, he was struck on the nose by a stone, which almost killed him. He participated in some later expeditions, including the conquest of Michoacan and perhaps the initial phases of the conquest of Guatemala, where he came to be considered one of the opponents of Cortés and Alvarado. By 1525 he had settled in Mexico City and became a *vecino*. In Mexico he was active in local commerce. According to at least one document of the time he did not know how to sign his name. He was married to Leonor de la Peña, and they had at least two children. Peña must have been

the woman Díaz del Castillo believes was the sister of Zamora. Gallego died in about 1534 (G: item 330). At some point he might have moved to New Galicia, where he was *encomendero* of Chocandiro. The Crown granted him a coat of arms in 1529 based on his taking the Aztec temple (HT, 185; Himmerich: item 144; Villar: item 12; see fig. 6.15).

89. *Alonso de Ojeda.* Ojeda signed the 1520 Segura de la Frontera letter. Díaz del Castillo only remembers one company member called Ojeda, a fellow who lost an eye in the conquest and eventually settled in the Zapotec region. Alonso Ojeda received some towns in *encomienda* (DdelC, 2:338; Himmerich: item 311). He was probably a native of Moguer in Andalucía. Other evidence indicates that Alonso de Ojeda had previous military experience, having served as a captain in the conquest of Cuba. He joined the Grijalva expedition and was wounded in Yucatan by an arrow, thus losing an eye, but gaining the nickname "the one-eyed," *el tuerto.* In the Cortés expedition he was put in charge of the Tlaxcallan native auxiliaries, especially in the confrontation with Narváez and later in the final siege of Tenochtitlan. After defeating Narváez, Cortés instructed Ojeda to oversee the collecting of the weapons of the defeated soldiers. After they swore allegiance to Cortés, Ojeda gave back the arms. Once returned to Tenochtitlan, he was responsible for acquiring provisions for the trapped Spaniards. In the Noche Triste he watched to see that no Spaniard was forgotten in their flight from the city. Ojeda was one of the men who supervised the transport of the brigantines from Tlaxcala to Texcoco. He also took a company of natives to retrieve two of the cannon which had been left in Veracruz. He participated in several later expeditions, including Honduras and Guatemala. By 1524 he was a *vecino* of Guatemala. He then moved to San Ildefonso de los Zapotecas, where he was a *vecino* and *regidor*. He shared the village of Tiltepec in *encomienda* with Rodrigo de Segura. Ojeda lived probably until about 1573. He might have been one of the principal informants for Francisco Cervantes de Salazar when Cervantes wrote his history of the conquest. Ojeda married Ana de Arcos in about 1536 and had six children, at least two of whom were sons. His sister married Nuflo Martín, one of the pilots of the expedition (G: item 721; HT, 100–101).

90. *Alonso Rodríguez.* Four men of this name signed the Veracruz petition (see signatures 4, 138, and 187). This Rodríguez may have been a settler on the island of Cuba, where he owned several productive gold mines. He joined the Cortés expedition but was killed in action during the conquest of Los Peñoles in the Mixteca Alta in 1520–1521 (DdelC, 2:350).

91. *Rodrigo de Castañeda.* Signed the 1520 Segura de la Frontera letter. Díaz del Castillo reports that Castañeda had the unique distinction among the conquerors of having learned the Nahuatl language. After the conquest he returned to Spain, where he died (DdelC, 2:338; G: item 208). Other sources contrib-

ute various bits of information: He was from the village of Valle de Carriedo in Santander. He sailed in the ship of Pedro de Alvarado in the Cortés expedition. He took a very active role in the conquest and remained in the company commanded by Alvarado for most of its duration. For example, he stayed in Tenochtitlan when Cortés marched out to engage Narváez. Castañeda also appears in native accounts of the conquest. The cockade of feathers in his hat and his feats of daring reminded the Tlaxcalan natives of their leader Xicotencatl, and so they gave Castañeda that nickname. His association with Alvarado likely tainted his view of Cortés. He served in later conquests, including the Alvarado expedition to Guatemala. Because of his friendship with Alvarado and enmity toward Cortés he was in the middle of the conflicts which disturbed Mexico in the years following the conquest. He was assigned and lost an early *encomienda*. By 1529 he had been recognized as a *vecino* of Mexico, where he continued to live and work, serving as an interpreter for the royal *audiencia*. Castañeda also served as *alguacil* for the city, and the royal government made him a local magistrate in several rural jurisdictions. In 1527 the Crown awarded him a coat of arms for his efforts in the conquest (Villar: item 9; see fig. 6.16). He was living in Mexico as late as 1557, but possibly died in Spain sometime after 1560. The Second Audiencia granted him a new *encomienda*, the village of Puctla far to the east and south of Mexico City, in recognition of his services to the Crown, in essence undoing the loss of the earlier grant in the turmoil after the conquest. He married Ana de León and they had eight children, six of whom were sons (HT, 27; Himmerich: item 82; G: item 208).

92. *Francisco de Granada.* Díaz del Castillo remembers a conqueror called Granado, a good soldier who tried hard (DdelC, 2:338).[4] Granada fought well during the conquest, and during the Noche Triste was shot in the face with an arrow, which Santos Hernández (signature 172) is said to have removed. Granada participated in several of the later skirmishes and battles, including those of the Guatemala expedition. He claimed that he lost his horse during the conquest, and asked for recompense from the Crown. He was one of the first *vecinos* in Mexico City. He was considered to be one of the enemies of Cortés and fled for a while to Guatemala. Nevertheless, he does seem to have supported Cortés during the latter's planned expedition to the South Pacific. He was a frequent witness when his fellow conquerors drew up testimony regarding their own exploits in the conquest and also filed his own request. Granada received a pension of 250 pesos from the Crown in 1547, and this was increased to 350 pesos in 1554. In further recognition of his service the Crown awarded him a coat of arms in 1532 (Villar: item 20; see fig. 6.17). He received an *encomienda*, which was lost in the turmoil following the conquest. He did own some estates in Jilotepec. All evidence indicates that he did not marry, but did father several

mestizo children. He died sometime around 1571 (Icaza: item 40; HT, 64; G: item 414).[5]

93. *Juan de Palacios*. Juan de Palacios left Palacios de Meneses in the province of Burgos and immigrated to the Indies in 1516 (BB: item 799). A Nicolás de Palacios signed the 1520 Segura de la Frontera letter (Dor, 346; G: item 757). There is some confusion as to whether this person might be the slightly better known Nicolás Palacios Rubios mentioned by Díaz del Castillo. Palacios Rubios probably did not arrive with the Cortés expedition but rather, in all likelihood, after the fall of Tenochtitlan. That conqueror's horse reportedly died because its body fat just melted away after it was ridden so hard in the Honduras expedition. A kinsman of Cortés, Palacios Rubios, broke his arm on that same expedition (DdelC, 2:208, 210).

94. *Cristóbal de Jaén*. Jaén was a carpenter in the company. According to Díaz del Castillo, Jaén was killed by the natives (DdelC, 2:347). He might have arrived in the New World in 1514 from Valladolid in Spain (G: item 495).

95. *Juan de Mora*. There was a conqueror with the surname Mora, who was a good soldier who died in a battle in the highlands of Guatemala (DdelC, 2:336). This might also be the conqueror Morales mentioned by Díaz del Castillo as the *alcalde ordinario* of Veracruz, who had been in the company of the *comendador* Solís. He was already old at the outset of the conquest and walked with a pronounced limp. As municipal judge he was fair and equitable (DdelC, 2:345). The 1520 Segura de la Frontera letter was signed by a Juan de Morales. Juan de Morales was not with the original Cortés company but joined them, along with his friend Diego de Camargo, after sailing in on the relief ships of Francisco de Garay. This means that he probably arrived too late to have signed the Veracruz petition. He fled Tenochtitlan during the Noche Triste. He later participated in Cortés's expeditions to Honduras and to California. By 1527 he had been granted a house lot in Mexico City and become a *vecino*. In 1529–1530 he returned to Spain to be married to Ana de Agüero. He served as a witness for other conquerors, testifying that he was illiterate. By 1540 he had moved to Puebla, where he was granted several house plots and rural land. He bought and sold several pieces of land there. He received the village of Ocuila in *encomienda*, along with Servan Bejarano. He lost that grant when he returned to Spain, but on his return the viceroy assigned him the village of Suchitepec. He died in about 1560–1561 without any known children (Icaza: item 138; G: item 669). Grunberg includes one conquistador with the surname Mora, Alonso, from Ciudad Rodrigo. He sailed with Cortés and then later stayed on in New Spain. Grunberg links him with the conqueror Díaz del Castillo describes as dying in Guatemala (G: item 666). Some of the sources mention a Morales Nedros, or Morales Netros, but with the given name Francisco (see signa-

ture 1). Morales Nedros participated in the final siege of Mexico, but left little trace after that (HT, 215; G: item 671).

96. *Juan de Medina.* Medina was a servant of Cortés. He distinguished himself in the conquest and received the village of Texupespa in *encomienda.* He initially settled in Mexico City in 1525, where he was a *vecino.* In 1542 he was elected as one of the two rural judges of city council, *alcalde de mesta.* At least one source indicates that he later moved to Pánuco. He was married to Juana Clavijo, and they had two sons and a daughter. Medina died in about 1545 (Icaza: item 284; HT, 88; G: item 631; Himmerich: item 270). Díaz del Castillo mentions another Juan de Medina, who arrived in one of the Garay companies in about 1523; this individual had only one eye, *el tuerto* (DdelC, 2:113).

97. *Pedro Lizato.* There is no information about this conqueror. The closest possibility is Juan de Lizana. In testimony after the conquest his widow claimed that he had arrived with Cortés and then received an *encomienda*, which eventually escheated to the Crown. They had four children (Icaza: item 904). (See also signature 39.)

98. *Diego Hernández Borrego.* None of the sources mentions a conqueror with this compound surname, although there are four men named Diego Hernández. The most famous of these came from a town called Saelices de los Gallegos in the province of Salamanca, and was a sawyer. He is credited with providing the boards used in the construction of the brigantines utilized in the final assault on Tencochtitlan. He was a very strong man, capable of hurling a rock like a cannon. He participated in later battles of the conquest, and eventually settled in Mexico City. He lost his sight, dying a natural death sometime around 1558. He married a mestiza, and had at least five children. He might have been a companion of Juan de Valladolid (signature 99, following this entry), since both were from villages in Salamanca (DdelC, 2:343; HT, 66–67; G: item 453; BB: item 2651). One need also consider the men listed with the surname Fernández. Diego Fernández Nieto also served under Cortés from the beginning. After the conquest he settled in Mexico City, and received the town of Turicato in Michoacan in *encomienda.* He was married with seven children. The Crown awarded him a coat of arms for his service (Himmerich: item 131). A Diego Fernández signed the 1520 Segura de la Frontera letter. Another Diego Hernández arrived with Narváez and distinguished himself in the conquest. He participated in later campaigns in Honduras and Pánuco (HT, 199, listing him as *encomendero* of Turicato). Thomas also mentions Diego Hernández Calvo as a conqueror (HT, 299). Because of the juxtaposition of this signature with those of Juan Rico and Juan Ruiz (signatures 100 and 101 below), both of whom might have come from Alanís, we infer that this individual might well be the conqueror named Diego Hernández de Alanís mentioned by Díaz del

Castillo (DdelC, 2:339). Another Diego Hernández also signed the Veracruz petition (see signature 132).

99. *Juan de Valladolid*. Two men with this surname are mentioned by Díaz del Castillo. Both died at the hands of the natives. One eventually settled in Colima, or Zacatula. The other was a good soldier, known as *el gordo*, "the fat one" (DdelC, 2:339–340). One Juan de Valladolid was from Alberca, Salamanca. He settled in Cuba in about 1518, and there joined the Cortés expedition. This might possibly be the conqueror who inscribed both this and the entry above, signing for Fernández, since both were from villages in the province of Salamanca (BB: item 2546). Two men named Valladolid signed the 1520 Segura de la Frontera letter: Rodrigo and Rodrigo Juan. The list in Dorantes has two of them named Juan, plus a Rodrigo (Dor, 350).

100. *Juan Rico*. Juan Rico also signed the 1520 Segura de la Frontera letter. Later sources list a Juan Rico de Alanís and Juan Ruiz de Alanís. Díaz del Castillo lists three fellows from Alanís in succession: Juan Rico de Alanís, Gonzalo Hernández de Alanís, and Juan Ruiz de Alanís. Juan Rico de Alanís was a good soldier who died at the hands of the natives (DdelC, 2:339). In all likelihood this conqueror is Juan Rico de Alanís, and he signed for both himself and Juan Ruiz [de Alanís], who follows. Juan Rico was from Alanís, in the highlands north of Seville. Grunberg writes that he died in the final siege of Tenochtitlan (G: item 859). Thomas held that Juan Rico de Alanís and Juan Ruiz de Alanís were the same individual, although Díaz del Castillo lists them together but as separate (HT, 112).

101. *Juan Ruiz*. Juan Ruiz de Alanís also signed the 1520 Segura de la Frontera letter. Clearly all of the information about Juan Rico (above) might well be applicable to Juan Ruiz, because of the confusion of their names. Thomas contended that they were the same man, but Díaz del Castillo describes them as different individuals (HT, 112). In all likelihood this conqueror is Juan Ruiz de Alanís. It seems that one person signed for both Rico and Ruiz. Ruiz de Alanís first sailed to Mexico with Hernández de Córdoba and then with the Cortés expedition. Others indicate that Ruiz de Alanís arrived with Narváez (Himmerich: item 398). He reportedly was one of the first conquerors to eat dog, as prepared by the natives, and liked it. He also claimed to have been one of the first Spaniards in New Spain to see the Pacific. It is not clear where he settled, but he did provide testimony for a few of his comrades. After the conquest he received half of the town of Tehuacan in *encomienda* along with Antonio Caicedo. He married Leonor de Castañeda, and they had at least one son. Ruiz died in about 1533 (HT, 112; G: item 921). There were other conquistadors named Juan Ruiz, including Juan Ruiz de la Parra, Juan Ruiz de Viana, and Juan Ruiz de Guevara. Juan Ruiz signed the 1520 Segura de la Frontera letter,

as did Ruiz de Alanís and Ruiz de Viana. Grunberg tells us that Ruiz de Guevara arrived with Narváez, and so we might be able to discount his presence in Veracruz (G: item 922). Díaz del Castillo recalls that Ruiz de la Parra settled in Colima or Zacatula where he died (DdelC, 2:340). Little is known of Ruiz de Viana, whose signature is on the 1520 Segura de la Frontera letter. Thomas indicates that he sailed in the Hernández de Córdoba expedition, and later served with Cortés, surviving the conquest (HT, 117). Thomas also lists Juan Ruiz Sedeño, who lived in Oaxaca, and Juan Ruiz de Mansilla. Ruiz de Mansilla, also known as Juan de Mansilla (see signature 274), was part of the group who opposed Cortés, but he nevertheless received an *encomienda*, half of the village of Atlatlauca. He sold his rights to the grant and returned to Spain (HT, 117; Himmerich: item 248: G: item 582).

102. *Martín de Solís.* While there are several men with this surname in the various sources, none is named Martín. Two men with the surname Solís, a Francisco and a Pedro (signature 215), signed the 1520 Segura de la Frontera letter. Díaz tells of a Solís known as *de la huerta* ("of the garden") because he had a rich garden from which he prospered, although Grunberg believed he was Francisco Solís (G: item 1007). Another Solís was known as *sayo de seda* ("silk coat") because he appreciated wearing silk (DdelC, 2:337). A Juan de Solís seems to have held some villages in *encomienda* in a type of joint tenancy with Cortés (HT, 122; Himmerich: item 442). One Martín de Solís arrived in Santo Domingo from Seville in 1511. He was a royal scribe. He served on the island of Hispaniola until 1517, when he went to Santiago de Cuba to serve as the secretary of the town council, which he did until 1525. He then returned to Santo Domingo, where he remained at least until 1529. It is highly unlikely that this particular Solís was our conqueror (BB: item 4027).
(*Between Solís and Lepuzcano a name has been scratched out.*)

103. *Rodrigo de Lepuzcano.* Thomas notes that this conqueror came from Guipuzcoa and was one of the first to settle in Colima (HT, 74; BB: item 1645e). Grunberg lists this conqueror as Rodrigo Guipuzcano. Guipuzcano/Lepuzcano/Guipuzcoano served in Italy prior to sailing to the Indies. He took part in the conquest of Cuba and then joined the Cortés company. He served in later conquests as well, taking part in events at Coatzacoalcos and New Galicia, the latter under the command of Nuño de Guzmán. He settled in Colima sometime before 1531, and died in about 1546. He was granted a village in *encomienda*: Milpa, in the Colima region. He held this along with an early settler, Pedro de Santa Cruz. He claimed that the income was so small that he could not dress in a manner appropriate for someone appearing in a Spanish village. Guipuzcoano married, and they had at least one son, Francisco Lepuzcano, who inherited the *encomienda* and eventually became a *vecino* of Puebla (G: item 428; Himmerich: item 182; Icaza: item 481).

104. *Alonso Cav . . . ; Alonso Alvarez, maestre.* This conqueror notes that he was a ship's master. Alonso Alvarez signed the 1520 Segura de la Frontera letter, and was probably killed in action before the fall of Tenochtitlan (G: item 45). Thomas mentions another Alonso Alvarez, who arrived with Narváez and who eventually joined those opposed to Cortés (HT, 163). Another Alonso Alvarez, also known as Alonso Alvarez de Espinosa, served with Cortés in the Honduras expedition, and in other conquests. He ultimately settled in Campostela, in New Galicia. He received the villages of Tintoc, Xiquian, and Izcuyuacan in *encomienda.* These were located in the far western district of Tepic (Icaza: item 1206).[6]

105. *Pedro de Alanís.* Alanís signed the 1520 Segura de la Frontera letter. This conqueror was a native of Marchena, in the province of Seville. He sailed to Santo Domingo in 1505, was in Cuba by 1518, and participated in the conquest of Mexico and later the conquest of Michoacan. He was known as a crossbowman (BB: item 3125; HT, 4; G: item 17). His signature appears in the same general section of this document as three other men from the village of Alanís, also near Seville (signatures 98, 100, and 101). He might possibly have been related to them. Although Marchena is in the Seville region, it is about one hundred kilometers from Alanís.

106. *Alonso Díaz.* Alonso Díaz is a very common name. Boyd Bowman lists seven men by that name. This conqueror might have been any one of them. It is unlikely that he survived the conquest (BB: items 1348, 1912, 2421, 3363–3365, and 4360). An Alonso Díaz de la Reguera arrived with the Alderete company in February of 1521, according to Díaz del Castillo (DdelC, 1: 471). Thomas includes him among both the Narváez and the Alderete companies. Díaz de la Reguera went on to the conquest of Guatemala, where he eventually settled (HT, 182, 280–81).

107. *Diego Bermúdez, piloto.* This conqueror signed with a note that he was a pilot. He also signed the 1520 Segura de la Frontera letter. It seems that he was from Palos, in Andalucía, and first sailed with Columbus in 1492. He also participated in the voyage of Ponce de León to Florida, as a ship's master. His brother was probably Juan Bermúdez, also a pilot, after whom the island of Bermuda is named. Diego probably died during the conquest (BB: item 1893; HT, 169; G: item 130).

108. *Diego Moreno.* This conqueror also signed the 1520 Segura de la Frontera letter. He was probably originally from Ecija, in Andalucía, sailing to the Indies in 1516 and on to Cuba in 1519 (BB: item 3062). A man of this name signed a letter in 1520 in support of Diego Velázquez and might have sailed with the Narváez expedition. He was known to have served with Juan Magallanes in leading a company of native auxiliaries after the defeat of Narváez. He also served under Alonso de Ojeda, carrying food to the troops who brought

the artillery up from the coast to Tlaxcala. He probably died in the final assault on Tenochtitlan (G: item 676).

109. *Gómez Merino.* No known conqueror has a similar name. A Juan Gómez Cornejo signed the 1520 Segura de la Frontera letter (see signature 111 for others with a surname of Gómez). Thomas lists him as Diego Gómez Cornejo (HT, 190).

110. *Francisco Montoya; Antonio Goya.* No known conqueror has either name. Both a Francisco Montaño and a Francisco Montejo played major roles in the conquest.

111. *Juan Gómez Jayolo.* Juan Gómez signed the 1520 Segura de la Frontera letter. Juan Gómez is one of the most common names in Spanish. Díaz del Castillo tells of one Juan Gómez who settled in Guatemala, became rich, and returned to Spain (DdelC, 2:340). This conqueror might also be Juan Gómez de Almazán, Gómez de Estarcena, Gómez de Herrera, or Gómez de Peñaparda, or Gómez de Sotomayor, although most of these individuals sailed with later companies. Juan Gómez de Herrera probably accompanied Cortés. He settled in Zacatula and the Second Audiencia awarded him the village of Arimao in Michoacan in *encomienda* (Himmerich: item 165; G: item 393). (See also signature 109.)

112. *Juan del Puerto.* Del Puerto signed the 1520 Segura de la Frontera letter. Díaz del Castillo remembers Juan del Puerto as a good soldier who contracted syphilis and was left crippled (DdelC, 2:342). Others indicate that he fought on one of the brigantines in the final siege of Tenochtitlan. He settled in the Pánuco region, and was granted an *encomienda*, Tanquera, perhaps in the Valles region. He died in about 1533 (G: item 826). Still others report that he was originally from El Puerto de Santa María, in Andalucía. He might have been a miner on the island of Santo Domingo. In 1512 he went with the expedition to the Darien region, south of Panama. After that he settled on the island of Cuba. He is reported to have died during the conquest (HT, 110).

113. *Bernaldino de Santiago.* Santiago served in the conquests of Mexico and Guatemala. He signed the 1520 Segura de la Frontera letter. Most sources agree that this conqueror was from Santiago de la Puebla, in Salamanca. He was wounded during the Noche Triste. He later fought in Tuxtepec and Guatemala, and received an *encomienda* in the Coatzacoalcos region, but by the 1540s there were no Indians in the village. In the 1520s and 1530s he gave testimony for other conquerors. Between 1535 and 1543 he served as a local magistrate in a variety of jurisdictions. Sometime around 1551 he sailed to Spain, but was shipwrecked and died after being rescued while being taken to Puerto Rico. In 1554 his widow, Mari López Contado, became a nun in the Madre de Dios convent in Mexico City (Icaza: item 42; G: item 981; HT, 149). Another conqueror

with this surname, originally from Huelva in Andalucía, became quite rich and also returned to Spain. The unknown Santiago was a friend of Pedro Ponce (signature 220) (DdelC, 2:348).

114. *Hernando de Solís.* None of the traditional sources mentions this conqueror. One does include a Garci Hernández de Solís, who was killed by the Aztecs during the Noche Triste. His brother, Francisco de Solís, was also a conqueror (Icaza: item 1278; G: item 1008). Two men named Francisco de Solís and a García Fernández signed the 1520 Segura de la Frontera letter. (Signature 102 lists the other Solís conquerors.)

115. *Martín de Laredo.* None of the traditional sources mentions this conqueror. Two men named Juan and one Diego de Laredo had immigrated to the Indies by 1519 (BB: items 2803a–2805).

116. *Diego Bardabo (Bardavo?).* This conqueror is probably Diego Bardales, who also signed the 1520 Segura de la Frontera letter. While he arrived with the Cortés expedition, he left New Spain and by September of 1521 was back in Santo Domingo. He left in the company of Diego de Ordaz shortly after the Spaniards entered Tenochtitlan. Ordaz had been sent out to pacify some of the provinces. After his absence, Bardales returned to settle in New Spain, receiving some property in Mexico City. He died in 1525 (G: item 116).

117. *Pedro Arias de Sopuerta.* Originally from Sopuerta in Vizcaya, Arias de Sopuerta had arrived in the Indies in 1516. It is not clear if he actually participated in the conquest of Mexico. He might well have left the company shortly after the founding of Veracruz. By 1524 he was serving as a lieutenant sheriff (*teniente de alguacil*) in Cuba (BB: item 4763; HT, 17; G: item 73). Another man from Sopuerta also participated in the conquest, Diego Sánchez de Sopuerta (see signature 119). Someone named Sopuerta was one of four pilots on the Cortés expedition, but that man was from the Huelva region, not Vizcaya (DdelC, 2:347). Nevertheless, if Díaz del Castillo were incorrect, or if Arias de Sopuerta was actually from Huelva, it might explain his absence from the record of the conquest: namely, that he was piloting one of the ships which left New Spain before the company moved inland.

118. *Rodrigo de Nájera.* Nájera signed the 1520 Segura de la Frontera letter. Díaz del Castillo probably had this conqueror in mind when he wrote of "Rodrigo de Jara," a hunchback (*el corcovado*) who died in Colima or Zacatula (DdelC, 2:339). Nájera sailed to New Spain with Juan de Salcedo, arriving just a few days after Cortés landed at Veracruz. He participated in all phases of the conquest, from the entrance into Tenochtitlan, to the Noche Triste, to the founding of Segura de la Frontera. He helped to construct the brigantines used in the final siege. Following the conquest, Gil González de Benavides hired him on as a miner in Michoacan. He provided testimony for a few other

conquerors, and eventually became a settler in Zacatula. He died sometime around 1544 (G: item 697; HT, 96). He might have been related to Francisco de Nájera (signature 143).

119. *[Diego?] Sancho (de) Sopuerta.* There might be a connection between this conqueror and Pedro Arias de Sopuerta (signature 117). Although he was originally from San Martín de Valdeiglesias in Madrid, he had settled in the Andalucian port town of Moguer. He sailed to the Indies in about 1502 and then lived on the island of Hispaniola. He later participated in the conquest of Cuba and received an *encomienda* for his services. He probably sailed on the Grijalva expedition. After that, sources differ on when he arrived in New Spain. Some say he sailed with the original Cortés company, and others say with Narváez, although his signature here confirms the former. He was badly injured during the Noche Triste. He later worked on the brigantines, participated in the fighting in Tenochtitlan, was injured, given up for dead, and finally rescued. He received the town of Talasco in *encomienda*. He settled in Mexico City in about 1524, and in 1528 became a *vecino* of the city. He married Anna Gutiérrez, possibly a native woman, after the conquest and they had at least two sons and a daughter. He died sometime around 1534. His brother, Alonso Sánchez de Sopuerta, a hatmaker, was also an early resident of Mexico City (HT, 237; G: item 969; Himmerich: item 419; Icaza: items 1108–1109).

120. *Diego Enos.* Although the signature seems clear enough, there is no one of this name or anything similar in the literature. The man named Cindo del Portillo comes close, also known as Jacinto, or Cinto, del Portillo (HT, 109). From León, Portillo arrived in the Indies in 1514 and in Cuba by 1518. He might have sailed with both Hernández de Córdoba and Grijalva before joining Cortés as a member of his personal guard. After the conquest he participated in two more explorations, one to the Gulf Coast and another to the Pacific. In about 1528 he was nearly killed when the natives and his slaves revolted to protest his mistreatment of them. The event changed his life. He attributed his rescue to God, gave up his slaves, and joined the Franciscan order. He served as porter for many years in the friary in Mexico City. In the 1560s he accompanied an expedition to Zacatecas, where he served as a missionary. He died in Nombre de Dios after being bitten by a poisonous spider, in 1566–1567 (HT, 109; G: item 820).[7]

121. *Francisco Donal.* Díaz del Castillo remembers a Francisco Donaire, a blacksmith, who accompanied the Sandoval expedition to Honduras. Donaire had a good horse, named "Motilla," who went with him. Díaz del Castillo praises this horse as the best in all of New Spain, and says that even the king had notice of it. It was a somewhat dark chestnut color, a good runner. It is not clear from Díaz del Castillo's comments whether Donaire was a member of the original Cortés company (DdelC, 2:243). This might be the same Francisco

Donaire (Donayre) who immigrated from Mérida along with his two brothers, Diego and Gonzalo, to the New World in 1513 (BB: item 479).

122. *Antonio Xuarez; Cristóbal Ortiz.* The signature is extremely difficult to interpret. None of the sources mentions an Antonio Juárez or Suárez. There was a conqueror named Cristóbal Ortiz (see signature 159). He is identified with the conqueror Ortiz described by Díaz del Castillo as a musician and dancer (DdelC, 2:349). Probably from Zalamea in Badajoz, he arrived in the Indies in 1517 and settled in Cuba in 1519. He signed the 1520 Segura de la Frontera letter. He was part-owner of a horse used in the expedition, along with his good friend Bartolomé García (signature 206). His absence from the documentation after 1521 leads one to conclude that he died during the conquest (G: item 744).[8]

123. *Juan de Vallejo.* A Juan de Vallejo from Barco in the province of Avila sailed to the New World in 1514 (BB: item 160). Otherwise no conqueror of this name appears in the literature. The only Vallejo known to have been in the Cortés company is Pedro. He settled in Cuba by 1514. He probably arrived after the fall of Tenochtitlan and went to Pánuco, where he was named the lieutenant governor by Cortés. By 1525 he was living in Mexico. He died in about 1528 of an arrow in a battle with natives in Pánuco (DdelC, 2:107–109, 117; G: item 1091).

124. *Cristóbal (de) Flores.* Flores signed the 1520 Segura de la Frontera letter. He is described as a worthy member of the company. Díaz del Castillo reports that he died of pneumonia in the expedition to Jalisco led by Nuño de Guzmán in 1531 (DdelC, 2:335). He was a native of Valencia de San Juan, and a relative of the conqueror Diego de Ordaz. Some sources indicate that he served as captain of one of the brigantines in the final assault on Tenochtitlan (HT, 55). He was an important member of the company and was elected one of the town councilmen, *regidores*, of Veracruz. He later settled in Mexico City, where he also served as a *regidor* (in 1524 and 1528 and beyond) and *alcalde ordinario* (in 1526 and 1527). Flores served the city council as an inspector of garden plots allocated to city residents. He received some prime land himself from the cabildo: a city lot on the Tacuba road. He also had as many as three other pieces of real estate in the city. The Inquisition imprisoned him on charges of blasphemy and apostasy, which were later dropped. There is no record of him having married, although he did have one daughter. He probably was granted the towns of Tenayuca and Chilapa in *encomienda*. Upon Flores's death, in about 1532, the *encomienda* escheated to the Crown, indicating that the daughter was probably illegitimate. In spite of what Díaz del Castillo reports, Flores must have briefly survived the Jalisco expedition, since he is credited with having written an account of the sojourn (G: item 310; Himmerich: items 319 and 460).[9]

125. *Bernardino (Bernaldino) de Tapia.* None of the traditional sources men-

tions a Bernardino or a Bernaldino de Tapia with no additional surname. Several other Tapias are well documented in the conquest. One of the first Spaniards in the New World was a Bernardino de Tapia, who sailed with Columbus in 1492 but was killed by the natives the next year (BB: item 2629). Sources mention Andrés, Hernando, Juan, and Pedro de Tapia in the Cortés company, but none of these appear in this letter. A drummer with this surname, described as a little crazy, is listed as a member of the Narváez company (DdelC, 1:374).

There is, however, a very famous member of the company with the name Bernardino Vázquez de Tapia. Vázquez de Tapia signed the 1520 Segura de la Frontera letter. He was one of the best-educated and most socially prominent of the conquerors. A native of Oropesa, he had one uncle who was a high-ranking inquisitor, and another who was a professor of theology at the University of Salamanca. Vázquez de Tapia attended the university, as a student in the Colegio Mayor de San Bartolomé. He sailed to the Indies in 1514, participating in the conquest and settlement of what is now Panama with Pedrarias Dávila. From there he became a settler in Cuba, gaining an *encomienda*. He participated in the voyage of Grijalva as the royal standard-bearer (*alférez real*), a position of very high status. He joined the Cortés expedition and served as a treasury officer, *factor*, after selling his possessions in Cuba to raise money. At Veracruz he was elected town councilman, *regidor*. He was one of the few horsemen in the conquest. He played a leading role in the conquest. He was a close advisor to Cortés and signed the certification of Cortés's third letter to the Crown in 1522 (Cortés, 202). As one of the officials of the expedition, he helped to legally establish Mexico City, was appointed *regidor*, and eventually received a lifetime appointment to that post from the Crown. He received several towns in *encomienda*, the most important of which was Churubusco, now a neighborhood of Mexico City, then an outlying village. He also participated in several of the later expeditions of conquest, including Pánuco. He was sent on two occasions (1526 and 1530) to represent the interests of the settlers of Mexico before the Spanish Crown. He was married twice and had at least one daughter and one son by the second marriage. He also brought three nieces from Spain to marry to other conquerors and early settlers. He died in 1559 (HT, 136–138; G: item 1104).[10]

126. *Hernando de Almonte*. A Fernando Almonte, from Seville, sailed to the Indies in 1517 (BB: item 3200). None of the traditional sources mentions a Hernando de Almonte taking part in the conquest of Mexico. There was an early settler by the name of Alonso Hernández de Almonte (Icaza: item 1151).

127. *Juan de Valdelamar (Valdelomar)*. Grunberg includes a man with the surname Valdelomar who was a resident of Santo Domingo in 1514 and who joined the Cortés company. He was probably killed in the conquest (G: item 1072).

128. *Hernando de Osma.* This conqueror had several adventures in the conquest. He was wounded several times and recovered. He was probably killed in action prior to the final siege of Tenochtitlan (G: item 747).[11] He might be the same person as the Fernando de Osuna who signed the 1520 Segura de la Frontera letter.

129. *Hernán Martín Herrero.* This conqueror was in fact a blacksmith, *herrero*, and that term is added here to his name, Hernán Martín. He is one of three blacksmiths listed by Díaz del Castillo; the others were Juan García and a man Díaz could not remember. He signed the 1520 Segura de la Frontera letter. Martín married a female member of the company called "La Bermuda," one of two by that nickname, probably Catalina Márquez. She and Martín eventually settled in Oaxaca (DdelC, 2:66, 347). He was probably from Palos near Huelva in Andalucía, since he was also known as Hernán Martín de Palos. As a blacksmith, Martín found many assignments during the conquest. He helped to dismantle the ships at Veracruz, saving their iron fittings. When the Narváez expedition arrived, he was building a new ship in Veracruz. He later helped to install the iron work on the brigantines used in the final assault on Mexico and was second in command to Martín López. After the conquest, he settled in Mexico City, where in 1524 he received a plot of land for a home from the city council. He was a *vecino* of Mexico City and continued to work as a blacksmith, although he also had contracts for working in precious metals and lead. He provided testimony for his fellow conquerors. He also sought repayment from Cortés for various bits of work he did during the conquest. In Mexico City he served as the steward of the hospital and sodality of Santa Vera Cruz. He later moved to Oaxaca, sometime before 1532. It is also possible that he moved to Puebla in about 1535. Martín received the town of Malinaltepec in *encomienda*. He died in about 1543, and the *encomienda* passed to his widow and her second husband, an early settler named Bartolomé Tofiño (G: item 602; Himmerich: item 260).

130. *Juan Darcos.* Juan de Arcos was originally from Niebla in the province of Huelva. He arrived in Panama in about 1515, and then passed to Cuba to become a member of the company. After the conquest, he received a house plot from the city council of Mexico City, in 1524. He probably died shortly thereafter (BB: item 1891; G: item 63).

131. *Fernando Donal.* There are no references to any conqueror with this name, or anything similar.

132. *Diego Hernández.* Another Diego Hernández signed the Veracruz petition before this one. A discussion of the various members with this name appears above (see signature 98).

133. *Juan Villa.* Díaz del Castillo remembers a conqueror named Villa who was married to a kinswoman of Cortés's first wife. That Villa was very strong

and worthy. He settled in Zacatula or Colima, where he died of natural causes (DdelC, 2:340; see also signature 287). Grunberg lists a conqueror Juan de Villar, who was probably killed by the natives in the conquest (G: item 1146). Villar also signed the 1520 Segura de la Frontera letter. Because the folio is torn immediately below this signature, the inscription might represent a longer surname, such as Villacorta or Villasana.

134. *Rodrigo de Moguer*. Moguer is one of three towns (Moguer, Palos, and Huelva) on the coast of Andalucía from which many of the original members of Columbus's crew came. This conqueror was probably from that village. Little is known of Rodrigo, other than the fact that he signed the 1520 Segura de la Frontera letter and appeared in a contract in 1528, after the conquest (G: item 648). Boyd Bowman has only two men with the name Rodrigo from Moguer: Rodrigo Pardo and Rodrigo Simón, both of whom served in the conquest of Mexico (BB: items 1854 and 1864).

FOLIO 5, VERSO

135. *Alvaro del Grado*. There are no conquerors known to have this name. He might be related to Alonso del Grado (signature F).

136. *Francisco López*. The only Francisco López mentioned by Díaz del Castillo arrived in a ship captained by Pedro Barba, sent by Diego Velázquez in 1520, before the Narváez expedition but after the founding of Veracruz. He eventually became a *regidor* in Guatemala (DdelC, 1:416). Other sources indicate that he had probably sailed earlier with Grijalva and possibly Hernández de Córdoba before joining Cortés. On one occasion he carried letters to Veracruz for dispatch on to Spain. Two men with this name signed the 1520 Segura de la Frontera letter. Probably one of them was a member of the original Cortés company. After the conquest López settled in Mexico as a *vecino*. He worked as a carpenter and as an accountant in the royal treasury for a while. He was active in local commerce, buying slaves and collecting debts. He also served some minor local magistracies, such as one in Ixmiquilpa from 1538 until 1542, but did not receive an *encomienda*. He seems to have married a native woman named Catalina López. They had three sons and two daughters. He died in about 1543, leaving his children under the guardianship of Jerónimo López, probably a kinsman (G: item 542; Icaza: item 228).

137. *Juan de Benavente*. There are no conquerors with this name in the traditional sources. There are some records of a Cristóbal and a Pedro de Benavente. Pedro signed the 1520 Segura de la Frontera letter, while Cristóbal served as a scribe (HT, 21, 68; G: item 124).

138. *Alonso Rodríguez*. Four men of this name signed the Veracruz petition (see signatures 4, 90, and 187).

139. *Juan Muñoz*. Muñoz signed the 1520 Segura de la Frontera letter. He probably did not survive the conquest, as there are few references to him after 1521. Others with the name Juan Muñoz also participated in later phases of the conquest or appear in documentation immediately afterward but do not seem to have been members of the Cortés company (G: items 692 and 693).

140. *Juan Larios*. Larios was probably from Lucena, near Córdoba (BB: item 1471). Díaz del Castillo reports that he was involved in many lawsuits over his *encomienda* and that he died of natural causes (DdelC, 2:340). Unfortunately he is not listed among the *encomenderos* compiled by Himmerich. In testimony he claimed to have climbed Popocatepetl with Montaño to collect sulfur for gunpowder, and also stated that he had served on the brigantines in the final assault on Mexico (HT, 73; see also signature 278). After the conquest he worked as a carpenter and received a house plot in Mexico City. He was also a *vecino* of Zacatula, on the west coast. He was appointed to several minor posts, such as *corregidor* of Pantla, indicating either that he did not receive an *encomienda* or that he had lost it for one reason or another. There is no indication that he was ever married. He died sometime around 1543 (G: item 516).

141. *Hernán de Arcos* (Hernandarcos). Thomas lists this conqueror as a member of the Garay relief expedition (HT, 150). A Juan and a Gonzalo de Arcos signed the 1520 Segura de la Frontera letter.

142. *Hernán de Olid; Hernán de Olea*. The only Olid traditionally included among the conquerors is Cristóbal. Hernán, or Hernando, de Olea probably died during the conquest (G: item 725). Just to confuse matters further, there was also a Cristóbal de Olea, sometimes known as Hernando. He was from Medina del Campo. A valiant fighter, he died in Tenochtitlan while protecting Cortés. He might have been a kinsman of Díaz del Castillo (HT, 101). Some insist that this other conqueror was neither Cristóbal nor Hernando de Olea, but rather Francisco (G: item 724).

143. *Francisco de Nájera*. Four Nájeras signed the 1520 Segura de la Frontera letter, but none of them was Francisco. Rodrigo appears before him on the Veracruz petition (see signature 118). There was a conqueror with a compound surname which might fit, Francisco González de Nájera. There is some confusion as to whether this individual was also known as Alonso, or if Alonso were a brother. Díaz del Castillo reports that he arrived with his son, Pedro González de Nájera, and two nephews with the surname Ramírez (see signature 236). Francisco González de Nájera survived the conquest of Mexico but died in a later action in Guatemala (DdelC, 2:340). It is possible that this conqueror was Juan and not Francisco. Díaz del Castillo mentions a Juan de Nájera who was a good soldier and marksman who served honorably in the conquest (DdelC, 2:338). He probably arrived in the Indies in 1517 and then settled in Cuba. He joined the Cortés expedition and served throughout the conquest and later

expeditions. He settled in Mexico and neither married nor received an *encomienda*. Because he remained unmarried he was given the nickname of "the hermit" (G: item 698).

144. *Juan Martínez Narices*. Also known as Juan Martín Narices. This conquistador is characterized as very lively. He left his home in Seville for Cuba in 1518 (BB: item 3723). Martín Narices worked as a carpenter during various moments of the conquest, especially during the construction of the four small boats used to sail up the coast shortly after the foundation of Veracruz. He remained in Tenochtitlan with Alvarado when Cortés left to confront Narváez. Stories indicate that Narices died when struck by a stone thrown by a native from the main temple in Tlatelolco during the final assault (HT, 85; G: item 617). He might have been a kinsman of Martín López, whom he accompanied as a servant and who signed the petition immediately below him (see signature 146).

145. *Francisco Hernández*. Several individuals of the era were named Francisco Hernández, although most used a compound surname: Hernández de Córdoba, Hernández Mirallo, Hernández Pérez, etc. The only person associated directly with the conquest was Hernández de Córdoba, who had organized one of the early expeditions to explore the coast. He did not serve in the Cortés company and so can be ruled out. Thomas includes a Francisco Hernández from Mairena, near Seville, who was one of the guards under Cortés and gave evidence following the conquest (HT, 67). Another Francisco Hernández appears in Díaz del Castillo, but he was sent to conquer Nicaragua by Pedrarias Dávila. Boyd Bowman lists nineteen men having the name Francisco Fernández or Hernández.

146. *Martín López*. López, a signatory of the 1520 Segura de la Frontera letter, was one of the most famous participants in the conquest; it was he who was appointed to supervise the construction in Texcoco of the thirteen brigantines that were used in the final assault on Tenochtitlan (DdelC, 2:338). López, the son of Cristóbal Díaz Narices and Estefanía Rodríguez, was raised in Seville as an hidalgo of the Osorio clan. Because of his father's surname, Narices, he might well have been a kinsman of Juan Martínez Narices (signature 144). López sailed to the Indies in 1516 with more supplies than he might have needed himself, probably intending a career as a merchant. He was one of the more wealthy conquerors, and traveled about with three servants to assist him, Miguel and Pedro de Mufla (both carpenters by trade) and Juan Martínez Narices (signature 144). He brought his own supplies on the Cortés expedition, which augmented the supplies of the company. He was not a shipwright, but he had skills which allowed him to oversee the complex process of building ships, and was wealthy enough to pay for the project. Early on he built four small vessels for Cortés, which were destroyed by the Aztecs. He also built a

seagoing caravel to ferry goods up the Gulf Coast. The original ships at Vera-cruz had been dismantled for their iron parts, which were used on these other ships and were also then carried up to the Valley of Mexico for use in the final assault. Timber was cut and the ships initially were fabricated near Tlaxcala, and then disassembled and carried over the pass to Texcoco, where they were reassembled. There is some debate as to whether López actually served as cap-tain of one of the ships or merely was on board. For his efforts he received part of the town of Tequixquiac in *encomienda* (Himmerich: item 236). He also received a noble coat of arms from the king in 1550 in recognition of his ac-complishments (Villar: item 96; see fig. 6.18). This is surprisingly little reward for a man who, as nearly everyone agreed, played a critical role in the Spanish success. He filed several petitions to the Crown for greater compensation for the costs he incurred in the conquest. Following the conquest, López became a *vecino* of Mexico City, and received several house plots from the city council, including one near the Aztec *templo mayor*. He returned to Spain to resolve issues surrounding the death of his wife. He remarried and brought his new wife to Mexico. López had some twelve children. He was very active among the conquerors in Mexico City, filing his own petitions for recognition and recom-pense for his services, and giving testimony for others to do the same. He filed numerous lawsuits seeking grants from the Crown. He died around 1575 (HT, 76–79; G: item 546).[12]

147. *Alonso García*. This is one of three conquerors with this name who signed the Veracruz petition (see also signatures 55 and 309). A conqueror of this name is one of the documented fatalities of the Cortés expedition in the battle with the forces of Narváez. Only one Alonso García signed the 1520 Se-gura de la Frontera letter. The other Alonso García was a surveyor and builder who worked in various construction projects in Mexico City after the conquest. He was granted the *encomienda* of Xilocingo until his death in about 1528 (G: item 344). There was also an Alonso García Bravo.

148. *Pedro Rodríguez*. This conqueror signed the 1520 Segura de la Frontera letter. Because this is an extremely common name, several conquerors shared it, although most had a compound surname: Rodríguez de Carmona or Rodrí-guez de Escobar. The simple Pedro Rodriguez is assumed to have died dur-ing the conquest (G: item 886). Pedro Rodríguez de Escobar settled in Cuba and participated in the Grijalva expedition. He joined the Cortés company and fought in the conquest. He was rewarded for his service with the village of Ixmiquilpan in *encomienda*. Because he settled in Guatemala, however, the grant was taken from him, in about 1525 (HT, 114–115; Himmerich: item 384; G: item 894). Pedro Rodríguez de Carmona arrived with the Cortés company, and was present in Texcoco for the final assault. After the conquest, he first settled in Mexico City and then later in Guatemala (G: item 893).

149. *Juan Sastre*. No conquerors with this name are listed in any of the traditional sources. There is one reference to a Martín Sastre (HT, 240). In 1515 a Pedro Sastre accompanied his employer, Francisco Verdugo, to the Indies (BB: item 4628).

150. *Alonso Fernández Pablos*. This conqueror signed the 1520 Segura de la Frontera letter. Elsewhere he is listed as a nephew of Alonso Hernández Puertocarrero. Nevertheless, Díaz del Castillo suggests that Fernández Pablos (whom he called Hernández Paulo or Palo) was the uncle and that he was already quite mature at the time of the conquest. Díaz del Castillo writes that Fernández Pablos was accompanied by two nephews, one of whom was also named Alonso Hernández. One of the nephews died in battle, while the uncle and the other nephew died of natural causes (DdelC, 2:342). Other sources indicate that Fernández Pablos died at the hands of the natives during the conquest (HT, 299; G: item 477). Two other men simply named Alonso Fernández signed the Veracruz petition (signatures 57 and 239).

151. *Miguel de Navarra*. (See also signature 77.) There were possibly three conquerors with this name or some variant, and teasing the different individuals' stories apart after five centuries is difficult. Thomas lists this conqueror as variously Miguel or Antonio, de Navarra or Navarro. He sailed to the Indies in 1513 and had settled in Cuba by 1519. In the conquest he served as a crossbowman. He settled in Puebla and held the villages of Guautla and Nanahuaticpac in *encomienda* (HT, 217–218). Himmerich lists the *encomendero* of Guautla and Nanahuaticpac as Juan, not Miguel or Antonio (Himmerich: item 300). Juan (Antonio) Navarro is listed as *encomendero* of Zayanaquilpa. He died in about 1545, when the grant passed to his widow, who in turn remarried (Himmerich: item 301). Grunberg lists Antonio de Navarra as the *encomendero* of Zayanaquilpa. He was a conqueror who arrived in the Narváez company (G: item 702). On the other hand Grunberg has the *encomendero* of Guautla as Juan Navarro (G: item 704). Strictly speaking, then, Miguel de Navarra is absent from the sources, while there are a Juan and an Antonio.

152. *Luis de Ojeda (Hojeda)*. This conqueror signed the 1520 Segura de la Frontera letter. Díaz del Castillo remembers a member of the company called Ojeda who lost an eye in the conquest and eventually settled among the Zapotecs, probably Alonso de Ojeda (signature 89) (DdelC, 2:338). Others indicate that Luis de Ojeda did not survive the conquest (HT, 145; G: item 723).

153. *Alonso de Navarra*. None of the sources mentions a conqueror of this name. He might possibly have been a kinsman of Miguel de Navarra (signature 151).

154. *Francisco Marqués/Márquez*. He signed the 1520 Segura de la Frontera letter. He probably died during the conquest (G: item 592). Some sources indicate that he was also called Juan. Juan Marqués set up a forge to melt down

the gold that had been collected by the company and stamp it with the royal tax stamp (HT, 208).

155. *Gonzalo de Alaminos.* While the pilot Antón de Alaminos is extremely famous (he played a key role in the Cortés expedition to New Spain and is credited with discovering the Gulf Stream), there is little record of Gonzalo. Thomas writes that he was one of Cortés's pages (HT, 161). Gonzalo may have been a kinsman of the more famous pilot (signature 243). His name is not found on the 1520 Segura de la Frontera letter, and thus he might have died by that date.

156. *Alonso de Estrada.* The most famous person involved in the conquest going by this name did not arrive in New Spain until considerably after the Veracruz petition was written. That Alonso de Estrada was the royal treasurer sent to supervise the collection of booty and to ensure that the king's share was removed before its distribution among the company. His appointment was dated October 15, 1522, when he was at court in Spain, and he arrived in New Spain in 1523. Consequently this signature must belong to someone else. Alonso de Estrada from Talavera de la Reina in the province of Toledo, who sailed to the Indies in 1516, might well be the conqueror in question (BB: item 4629). The only other Estrada found among the conquerors was Francisco de Estrada. He originally sailed to the Indies in 1502 with Columbus. He participated in various expeditions in the New World until joining Cortés, perhaps as part of the Narváez expedition (G: item 303).

157. *Pedro Hernández.* This conqueror might have a compound surname, but the lower portion of the folio was destroyed. (See also signature I.) Three men named Pedro Fernández signed the 1520 Segura de la Frontera letter. Two men with this name worked on the brigantines in the final assault. One was a carpenter and had known Martín López in Spain. Some say that he was the assistant construction manager after López (HT, 68; G: item 461). The other was a blacksmith who worked with the iron fittings for the boats. After the conquest he settled in Zacatula (HT, 68; G: item 459).

158. *Andrés de Mola.* Díaz del Castillo refers to this conqueror as Andrés de Mol, originally from Spain's eastern Mediterranean coast, who died at the hands of the natives (DdelC, 2:350; HT, 303; G: item 649). He signed the 1520 Segura de la Frontera letter.

159. *Luis Ortiz.* None of the traditional sources list this conqueror. It is possible that he is the person referred to by Díaz del Castillo as the "musician." Other sources, however, associate the label with Cristóbal Ortiz (signature 122).

160. *Miguel Gómez.* This conqueror signed the 1520 Segura de la Frontera letter. Since little else is known of him, it is assumed that he died during the conquest (G: item 384). Thomas includes him among the members of the Narváez expedition (HT, 189).

161. *Sebastián Rodrigo.* A Sebastián Rodríguez signed the 1520 Segura de la Frontera letter. Díaz del Castillo indicates that Rodríguez was a good crossbowman who became a trumpeter after the conquest, and eventually died of old age (DdelC, 2:348). There may have been two distinct men who went by the name Sebastián Rodriguez. One of these was a crossbowman in the conquest. He was originally from Oliveira, in Portugal. He was a member of the Cortés company and in the later expedition to Honduras. After the conquest he first settled in Mexico City, but later moved to Puebla, in 1533, where he became a town council member, *regidor*, the following year. He was granted several tracts of land around the village of Atlixco. He received the villages of Chocaman and Tozongo in *encomienda*. He was prominent in local society and became the majordomo of a charity hospital. He was also active in buying and selling real estate in Puebla. He married María de Villanueva, and they had two children, a son and a daughter. He died in about 1560 (Himmerich: item 385; G: item 888). Another conqueror who went by the name Sebastián Rodríguez received the town of Malinalco in *encomienda*. He was also known as Cristóbal Rodríguez de Avalos. His wife, Isabel Rodríguez, was also a member of the Cortés company. She played an important role in the conquest by serving as a nurse to the wounded.[13] This other Sebastián served as a trumpeter in the conquest. This conqueror died in about 1542 (Himmerich: item 369; Icaza: item 522; G: item 892).

162. *Benito (de) Venegas.* None of the traditional sources mentions this conqueror. Grunberg lists a Vanegas who was probably killed by the natives during the final assault on Mexico (G: item 1093).

163. *Pedro de Guzmán.* Guzmán signed the 1520 Segura de la Frontera letter. Díaz del Castillo characterizes this conqueror as a good man. He married a woman from Valencia, doña Francisca de Valterra. After the conquest they moved to Perú, where the two of them froze to death in an accident (DdelC, 2:342). Other sources indicate that Guzmán was originally from Zamora and was a servant in the household of the Conde de Liste. Guzmán sailed to the Indies in 1510 (HT, 66). Immediately following the conquest of Mexico, Guzmán participated in the conquest of Pánuco and New Galicia, as part of the expedition of Nuño de Guzmán, possibly a relative. Some sources indicate that Pedro Guzmán was originally from Toledo in Spain and a member of the petty

nobility, an *hidalgo*. He traveled to Peru as part of a contingent organized by Pedro de Alvarado (G: item 446).

164. *Cristóbal Cárdenas*. Díaz del Castillo mentions a conqueror named Cárdenas who died during the conquest; he was a grandson of the famous *comendador mayor* Cárdenas[14] (DdelC, 2:343). Others indicate that this was Juan de Cárdenas (see signature 228).

165. *Francisco de Terrazas*. Díaz del Castillo characterizes this conqueror as a very prominent person and one of the men who served as majordomo to Cortés. He died of natural causes after the conquest (DdelC, 2:336). This well-known conqueror was originally from Fregenal de la Sierra. His father was university educated. Terrazas sailed to the Indies before 1518. He joined the Cortés expedition and played a prominent role in the conquest, serving as the captain of the guard keeping watch over Narváez after his defeat by the forces loyal to Cortés. In recognition of his service, Cortés made him his majordomo, in which role he served from 1524 until about 1526. He received the villages of Igualtepec and Tulancingo in *encomienda*. He settled in Mexico City and received both garden and house plots. He owned several gardens in the environs of the city. He continued as Cortés's majordomo after the conquest. He also participated in the business life of the city, buying and selling goods and land. He served on the Mexico City council as *alcalde* in 1538 and 1549. He provided testimony for several other conquerors who sought recompense from the Crown. Terrazas was married in Spain prior to the conquest. By that marriage he had four sons and a daughter. Three sons were already adults at the time of the conquest, including Francisco, Hernando, and possibly Diego de Terrazas. Terrazas married for a second time in Mexico to a widow, Ana de Castro, and they had four children. He also had at least three children out of wedlock. The most famous of Terraza's children, also named Francisco, gained fame as Mexico's first poet. The conqueror Terrazas died in 1549 (HT, 130–131; Himmerich: item 455; G: item 1040).[15]

166. *Martín Díaz Peñalosa*. Díaz del Castillo mentions a crossbowman with the surname Peñalosa, a friend of Sebastián Rodríguez (signature 161) (DdelC, 2:348). Thomas lists a Rui Díaz Peñalosa as a member of the Narváez expedition (HT, 182). A Martín Díaz, from Cobeña near Madrid, sailed to the Indies in 1515 (BB: item 2265).

167. *Melchor Dálava; Martín López Dálava (de Alava)*. Díaz del Castillo describes a Melchor de Alavés who settled in Oaxaca after the conquest; he died there of natural causes (DdelC, 2:338). Others give several variants of this conqueror's name: Alanés and Alavez. Various sources indicate that Melchor was from Teruel, had arrived in Cuba by 1517, and served in the Grijalva expedition. During the conquest, he helped transport the brigantines from Tlaxcala to Tex-

coco. He also went in search of the gold which Cortés had demanded that the ruler of Texcoco, Cacamatzin, turn over to the Spaniards. He participated in several of the later minor expeditions, including the one led to Guatemala by Pedro de Alvarado. Alava was one of the first settlers in Oaxaca. He provided testimony for several other conquerors. He received the village of Patlahuistla-huaca, near Yanhuitlan, in *encomienda*. He married María de Salas, the daughter of Juan Rodríguez de Salas, also a conqueror. They had some ten children. He died sometime before 1567 (HT, 4; Himmerich: item 9; G: item 19).

168. *Fernando Bargueño.* No conqueror bearing this name appears in any of the traditional lists. There is a Fernando de Bargas (Vargas) listed as a conqueror of Mexico (signature 293).

169. *Mendo Xuárez (Suárez). (See fig. 6.8.)* Xuárez sailed to the New World with his brother Alonso in 1512. From Benavente in the province of Zamora, he had arrived in Cuba by about 1519, intending to join the Cortés expedition. He signed the 1520 Segura de la Frontera letter. Traditional sources indicate that he was a member of the Narváez company (HT, 245; BB: item 4834). He settled in Mexico City after the conquest, becoming a *vecino* before 1525. He was involved in some minor business transactions. He died sometime around 1528, leaving behind only one daughter. His son-in-law, Benito Muñoz, mentions that Suárez participated in the Guatemala expedition, and had eventually received two villages in *encomienda* (G: item 1026; Icaza: item 899).

170. *Andrés de Paredes.* Díaz del Castillo remembers a conqueror named Paredes who was already old at the outset of the expedition; he was the father of an early settler in Yucatan. The elder Paredes died at the hands of the natives (DdelC, 2:347). Some five men with the surname Paredes are listed as conquerors, but none with the given name Andrés or even Antón.

171. *Bartolomé de Loja (Loxa).* No known conqueror with this name is listed.

172. *Santos Hernández.* This conqueror was already a mature man at the start of the conquest. The other members of the company gave him the nickname of the "Good Old Fellow" (*buen viejo*). He was a horseman who survived the battles and died a natural death (DdelC, 2:338). He was originally from Coria in the province of Cáceres, and his father had served the Catholic kings in the war in Granada. He arrived in the New World in 1502, settling first on the island of Hispaniola. He also claimed to have participated in the conquest or settlement of Tierra Firme (Panama), Cuba, Jamaica, Puerto Rico, Cartagena, and Santa Marta. Santos fought notably in the conquest of Mexico, especially in the Noche Triste when he was credited with removing an arrow from the face of Francisco de Granada (signature 92). He fought with several later companies, including the Pánuco, Michoacan, Zapotecas, and Guatemala expeditions. He eventually received the village of Petlalcingo in *encomienda*. He settled in Mexico City, becoming a *vecino* in 1525, and provided testimony re-

garding the service of several of his comrades. He owned land both in and around Mexico City and along the road to Veracruz, near Perote. By 1547 he was a *vecino* of Oaxaca. He died sometime around 1558. He had at least two children, a son and a daughter (BB: item 941; HT, 68; G: item 463; Himmerich: item 200).[16]

173. *Antón de Veintemilla.* Veintemilla was probably from the town of the same name, Ventimiglia, west of Genoa. As such he was one of a very few non-Iberian members of the company. He arrived in Cuba in about 1518, and then joined the Cortés expedition. He signed the 1520 Segura de la Frontera letter. He was a crossbowman in the conquest. Some sources incorrectly indicate that this conqueror was a member of the Narváez expedition (HT, 251). He participated in the conquest of Michoacan, and then settled in Santiago de Guatemala, where he died sometime around 1528 (G: item 1107).

174. *Hernando Alonso.* The one Hernando Alonso mentioned in many accounts was a blacksmith, *herrero,* and appears so frequently with this epithet that it is used as his second surname: Hernando Alonso Herrero. Opinions differ, with some authors placing him in the Narváez expedition. Testimony regarding him, collected well after the conquest, indicates that he was from Moguer near Huelva and that he emigrated first to Santo Domingo. It seems that his wife, Isabel de Ordaz, accompanied the Narváez expedition. Isabel might have been the sister of another conqueror, Diego de Ordaz. Nonetheless, she died early in the conquest and was buried in Cholula, or Tepeaca. Soon thereafter Alonso married a woman named Ana, who also died in the conquest. He assisted in the construction of the brigantines for the final assault on Mexico. He was a member of several of the later conquest expeditions before finally settling in Mexico in about 1524. He set up his forge to work as a blacksmith. In recognition of his service in the conquest, he received the town of Actopan and part of Guaniqueo and Pungaravato in *encomienda.* Alonso was an active businessman and also ran slaughterhouses, regularly bidding on the right to supply Mexico City with meat. He also dealt in real estate, buying and selling both urban and rural parcels. He married Isabel de Aguilar, the daughter of a one-eyed tailor. Alonso had two or three children, possibly by his first wife, since they are described as being older. Alonso was eventually denounced to the authorities for supposed "Jewish practices." The prosecution applied judicial torture, during which Alonso confessed to being a Jew and practicing Jewish rites. He was found guilty and burned on orders of the Inquisition in 1528 (HT, 162–163; G: item 34; Himmerich: item 16).[17]

175. *Francisco López de Nambroca; Francisco López de Marmolejo.* There were two conquerors with the name Francisco López, both of whom signed the 1520 Segura de la Frontera letter (see also signature 136). Another Francisco López, routinely associated with the Narváez expedition, had earlier sailed with Her-

nández de Córdoba. During the conquest he carried messages from the Valley of Mexico to Veracruz. He later joined Pedro de Alvarado for the conquest of Guatemala, where he eventually settled. He lost most of his possessions and several family members when an earthquake struck the city of Santiago de Guatemala in 1541. He received portions of several villages in *encomienda* in recognition of his service (HT, 261; G: item 541).

176. *Domingo Hernández*. There was one Domingo Hernández, from Los Ojos in Murcia, who sailed to the Indies in 1512. There are no recorded members of the Cortés company with this name.

177. *Rodrigo Díaz*. This is a very difficult signature to decipher. There are no conquerors of this name listed in the traditional sources. Two men with this name immigrated to the Indies. One, from the city of Avila, son of Juan de Bonilla and Isabel Díaz, sailed in 1517 (BB: item 133). The other, the son of Juan Díaz and Inés del Cerezo, from the city of Salamanca, sailed in 1513 (BB: item 2666).

178. *Martín Bajerol; Martín Gonzalo Heroles*. Damage to the folio and other factors make this a difficult signature to decipher. While few men of the era had the given name Martín, there was a conqueror by the name of Martín Barahona who signed the 1520 Segura de la Frontera letter. By 1526 he had settled in Mexico City. The next year he moved to Zacatula, and probably died by 1528. He might have been related to another conqueror, Sancho de Barahona (G: item 110).

179. *Lorenzo Xuárez (Suárez). (See fig. 6.9.)* Suárez was originally a Portuguese from Evora. He sailed to the Indies with Fray Nicolás de Ovando in 1502. He participated in several expeditions in the Caribbean before taking part in the conquest of Cuba with Diego Velázquez. He received grants of land and Indian labor on the island of Cuba, which he abandoned in order to join the Cortés expedition. He claimed to have provided a horse and a crossbow to the Cortés expedition. Among the members of the company he was known as the "elder" (*el viejo*), indicating he was older than the average or that there was another Xuárez who was younger than he was. After the war he settled in Mexico City, where he became a *vecino*. He received the village of Tlanocopan in *encomienda*. He was active in postconquest Mexico City, buying and selling land and slaves. His house was next door to the monastery of the Franciscans. He gave testimony in support of claims for assistance for several of his colleagues from the conquest, although it was noted that he could not read or write. He married María de Salazar, held to be a member of a petty noble family in Burgos, with whom he had a son, Gaspar Suárez. He also had an illegitimate child by a native woman in Cuba. In 1527 he sent a colleague, Alonso Botel, to go look for the child. His marriage was a difficult one, and Lorenzo killed his wife with a grinding stone. The court stripped him of his *encomienda*, although

later it was granted to his son Gaspar. In penance for the murder, Lorenzo renounced the world and became a friar (DdelC, 2:340; HT, 124; G: item 1025; Himmerich: item 449).[18]

180. *Cristóbal Díaz.* This conqueror signed the 1520 Segura de la Frontera letter. He arrived in the Indies in 1516. Díaz del Castillo notes that Cristóbal was from Colmenar de Arenas (now Mombeltrán) in Avila, and was a good crossbowman. He died of natural causes after the conquest (DdelC, 2:342). He settled in Coatzacoalcos and worked as a teamster and muleteer. At one point he was accused and convicted of blasphemy by a local ecclesiastical court. His punishment consisted of a ten peso fine and penance (G: item 258). It is just possible that he was related to Díaz del Castillo, whose signature follows.

181. *Bernal Díaz.* This is the signature of the most famous member of the company, Bernal Díaz del Castillo. Much of what we know about him comes from his own pen in his famous work, *Historia verdadera de la conquista de la Nueva España.* In 1514 he sailed for the Indies with Pedrarias Dávila and came to what is now Panama. He next arrived in Cuba, where he became a retainer of Diego Velázquez. When he received no Indians in *encomienda* from the governor, he joined various expeditions, including the Hernández de Córdoba and Grijalva voyages to what is now Mexico. He joined the Cortés expedition and, in spite of his ties to Velázquez, sided with the faction which sought to break away from the governor, establish a permanent trading post, and go on to conquer the region. During the conquest he was wounded in the flight from Tenochtitlan on the Noche Triste. After the conquest he settled first in Coatzacoalcos, and became a town councilman there. He traveled to Spain in 1539, returning in 1541, when he moved to Santiago de Guatemala. His first wife was Teresa Becerra, and after her death he remarried in Guatemala. He received four small villages in *encomienda.* He returned to Spain again in about 1550, as an agent for the city council of Santiago de Guatemala. He was appointed a permanent city council member, *regidor,* by the king in 1551. His famous work was composed while he lived in Guatemala, in about 1568, as a very old man, in reaction to the history of the conquest written by Cortés's private secretary, Francisco López de Gómara. He died in 1584 (G: item 268; HT, 52–54).

182. *Diego Ramírez. (See fig. 6.3.)* This conqueror signed the 1520 Segura de la Frontera letter. Ramírez was a carpenter, and was originally from Jerez de la Frontera, in Andalucía. He sailed to the Indies before 1505. He worked as a carpenter on the island of Hispaniola before moving to Cuba. While living on Hispaniola, he was already married, to Ana de Acosta. His skills as a carpenter were utilized in building the first fort at Veracruz and later during the conquest, specifically on the thirteen brigantines assembled in Tlaxcala and used in the final assault. After the conquest he settled in Mexico City and had become a *vecino* there by 1525. He ran a mill in Chapultepec. He was an active busi-

nessman in the city, buying and selling land and slaves until his death in 1546. In testimony taken during the investigation of Cortés's rule of Mexico, it was noted that Ramírez was illiterate. He received half of the town of Atengo in *encomienda*. Although he had children, they seem to have predeceased him, since his *encomienda* passed to the Crown upon the death of his widow in about 1556 (HT, 111; G: item 839; Himmerich: item 359).

183. *Diego de ???* The folio is torn, obliterating the surname.

184. *Andrés Farfán.* This conqueror signed the 1520 Segura de la Frontera letter. He probably came from Seville and arrived in Cuba by 1519. The absence of any further information about this conqueror implies that he died during the conquest (G: item 306; HT, 55).

185. *Arias de Ribera.* Arias de Ribera, from Medina de Rioseco in the province of Valladolid, sailed to the Indies in 1517. He was the son of Alvaro González and María Fernández (BB: item 4555). Otherwise, nothing is known about this conqueror.

186. *Alonso de ???* The folio is torn, obliterating the surname.

FOLIO 6, VERSO

187. *Alonso Rodríguez.* Four men of this name signed the Veracruz petition (see signatures 4, 90, and 138).

188. *Alonso de Argüello.* Díaz del Castillo mentions an Argüello from León, a good fighter who died in the conquest (DdelC, 2:343). This information could possibly also refer to Domingo de Argüello (signature 276), although others list a Juan or Hernando (HT, 17). Alonso de Argüello was from Torre de Mormojón in the province of Palencia, and probably a kinsman of Fernando de Argüello, town councilman on the island of Hispaniola in the town of Guahava. He sailed to the New World in 1514 (BB: item 2499). There is no other indication that he participated in the conquest of Mexico, and so he might be assumed to have died early on.

189. *Juan de Alcántara.* Alcántara, probably from the village of the same name in Cáceres, was considered one of the captains of the expedition, in that he had a small contingent assigned to his leadership. He was one of the leaders of the group who remained in Veracruz when the main force moved inland. After the Noche Triste Cortés ordered that he accompany the gold, silver, and other booty back to the coast from Tlaxcala, where the main body of the company was encamped. His company included some forty-five footmen, five horsemen, and around two hundred native auxiliaries from Tlaxcala. Unfortunately he and his fellows were ambushed, killed, and robbed by natives near the town of Calpulalpan (DdelC, 1:379, 402, 405, 424). He was known as "the elder" because another conqueror of this name arrived with the Narváez expe-

dition (G: item 24). The other Juan de Alcántara, from the Narváez company, was the one who signed the 1520 Segura de la Frontera letter—by that date Alcántara "the elder" was probably already dead.

190. *Antón Darco; Antón Crespo*. There are no recorded members of the Cortés company with these names. There was an Alonso Martín Crespo of village of Llerena in the province of Badajoz who sailed to the Indies in 1514 (BB: item 431).

191. *Juan Hedivo; Juan Sedeño*. There are no recorded members of the Cortés company with the surname Hedivo. According to Díaz del Castillo there were three men named Juan Sedeño in the expedition, and their biographies could well be intertwined and confused (see signature 218). One of them signed the 1520 Segura de la Frontera letter. Díaz del Castillo mentions that one lived in the town of Santo Espíritu in Cuba and joined the expedition when Cortés put out a call for more men. The other Sedeño was a fairly wealthy merchant from Havana who brought a ship to Trinidad laden with cassava bread, bacon, and other provisions which he had intended to sell in a nearby mining district, but instead he sold his cargo to Cortés and became a member of the company himself. The rich Sedeño died of natural causes and was a very prominent person (DdelC, 1:86–87, 2:343). One of these men married an Indian woman named Isabel Sedeño and settled in Veracruz. He had initially been granted the town of Jilotepec, located near Veracruz, in *encomienda*, but it escheated in 1531. He lost the town because the natives complained, rightly or wrongly, about extreme maltreatment at the hands of Sedeño (G: item 991; Himmerich: item 433). Another Juan Sedeño followed Alvarado to Guatemala, where he settled. He received several villages there in *encomienda*. In 1535 he sailed to Spain, never to return to the Indies. His son became a member of the entourage of the viceroy Martín Enriquez and sought recognition of his father's accomplishments (G: item 992). This might be the Sedeño identified by Díaz del Castillo as the rich man, although Díaz does not mention that he had returned to Spain.

192. *Sebastián de Grijalva*. This conqueror might be a kinsman of the explorer Juan de Grijalva, since the Cortés expedition had been sent out ostensibly to look for the Grijalva expedition. Sebastián signed the 1520 Segura de la Frontera letter. After the conquest he first settled in Mexico City. In 1524 he received a house lot from the city council and by 1527 was considered a *vecino*. He became involved in the mining business, entering into several partnerships. By 1537 he had moved to Oaxaca, where he became a member of the city council. He received the towns of Sosola and Tenexpa in *encomienda*. He married a woman named Beatriz Hernández, and they had several children, two of whom were girls who married early settlers. He died in about 1549 (HT, 196–197; G: item 419; Himmerich: item 178).

193. *Blas (Pablo?) de Retamales.* Díaz del Castillo remembers a member of the company named Retamales who died at the hand of the natives in Tabasco (DdelC, 2:342). Other sources mention a Pablo de Retamales from Seville. Pablo later gave testimony regarding his activity in the conquest. He was granted half of the town of Mizquiahuala in *encomienda.* He married Isabel Rodríguez, the widow of Miguel de Guadalajara, and they had several children. As opposed to the recollections of Díaz del Castillo, Pablo de Retamales seems to have died in Mexico City in about 1536 (HT, 112; G: item 855; Himmerich: item 363).

(*The next several signatures seem to have been executed by the same person.*)

194. *Francisco Gutiérrez Coguyos.* There were several conquerors with the name Francisco Gutiérrez. A man named Francisco Gutiérrez signed the 1520 Segura de la Frontera letter. Díaz del Castillo lists a man called Francisco Gutiérrez, a resident of Havana, who joined the expedition and who died in the conquest (DdelC, 2:340). One of the conquerors named Francisco Gutiérrez was from Villadegota in Cáceres. He served as a blacksmith, although he had not actually trained in that occupation. He settled in Zacatula and was assigned half of the village of Chilapa in *encomienda.* He continued to work as a blacksmith. Upon his death the *encomienda* escheated to the Crown (G: 433; Himmerich: item 187). Another Francisco Gutiérrez, from Lebrija in the province of Seville, arrived in the Indies in 1517. After the conquest and the death of his first wife, he married a native woman and settled in Mexico City. He received half of a village in Michoacan in *encomienda* (G: item 434).

195. *Alonso de Monroy.* Díaz del Castillo says this conqueror was the son of one of the officers in the military-religious Order of Santiago, the *comendador* of Santisteban. As a result of this, the men gave him the nickname of "Salamanca," perhaps his city of birth. Similarly, he might have been known as Alonso de Salamanca. He was a squire for Cortés. During the Noche Triste, while he accompanied Cortés in the flight from Tenochtitlan, he was able to escape an ambush, since he was a young and agile man. Nonetheless, he later was captured by the natives and sacrificed (DdelC, 1:490, 2:341). Monroy was an early settler on the island of Hispaniola, holding land from 1514 (G: item 657; HT, 91).

196. *Juan Méndez.* This conqueror signed the 1520 Segura de la Frontera letter. A conqueror with this surname mentioned by Díaz del Castillo was already quite old at the outset of the expedition and died during the conquest (DdelC, 2:349). There was a Juan Méndez who survived the conquest and who settled in Mexico City. He was originally from the village of Las Garovillas, in Cáceres. He arrived in the New World sometime around 1516. He was a *vecino* of Mexico City by 1526, when records indicate he rented out some tools and a garden plot to another man. In the ensuing years he continued to engage in small rentals

and other contracts. He married Catalina Vargas, and their son went on to be an interpreter in the royal courts. Méndez was granted an *encomienda* of several very small villages (G: item 637). This might be the man known elsewhere as Juan Méndez de Alcántara, who seems to have participated throughout the conquest (HT, 88).

197. *Sebastian de Porras*. This conqueror signed the 1520 Segura de la Frontera letter. Díaz del Castillo recalls a man with reddish blond hair (*bermejo*) surnamed Porras who was a very good singer, and who died at the hands of the natives (DdelC, 2:349). Sebastián de Porras was one of the Cortés company who spied on Narváez prior to the confrontation between the two armies (G: item 818). There are no records of him after the conquest, and so one can assume that he died during the conflict.

198. *Juan Gango*. There are no recorded members of the Cortés company with the surname Gango. There were members named Juan Sánchez and Bartolomé Sancho (see signature 207). This might be the man known as Juan Sánchez Galingo/Galindo, originally from Carmona, near Seville. He served in various expeditions prior to the voyage to Mexico, including accompanying Ponce de León to Florida. Some sources indicate that he arrived even after the Narváez expedition. He played an important role in the siege of Tenochtitlan as a crossbowman. He also served on one of the brigantines, commanded by Antonio de Carvajal. He was a member of the group who captured the children of Moteuczoma. He took part in several later conquests as well. He had settled in Mexico by 1525, becoming a *vecino*. He gave testimony for several other conquerors seeking recompense from the Crown. He married Elvira Rodríguez in 1527. She was the sister of an early settler, the armorer Diego Rodríguez. She seems to have died early in the marriage, and he then took an Indian wife. Galingo was granted half of the village of Nestalpa in *encomienda*. He died sometime before 1547 (G: item 972; Himmerich: item 142).

199. *Miguel de Anos (Llanos?); Miguel de Canos*. There are no recorded members of the Cortés company with these names. There were three men with the surname Cano: Alonso, Juan, and Luis.

200. *Gonzalo de Jaén*. A Gonzalo de Jaén, merchant from Seville, sailed to the Indies in 1510. He was born in Utrera, in the province of Seville (BB: item 4175). This conqueror signed the 1520 Segura de la Frontera letter. There are no records of him from after the conquest, and so one can assume that he died during the conflict (G: item 496).

201. *Antonio Alonso*. There is no record of a member of the Cortés company with this name. Two men named Andrés Alonso signed the 1520 Segura de la Frontera letter (see signature 279). Hernando Alonso signed the Veracruz petition (see signature 174). A Luis and a Rodrigo Alonso are also listed as members of the company (G: items 35–36).

202. *Manuel Verdugo*. There is no record of a member of the Cortés company with this name. A Manuel Verdugo sailed to the Indies in 1516, along with his uncle, Bartolomé de Cueva, and cousin, Juan. He was from the village of Cogeces de Iscar in Valladolid (BB: item 4487). A Francisco Verdugo played a major role in the conquest. He was a close ally of Diego Velázquez who, rather than trying to stop the Cortés company, joined it (G: item 1126). Manuel and Francisco might well be relatives, since they were both from Cogeces de Iscar (BB: item 4486).

203. *Juan Jiménez*. As noted earlier, there were several conquerors with the surname Jiménez, and two men named Juan Jiménez signed the Veracruz petition (see signature 13).

204. *Gaspar de Polanco*.[19] Díaz del Castillo notes that Polanco was originally from Avila and later settled in Guatemala, where he died a natural death (DdelC, 2:340). Polanco sailed to the Indies in 1518 and settled in Cuba. Some commentators believed he sailed with Narváez. During the conquest he received a punishment of one hundred lashes for having stolen clothing from a native. He settled in Guatemala, and probably died sometime before 1528 (HT, 109; G: item 809).

205. *Rodrigo de Medellín*. This conqueror emigrated to the Indies from his home in Las Garrovillas in the province of Badajoz in 1512. Nothing else is known about him. In all likelihood he died during the conquest (BB: item 391).[20]

206. *Bartolomé García*. This conqueror signed the 1520 Segura de la Frontera letter. According to Díaz del Castillo, García was a miner in Cuba. He and a friend called Ortiz (signature 159) brought the best horse in the company, which then was purchased by Cortés. Both Ortiz and García died at the hands of the natives (DdelC, 2:349). The absence of García from postconquest documents tends to confirm Díaz del Castillo's statement (G: item 348).

207. *Bartolomé Sánchez*. This conqueror signed the 1520 Segura de la Frontera letter. He was wounded by an arrow toward the end of the final assault on Tenochtitlan. He participated in several other expeditions after the conquest, and served as a witness for other conquerors as they sought preferment from the Crown. Immediately after the conquest he supervised mines owned by Cortés and worked in the mining industry. He became a *vecino* in Mexico City before 1529, and then in Oaxaca, eventually becoming a town councilman (*regidor*) there. In 1547 he petitioned the king to appoint him to a town council in either Mexico City or Puebla because the climate of Oaxaca was injurious to his health. He probably settled in Puebla in 1548, becoming a *vecino* there. He received several villages in *encomienda*. At first Cortés assigned him the village of Zola, which was then taken away, and he was reassigned the town

of Coyotepec and four smaller places. Sánchez died sometime around 1565, and only Coyotepec was inherited by his heirs (Himmerich: item 418). In 1562 he received a coat of arms from the Crown in recognition of his services (Villar: item 103; see fig. 6.19). His first wife was a native woman. Upon her death he married a Spaniard, Inés de Cabrera, and they had two children. Grunberg lists Sánchez Coyote as an alternate surname (G: item 959; HT, 118).

208. *Juan Castaño*. Very little is known of this conqueror. He may have been the Portuguese crossbowman who very early sailed to the Indies (BB: item 5250a). During the Noche Triste he is reported to have announced (in error) the death of Cortés to the rear guard as the Spaniards fled Tenochtitlan. He participated in a few later expeditions. In the period following the conquest he remained loyal to Cortés when factions formed that supported or opposed him. As a result, an *encomienda* he had been granted was taken from him when Cortés's detractors gained the upper hand. He probably died before 1530 (HT, 175; G: item 209).

209. *Gonzalo García. (See fig. 6.4.)* It is possible that he originally came from Seville and sailed to the Indies in 1517. He first settled in Cuba and then joined the Cortés company (BB: item 3541). This conqueror signed the 1520 Segura de la Frontera letter. His absence from any further documentation implies that he died in the conquest (G: item 353). There are at least five other early settlers in the Indies with this name.

210. *Luis de Frias*. This conqueror signed the 1520 Segura de la Frontera letter. There might have been more than one conqueror with this name (BB: items 3513–3514). His absence from any later documentation implies that he died in the conquest (G: item 321).

211. *Hernán López Dávila (also known as Hernando López de Avila)*. Díaz del Castillo mentions this conqueror immediately after Gaspar de Polanco (signature 204), since both came from the city of Avila in Spain. López Dávila became the official charged with managing the estates of those who died intestate (*tenedor de bienes de difuntos*). He became quite rich and returned to Castille (DdelC, 2:340). Some sources indicate that he owned one of the horses used in the expedition. He participated in later expeditions, including the one led by Cortés to what is now Honduras, but had to return to Mexico due to illness. He settled in Mexico City, becoming a *vecino* by 1526. He held various offices for the city government, serving as majordomo, councilman (*regidor*), and constable (*alguacil*). In his position as curator for the estates of those who died, he briefly took control of Cortés's properties during a later period when it was believed that the conqueror had died in an expedition. He took over the duties of constable from Diego Hernández Proaño, to whom he paid 600 pesos for the office. He was assigned the village of Capula in *encomienda*. He prob-

ably returned to Spain and died shortly after arrival, sometime in 1528. Several authors indicate that he suffered from a skin ailment, possibly syphilis, which prompted his departure (HT, 79–80; G: item 550).

212. *Alonso de Valencia.* A man of this name from the province of Extremadura sailed to Santo Domingo in 1517 (BB: item 5111). He participated in the conquest of Mexico. Afterward he claimed that he was poor and requested a house plot from the city of Mexico (G: item 1082).

213. *Martín de Monjaraz.* Several members of the Monjaraz family joined the Cortés expedition. Díaz del Castillo tells of the brothers Andrés (signature 230) and Gregorio (signature 233), who were with Cortés from the start. They were later joined by their uncle, whose name he could not remember, but which other sources indicate was also Andrés (possibly signature 230). It is not exactly clear if Martín de Monjaraz was related to these others, although Boyd Bowman lists him, under the name of Martín Ruiz de Monjaraz, as an uncle of Gregorio and Andrés. It has been assumed that he and Martín de Monjaraz were one and the same person (BB: item 4722). This conqueror was probably from Durango in Vizcaya. Martín participated in several later expeditions, especially in the west: Zacatula, Colima, and Jalisco. He fought as a foot soldier under the command of Cristóbal de Olid. He eventually settled in Colima, probably as one of the very first residents there, being recognized as a *vecino* by 1532. He served as a local magistrate in various districts. He also provided testimony for various other conquerors. Ruiz de Monjaraz received several villages in *encomienda*. He was married to a Spanish woman, and they had five children. He died sometime before 1564 (G: item 655; Himmerich: item 400).

214. *Juan Ruiz Canias (Cangas?).* A Juan Ruiz signed the 1520 Segura de la Frontera letter (see signature 101). This conqueror might possibly be Juan Cansino. From Palos, near Huelva, Cansino arrived in Cuba by 1513. He became associated with Cortés and joined the expedition. During the conquest he was arrested for having seduced an Indian woman and then branding her on the face. He was tried but acquitted thanks to the efforts of his lawyer, the *bachiller* Alonso Pérez (see signature 65) (HT, 26; BB: item 1899a).

215. *Pedro de Solís.* A conqueror with this name signed the 1520 Segura de la Frontera letter. Pedro de Solís was an important member of the company, possibly also known as Pedro de Solís Barraso. This might be the Pedro de Solís whom Díaz del Castillo calls "tras la puerta" ("behind the door") because he liked to stand behind the door of his house, located across the corner from the monastery church of San Francisco, peering out to see who passed by (DdelC, 2:337). Grunberg lists Pedro Solís as also going by the name Francisco Solís. He was in the first company sent to confront Narváez. Upon returning to Mexico, his horse started and threw him in the water, which was taken as a bad omen by

the other members of the company. This anecdote tells us that he was one of the few horsemen of the company. In October 1520 he went to Jamaica for additional horses for the company. He participated in some later expeditions, especially to Chiapas, where he became a resident of Ciudad Real (G: item 1006). Other sources provide varying pieces of information: Pedro Solís Barraso was generally identified as "behind the door." Solís sailed to the New World with Pedrarias Dávila, after which he went to Cuba. During the conquest he was a member of the company headed by Gonzalo de Sandoval. In Tenochtitlan he was one of the guards for Moteuczoma and had general security responsibilities. After the conquest he settled in Mexico, where he received land for houses and gardens. He married Leonor de Orduña, daughter of Francisco de Orduña, also a conqueror. They had some eight children. He received the town of Acolman in *encomienda*. He died sometime around 1567, some say in Guatemala. Thomas holds that Pedro de Solís and Pedro de Solís Barraso were the same man (G: item 1009; Himmerich: item 443; HT, 123).

216. *Román López.* A Ramón López signed the 1520 Segura de la Frontera letter. That conqueror, according to Díaz del Castillo, was a prominent person and lost an eye in an accident after the conquest. He died in Oaxaca (DdelC, 2:338). Others agree that he was known variously as Román or Ramón, López or Lópes, or López de Solís. Because of the last possible surname, he might have been related to the Solís family (signature 215). He came from Toro in the province of Zamora. During the conquest he served in the company of Andrés de Tapia as the standard-bearer (*alférez*). He also participated in later expeditions, including Guatemala. López was a *vecino* of Medellín in 1525; of Mexico City in 1528; and of Oaxaca in 1531. He served as a witness for several other conquerors after the conquest. He received the villages of Zola and Istayutla in *encomienda*. By the time he was living in Oaxaca he was married to Inés de Guzmán, and they had six children. He died sometime around 1562 (HT, 79; G: item 548; Himmerich: item 239).

217. *Martín de Xerez (Jerez); Martín Pérez.* There are no references to a Martín de Xerez or Jerez, although an Alonso (see signature 280), a Hernando, and a Juan appear. A Martín Pérez signed the 1520 Segura de la Frontera letter. Witnesses after the conquest recall Martín Pérez as having been a good carpenter who worked on the brigantines for the final assault. He settled in Mexico City after the conquest, becoming a *vecino* in 1525. He was involved in the management of the famous inn at Perote, on the Mexico–Veracruz road, work giving rise to several contracts and court appearances. He received the town of Xalacingo in *encomienda*. Some sources indicate that he was married, in Spain, to Juana Rodríguez, but they do not appear to have had children, and so his *encomienda* escheated to the Crown upon his death in about 1536. Others

hold that the husband of Rodríguez was a different Martín Pérez (HT, 107; Himmerich: item 347; G: item 789).

218. *Juan (de) Sedeño*. According to Díaz del Castillo, no less than three men of this name were members of the Cortés expedition (see also signature 191).

219. *Miguel de Losa*. Only a Juan de Losa appears on lists of conquerors. That conqueror arrived with Cortés and was known as a very accurate crossbowman. He eventually settled in Mexico City. He received half of two towns in *encomienda*, but he was stripped of the grant shortly after it was given (G: item 559).

220. *Pedro Ponce*. Díaz del Castillo remembers a member of the company with this surname. Ponce was a companion of a man called Santiago from Huelva (see signature 113). He died during the conquest (DdelC, 2:348–349). Nothing more is known of this conqueror.

221. *Rodrigo Ronquillo*. There are no members of the Cortés company known by this name. The signature is damaged.

222. *Juan González de Heredia*. This was probably the company member known as the "elder" Heredia (*el Viejo Heredia*). Heredia was a native of Vizcaya, and had a knife scar on his face, a bad eye, a full beard, and a limp in one leg, and knew how to use a gun. He bore the wounds of an experienced soldier, having already served in Italy. He was considered a close supporter of Velázquez (DdelC, 1:84, 154–155). He was sent with a relative of Cortés, Diego Pizarro (see signature 76), to look for gold mines. He also helped in the transport of the dismantled brigantines from Tlaxcala to Texcoco. He probably died during the conquest (G: item 405).

223. *Juan Enríquez*. Díaz del Castillo tells of one member with the surname Enríquez, originally from Palencia, who drowned because he was tired from the weight of his armor and fatigued because of the heat (DdelC, 2:347; see also signature 238). The signature is damaged.

224. *Alonso Coronado*. There is reference to an otherwise unknown conqueror with the surname Coronado who arrived with a contingent of some fifty men. He was killed in battle at Tepeaca in 1520 (G: item 241).

FOLIO 7, RECTO

225. *Rodrigo de Guevara*. Díaz del Castillo mentions only one person by this surname: Pedro de Guevara, a priest who accompanied the Narváez expedition (DdelC, 1:338). Three individuals with this surname are known to have immigrated to the New World, but none is named Rodrigo.

226. *Francisco Martín*. This conqueror signed the 1520 Segura de la Frontera letter. Díaz del Castillo remembers one Francisco Martín who had also settled in Coatzacoalcos and who participated with him in an expedition to Chiapas

in a company led by Juan Marín. He describes Martín as coming from Vizcaya, or at least as being half Vizcayan. On one occasion Díaz and Martín were wounded but escaped death by jumping into a canoe commanded by native allies (DdelC, 2:132–133). Martín had at least one daughter, who was married in 1538, although Martín himself probably died sometime around 1526 (G: item 598). There were other conquerors of this surname, including a page to Cortés who was captured and sacrificed by the natives (G: item 599).

227. *Juan de Espinosa*. There were at least three conquerors with this surname. One was from Vizcaya and died in the conquest. The second was given the nickname "the good benediction" (*la buena bendición*) because he always had some good words to share in the form of a benediction. He died of natural causes. The third Espinosa was a native of Espinosa de los Monteros in the province of Burgos, in Spain, and died at the hands of the natives (DdelC, 2:344). Others have identified this last Espinosa from Espinosa as Juan (HT, 55). He might have later served in the conquest of Michoacan (G: items 296 and 297).

228. *Juan de Cárdenas*. A conqueror with this name signed the 1520 Segura de la Frontera letter. Díaz del Castillo mentions a conqueror named Cárdenas who died during the conquest and was a grandson of the famous *comendador mayor* Cárdenas, generally identified as this conqueror (DdelC, 2:343; see also signature 164). He was an early settler on the island of Hispaniola. He probably died in the conquest, since no references to him appear afterward (G: item 185; HT, 26).

229. *Diego Pérez*. Although this is an extremely common Spanish name, there do not appear to be any conquerors who went by it. Boyd Bowman lists six men of this name as emigrants to the Indies before 1519, any of whom might be this conqueror (BB: items 384, 598, 1726, 3863–3864, and 4608).

230. *Andrés de Mucharaz; Andrés de Monjaraz*. Two men by this name (Andrés de Monjaraz, or Mocharás, Mucharaz, etc.) are known to have been members of the company. One signed the 1520 Segura de la Frontera letter. Díaz del Castillo provides a rather complete description of him. He was of average height, with a happy face, possessed of a dark beard, and good in conversation. He eventually died of plague, yaws, or syphilis, but had suffered from some affliction which enlarged his lymph glands (*bubas*) (DdelC, 2:354). This conqueror was from Escalona in Toledo. One of the men named Andrés was the uncle of the other. The ship on which he sailed from Cuba was separated from the rest of the fleet, so he and his fellows missed some of the exploration of Cozumel and the Yucatan coast. The uncle did not participate in any battles because upon arrival he was quite ill, probably with the swollen glands. When he had recovered, he envisioned himself as very brave and a warrior. In a subsequent encounter with the natives, he climbed one of the temples, only to be

captured. Díaz del Castillo did not know how he ultimately died, but thought it was probably divine retribution, since the uncle had killed his very lovely and honorable wife, and afterward asked witnesses to perjure themselves when he was accused (DdelC, 1:435–436). It seems that Díaz del Castillo conflates the biographies of the two men, since one died of his illness, and the other died at the hands of the natives. Another nephew, or possibly brother, Gregorio, also participated in the conquest (signature 233). Martín de Monjaraz, yet another conqueror, also was probably a kinsman (signature 213). The Andrés who survived the conquest had been an ally of Cortés in the conquest. He was a captain in the company under the command of Pedro de Alvarado. Monjaraz became a leader in the new city of Medellín. In the period immediately following the conquest, he eventually became one of Cortés's detractors. He lived for a time in Tlaxcala and then in Mexico. He provided testimony for several fellow conquerors. He was a *vecino* of Mexico by 1527. He invested in at least one mine and participated in explorations for more in company with others. By 1528 he was listed as a "great and capital enemy" of Cortés. In 1529 he received a plot of land for a house in Mexico City. He first was assigned the village of Coatlan in *encomienda*, along with his brother, Gregorio (signature 233). That grant was later rescinded, but they then received the villages of Jaso and Teremendo. This Andrés was the one who died from syphilis, yaws, or plague in about 1534 (HT, 90–91; G: item 653; Himmerich: item 282).

231. *Juan de la Pera.* There was a Pedro Perón or Pedro de Peral, but no Juan de la Pera among the known conquerors.

232. *Pedro de Alcántara.* A Juan de Alcántara (signature 189) signed the 1520 Segura de la Frontera letter. A Pedro Valencia de Alcántara sailed to the Indies in 1513, with his brother Fernando (BB: item 1110).

233. *Gregorio de Monjaraz.* This conqueror was the brother and nephew of Andrés de Monjaraz, and probable kinsman of Martín de Monjaraz (see signatures 213 and 230). Gregorio, also from Escalona in Toledo, participated in all aspects of the conquest. He was rendered deaf as a result. As such he was known as "the deaf Monjaraz" (Monjaraz, *el sordo*). By 1527 he had settled in Mexico City and was a *vecino* there. He fell under the scrutiny of the Inquisition and was found guilty of blasphemy. He later settled in Oaxaca. He was married and had at least two sons. He received some villages in *encomienda*, but because of the confusion in the sources regarding his other kinsmen, it is not entirely clear who received what. It seems that he received Exutla, Coatlan, and Miaguatlan, but some of these were shared with other conquerors, probably his brother, Andrés. He might have also shared Jaso and Teremendo with Andrés (signature 230) (G: item 654; Himmerich: item 283; HT, 91).

234. *Sebastián de la Peña.* There are no known conquerors by this name, although other men with the surname Peña do appear in the record. Díaz del

Castillo refers to a man with this surname who served as a messenger for and friend of Pedro de Alvarado. Peña carried news regarding the conspiracy of Francisco de las Casas, Rodrigo de Paz, and Lic. Zuazo back to Spain (DdelC, 2:237).

235. *Juan de Limpias.* This conqueror is generally known by his full name, Juan de Limpias Carvajal. Díaz del Castillo reports that he was a good soldier who served as captain of one of the brigantines in the final assault. He became deaf as a result of an injury during the war, eventually dying of old age. He was known as "the deaf one" (*el sordo*). The brigantine he commanded was the first to break the stockade the natives had thrown up around the city. He fought so valiantly that he inspired his forces to break through. After the conquest he settled in Puebla (DdelC, 2:35 and 338). Limpias Carvajal arrived in the Indies in 1513, a native of Seville. He settled in Cuba. He was sent by Velázquez and Cortés to collect provisions for the expedition in Jamaica. In other details from the conquest, Limpias Carvajal emerges as a faithful captain for Cortés, leading and participating in many minor actions. He joined Francisco de Montejo in the expedition to explore the coast north of Veracruz. He even served as a spy, collecting information about the Narváez expedition for Cortés. His participation in the siege and final battle of Tenochtitlan guaranteed his place in history, and earned him his nickname, since it left him deaf. He participated in several of the later conquests, going as far south as Honduras. He lived in Mexico City first and later, sometime around 1546, settled in Puebla, where he served as the sheriff (*alguacil*). He gave testimony for several other conquerors in their quest for royal largesse. He and his brother, Hernando, were active in the business world, especially in the 1530s. Limpias Carvajal married María Alcazar, and they had at least six children. He was granted the village of Quechula in *encomienda* along with his brother, Hernando. That grant was taken away, and Limpias then received Oatitlan in *encomienda* (HT, 74–75; G: item 529; Himmerich: item 226). His brother, Hernando de Carvajal, is also mentioned as a conqueror, probably a member of the Narváez expedition (G: item 201).

236. *Juan Ramírez.* There were several conquerors with this surname, yet none clearly identified as Juan. The page or equerry (*mozo de espuelas*) who served Cortés on the expedition was a Ramírez. He died during the course of the conquest (HT, 111). Two young men of this surname, brothers, served along with their uncle, Francisco (Alonso) González Nájera, in the conquest (see signature 143). They died either during the Noche Triste, on the bridges fleeing the city, or slightly later, in a massacre of some fifty Spaniards. The record, however, is silent regarding their given names (DdelC, 2:340; G: items 844 and 845).

237. *Francisco de Manzanilla.* A Juan de Manzanilla signed the 1520 Segura de la Frontera letter. Other sources mention a Juan and a Pedro de Manzanilla, but no Francisco (G: items 584–585).

Biographies OF THE *Signatories*

238. *Juan Enríquez.* Another conqueror by this name appears earlier (signature 223). This signature is extremely difficult to decipher.

239. *Alonso Fernández.* (See also signature 57.) This could be either Fernández or Hernández. Several conquerors had this name, including Alonso Fernández Diosdado, Alonso Fernández Paulo, Alonso Fernández Puertocarrero, and simply Alonso Fernández.

240. *Francisco de Horozco (Orozco).* This conqueror signed the 1520 Segura de la Frontera letter as a councilman (*regidor*) of the town of Segura de la Frontera. Díaz del Castillo notes that Orozco was a veteran of the Italian campaigns prior to his arrival in the Indies. He suffered from swollen lymph nodes (*bubas*), possibly syphilis. Díaz del Castillo confirms that Orozco had been an important figure in Tepeaca (Segura de la Frontera) while the main body of the expedition was in Tenochtitlan, calling him a captain (DdelC, 2:341). Orozco arrived in the Indies in about 1513. By 1519 he was in Cuba. Because of his military experience he served as a captain of the artillery brigade of the Cortés company, a very small unit. He served as a scout in the expedition against Narváez, along with Juan de Limpias (signature 235). He remained in Segura de la Frontera with the wounded members of the company when the main body of the company returned to Tenochtitlan for the final siege. In one of the later expeditions of the conquest he founded the Spanish city of Oaxaca, where he had died by 1524. He received the village of Tecuicuilco in *encomienda*. Upon his death it was assigned to Martín de la Mezquita, and later escheated to the Crown (Himmerich: item 277; G: item 738).

241. *Antón Rubio.* No conqueror of this name appears in any of the traditional sources, although a Juan and a Diego Rubio are mentioned (G: item 917; HT, 233). Juan signed the 1520 Segura de la Frontera letter. An Alonso Rubio, from Santa Cruz de la Sierra in the province of Cáceres, immigrated to the Indies in 1517 (BB: item 1179).

242. *Cristóbal Bravo.* There is confusion as to whether this conqueror signed the 1520 Segura de la Frontera letter. Although Thomas believes he did, only Juan Bravo seems to appear on most lists (HT, 171). Thomas posits that Cristóbal died at Tlayacapan in 1521. Díaz del Castillo indicates that a conqueror surnamed Bravo died in that region (DdelC, 1:474; G: item 150).

243. *Antón de Alaminos.* Alaminos is the name of two of the most famous members of the company. They were father and son. Alaminos was the chief pilot of the expedition. Originally from Palos, near Huelva, he first sailed to the Indies with Columbus as a cabin boy on the fourth voyage, in 1502. He is credited with serving as a pilot for Ponce de León in his expedition to Florida in 1513. He also served as the pilot for the two early expeditions to Mexico under Hernández de Córdoba and Grijalva. Quite simply, he knew more about the Gulf of Mexico than any Spaniard of his era. After the landing at Veracruz he

was sent along with Francisco de Montejo to explore the north coast, and they went as far as Pánuco. He was sent to Spain to carry the Veracruz petition to the king in July 1519. He did not return to Mexico until about 1522 (DdelC, 2:347; HT, 3–4; G: item 15). He served only briefly in Mexico after his return. He soon sailed back to Spain, taking his son with him. It is possible that this signature is that of his son, of the same name, especially because the senior Alaminos was probably in Pánuco with Montejo when this letter was signed, although other members of that expedition, such as Juan de Limpias, also signed the letter (signature 235). He might be related to Gonzalo de Alaminos (signature 155).

244. *Hernán Martínez.* Both a Hernán Martín (see signature 129) and a Hernando Martínez signed the 1520 Segura de la Frontera letter. Fernán Martínez, from Guaza in the province of Palencia, sailed to the New World in 1512 with his two brothers, Gaspar and Marcos (BB: item 2459). Hernando Martínez signed the Veracruz petition (see signature 298).

245. *Juanes de Fuenterrabia.* Díaz del Castillo recalls that this member of the company joined the expedition in the town of Trinidad in Cuba, along with Pedro de Alvarado and several others (DdelC, 1:86). After the conquest of Mexico he continued on to Guatemala with Alvarado; he eventually settled there, becoming a *vecino*. He died in about 1524 (G: item 323).

FOLIO 7, VERSO

246. *Rodrigo Alvarez Chico.* Rodrigo was one of three men, along with Francisco (see signature 260) and Juan (signature 28 or 37), with this compound surname. It is quite possible that the three were brothers who all participated in the conquest. More certain is that Francisco and Rodrigo were brothers, since both came from Fregenal, near Badajoz, in Extremadura, although Díaz del Castillo recalls that Juan and Francisco were brothers (DdelC, 2:336). Rodrigo signed the 1520 Segura de la Frontera letter and served as one of the founders of the town. Early in the conquest he was sent with Montejo to survey the coast north of Veracruz.[21] Later he was one of the men charged with guarding the Aztec emperor, Moteuczoma. He served as overseer, *veedor*, of the royal treasury. He was sent by Cortés to negotiate with Narváez, who imprisoned him. Others say that he was one of the leaders of the attack on Narváez. He settled in Mexico City, owning houses on the principal street. He became a city councilman, *regidor*, in 1526. Also in 1526, he led an expedition to explore and conquer the Pacific coast north of Acapulco, where he was killed by natives in Colima (HT, 15; G: item 50).

247. *Francisco Flores.* This conqueror signed the 1520 Segura de la Frontera letter. Díaz del Castillo considers him to be a noble person. He settled

in Oaxaca, where he died a natural death (DdelC, 2:336). He was probably from a little village, Encinasola, in the province of Huelva. Flores played an important role in the conquest and provided eyewitness testimony regarding the moment when Moteuczoma handed power over to the Spaniards. He also provided more testimony regarding the temples of Tenochtitlan. He witnessed the massacre of the Aztec nobles by the men under the command of Pedro de Alvarado. He claimed to have been one of the last horsemen to flee the city on the Noche Triste, when he was wounded (HT, 55–58). He settled in Mexico City, where he became a city councilman, *regidor*, in late 1529 through a royal decree. Because of his service to the city, he appears frequently in the historical record. He served until his death in about 1545.[22] He provided testimony in numerous cases when his fellow conquerors petitioned the Crown for remuneration for their services. At some point he might well have lived in Oaxaca, as suggested by Díaz del Castillo. Grunberg believes this occurred in the late 1530s and early 1540s, since after 1537 Flores does not appear in the Mexico City records. Flores married Francisca de la Cueva. They had at least one son. Flores was given several small villages in the Oaxaca region in *encomienda* (G: item 311; Himmerich: item 137).

248. *Pedro Gutiérrez de Valdedueñas.* A Pedro Gutiérrez de Valdelomar signed the 1520 Segura de la Frontera letter. He was probably from Illescas in Toledo. Since nothing is known of him following the conquest, it is assumed that he died during the hostilities. One conqueror credits him with gouging out Narváez' eye (G: item 443; HT, 65). A Pedro Gutiérrez in the company was a royal notary. That conqueror first settled in Mexico City, but left for Guatemala in about 1528 (G: item 441).

249. *Juan Ramos de Lares.* Juan Ramos de Lares signed the 1520 Segura de la Frontera letter. Díaz del Castillo lists Martín Ramos de Lares as a member of the company. Martín Ramos de Lares was one of the men who were personal retainers of Diego Velázquez who joined the Cortés expedition (DdelC, 1:84). Thomas indicates that Juan and Martín were either one and the same man, or possibly brothers, originally from Vizcaya. Grunberg holds that the two were relatives. Juan fought extraordinarily fiercely during the Noche Triste (HT, 111). After the conquest Juan, who was illiterate, gave testimony for Francisco Flores (item 247). In 1527–1534 Juan was living in Mexico, becoming a *vecino* in 1528 (G: item 847). Martín participated in the Hernández de Córdoba expedition, and probably died during the conquest (G: item 848).

250. *Pedro Vizcaíno.* This conqueror signed the 1520 Segura de la Frontera letter. Vizcaíno was a crossbowman during the conquest. He participated in several expeditions after the conquest of Mexico, as a crossbowman in the conquest of Michoacan and in the pacification of Chiapas. In 1528 he settled in

Villa Real, Chiapas (G: item 1157). As his surname indicates, he was probably from Vizcaya.

251. *Cristóbal Rodríguez.* This conqueror signed the 1520 Segura de la Frontera letter. According to Thomas, he was originally from Vizcaya and worked as a ship's carpenter (HT, 113). Grunberg includes a conqueror by this name, but notes that he arrived in Mexico with Narváez (G: item 880). Several conquerors carried this name. Boyd Bowman lists five early settlers in the Indies by this name (BB: items 180a, 1684, 1857, 4687, 4799).

252. *Pedro Montefrío.* None of the standard reference works list this conqueror.

253. *Pedro López de Belvas.* (See also signature 27.) The name Pedro López was extremely common. If one includes all the possible conquerors with compound surnames, there are as many as seven. Díaz del Castillo mentions four who were simply "Pedro López": one was a physician; another, a pilot; and the last two, crossbowmen (*ballesteros*). This conqueror, also known as Pedro de Balvas, seems to have come from Alcaraz in the province of Albacete, in south-central Spain. He sailed on the Grijalva expedition. Immediately after the conquest he sailed to Spain, ostensibly carrying news of the conquest, but was captured by French corsairs. He was able to gain his freedom and return to Santo Domingo in about 1525. He went to Spain before returning to Mexico. His wife and three children seem to have remained in Spain. By 1548 he was a *vecino* of Mexico. Whatever *encomiendas* he might have received were lost when he went to Spain. Yet he also seems to have received a royal pension worth 250 pesos a year. He later served as a local magistrate (Icaza: item 35; G: item 106; HT, 19).

254. *Alonso Muñoz.* (*See fig. 6.5.*) This conqueror might have been illiterate, and the sign of a key was his signature. Someone else might have put his name under it. Two men by this name sailed to the Indies before 1519. One was from the village of Guadalupe in Cáceres, who sailed in 1515. The other, from Aguilar de Campoo, in Palencia, sailed in 1517. None of the standard reference works list this conqueror.

255. *Francisco Quintero.* This conqueror signed the 1520 Segura de la Frontera letter. He might well have supplied the name of Alonso Muñoz under his sign (signature 254). Díaz del Castillo mentions a man named Quintero who was a ship's master and good member of the company and who died during the conquest (DdelC, 2:350). Quintero was originally from Huelva. He might have made several trips to the Indies, as early as 1504 but certainly by 1517. He was either injured or fell ill during the conquest and missed some of the battles. He was a member of the Veracruz town council in the summer of 1519. He fought in the conquests of Pánuco and Guatemala, after Mexico. After the conquest he lived in Mexico City and married a Spanish woman. He was a *vecino* of Mexico

City in 1528, but five years later he had taken up residence in Puebla, only to return to Mexico in 1537. In that year he rented the labor of the natives in his *encomienda* to other conquerors. At some point he traded his grants with others, so that it is difficult to deduce exactly which villages provided him with rents at what time. He left New Spain for Peru sometime around 1548 (HT, 110; G: item 835; Himmerich: item 358).

256. *Juan Ceciliano (Siciliano)*. Díaz del Castillo remembers Siciliano as an artilleryman in the company that participated in the battle with Narváez. He settled in Mexico and died of natural causes (DdelC, 1:370; 2:342). Born in Sicily, he sailed to the Indies with governor don Nicolás de Ovando in 1502. He ended up in Cuba and joined the Cortés expedition. In one expedition to Pánuco he was shipwrecked along with his companions. They salvaged some of the ship's timbers to make a raft and were able to reach an island. They were then picked up by a relief vessel sent by Cortés. He settled in Mexico City in 1525 and was listed as a *vecino* in 1528. He was active in the life of the city, giving testimony for his fellow conquerors. He filed a claim on a mine in Pachuca called "La Ceciliana." He received the villages of Tlahuelilpa and Atitalaquia in *encomienda*, but lost them to the First Audiencia. Because of this he served several times in the 1530s as a local magistrate for various districts. He was married to Juana Rodríguez, a Spanish woman, and they had at least a son and a daughter. He died sometime before 1560 (HT, 28; G: item 218; Himmerich: item 439; Icaza: item 36).

257. *Alvaro Velón*. None of the standard reference works lists this conqueror. One of the sailors of the company was known simply as Alvaro. Díaz del Castillo writes that the fellow known as Alvaro was originally from Palos. Soldiers' tales about him recounted that he had numerous children by several native women. He continued in later expeditions and eventually died in what is now Honduras (DdelC, 2:348). Alvaro was not a common name. Among the 545 men who signed the 1520 Segura de la Frontera letter, only 4 had the given name Alvaro.

258. *Juan Díaz Carpintero*. There were several members of the company named Juan Díaz. This conqueror further identifies himself as a carpenter. Díaz del Castillo ignores the occupation of the Juan Díaz he remembers. That conqueror had a clouded eye: either a cataract or the white of the eyeball had spread over the iris. He was a native of Burgos and was charged with transporting the supplies and booty which pertained to Cortés. He died during the conquest (DdelC, 2:343). He sailed to the New World in 1512 and had arrived in Cuba by about 1519 (BB: item 687; G: item 264).

259. *Hernando Sánchez; B. Hernández*. This might be the conqueror known as Hernán Sánchez Ortigosa. He sailed to the Indies in 1508, participated in an expedition to Puerto Rico, and then joined the Cortés expedition. Following

the conquest he returned to Spain for his wife, Leonor Vázquez de Vivanco, and two daughters. Returning to Mexico City, he became a notary, merchant, and businessman. He received the town of Chiapatongo in *encomienda*. Unfortunately many sources indicate that this conqueror was a member of the Narváez expedition (HT, 236; G: item 968; Himmerich: item 420). It is possible that this signature is in fact B. Hernández. Bartolomé and Blasco Hernández were also both conquerors. Bartolomé, also known as Hernández de Nava, was a sailor and a member of Cortés guard. In the conquest he served on one of the brigantines in the final assault. He received part of the village of Ocuiltuco and Iztacquimaxtitlan (Castilblanco) in *encomienda*. He first lived in Mexico City and received a permit to operate the inn at Perote on the Veracruz road along with Martín Pérez (signature 217). He later settled in Puebla, where he became active on the city council. Later he also served as a magistrate in several districts (HT, 66; G: item 471). Blasco Hernández served in the conquest of Mexico. Afterward he took up residence in Mexico City, where he was sheriff (*alguacil*) on occasion and also served as the officer in charge of weights and measures in the city (*fiel*). He supported himself also through gardens and small farms in the environs of the city (G: item 450).

260. *Francisco Alvarez.* The most famous man of this name was Francisco Alvarez Chico, one of the officials of the town of Veracruz. (See signature H.) None of the standard references lists another Francisco Alvarez. He might be related to the other men named Alvarez, cousins of Francisco de Terrazas (see signature 165).

261. *Juan de Valdivia.* There was a conqueror identified just by his surname, Valdivia, who arrived with Cortés. He took part in the expedition against Narváez. He was one of three members of the company captured and sacrificed by the natives in June 1520 (G: item 1079).

262. *Arriego de Alva.* None of the standard reference works lists this conqueror.

263. *Luis de Cárdenas.* This conqueror is identified as one of Cortés's pilots. He signed the 1520 Segura de la Frontera letter. He stands as one of the major opponents to Cortés within the expedition. He was very disgruntled about his share of the booty collected in Mexico. He gained the nickname of "the talker" (*el hablador*). Originally from the Triana neighborhood of Seville, he had sailed to the Indies to enrich himself. He participated in the early stages of the conquest of Mexico but became disillusioned when the booty was divided. Twenty percent went to the king and a similar portion to Cortés. At the first opportunity Cárdenas returned to Cuba, and he continued to complain. When Cortés heard of it, he sent him an additional sum of money, but that only mollified Cárdenas for a short time. He returned to Spain to lodge petitions before the court against Cortés and in his own favor. As a result of this the Crown eventu-

ally granted him a stipend of one thousand pesos on the Mexico City treasury. At that point he seems to have returned to New Spain and received a house lot in Mexico City. He even received the village of Tepeucila in *encomienda*. He either died or left New Spain sometime around 1541 (DdelC, 1:325–326, 431; 2:152–154, 159, 161; HT, 26; G: item 186; Himmerich: item 73).

264. *Martín*. This signature is damaged. At least twenty-one men named Martín signed the 1520 Segura de la Frontera letter.

265. *Sancho*. This signature is damaged. Only two men named Sancho signed the 1520 Segura de la Frontera letter: Sancho de Barahona and Sancho de Salcedo. Barahona is believed to have sailed with Narváez because he was wounded during the Hernández de Córdoba expedition and was unable to sail with Cortés (G: item 111). Salcedo in all likelihood died in the conquest, because nothing further is known about him (G: item 941). Because the signature here ends with "-do" this conqueror could in all likelihood be Salcedo.

266. *Juan Bautista Maestre*. The "maestre" might represent either a surname or a profession, such as ship's master, or someone with a university degree. This might be the conqueror who signed the 1520 Segura de la Frontera letter simply as Juan Bautista. There was a conqueror known as Juan Maestre in the Cortés expedition who served as the physician to Cortés. He also ministered to the wounds of Narváez and his captains after the battle with Cortés. After the conquest he seems to have continued as a physician, charging exorbitant rates for his services. He might have originally been from Valencia and immigrated to the Indies in about 1513 (BB: item 4462; G: item 571).

FOLIO 8, RECTO

267. *Gonzalo de Sandoval*. Sandoval was one of the major figures of the conquest. He signed the 1520 Segura de la Frontera letter. Sandoval was from the city of Medellín in Extremadura. Díaz del Castillo describes him as being not too tall, but well proportioned, with a broad and high chest, stalwart, a bit bowlegged, and a good horseman. He had a rather rugged face, with chestnut brown hair and beard. His speech was ragged and not at all clear, and he lisped from time to time; he was not well lettered; he was not a greedy man, but a very good captain who always got along well with the men. He dressed very plainly but rode the best horse in the company, a chestnut with a white star on his forehead and a white left front hoof, named Motilla (DdelC, 2:352). He was originally from the Medellín, near Badajoz. Sandoval became one of the most important captains in the conquest. He was one of the first four town councilmen in Veracruz. He took on several important charges during the conquest. Sandoval was the captain of one of the companies during the battle with Narváez.

Cortés had lost much faith in Pedro de Alvarado's abilities after the massacre of the Aztec nobles, and so Sandoval emerged as one of his closest advisors. Sandoval was placed in command of the rear guard during the flight from Tenochtitlan on the Noche Triste. Later he was one of the overall commanders of the brigantines. He led several of the later expeditions of discovery and conquest, notably to Honduras. He received several *encomiendas*. In the conflicts following the conquest he was a strong supporter of Cortés. In 1528 he returned to Spain with Cortés and Andrés de Tapia. Shortly after his arrival he was robbed and murdered in Palos, near Huelva[23] (HT, 120; G: item 975; Himmerich: item 425). For reasons unknown Thomas lists him as "Gustavo."

268. *Simón de Frias. Fernando de Frias.* Simón de Frias does not appear in any of the traditional sources. Fernando de Frias signed the 1520 Segura de la Frontera letter. Fernando left Olmedo in the province of Valladolid for the Indies in 1513, along with his wife, Ana de Morales. He does not appear in any of the documentation following the conquest and so it is assumed that he died in the hostilities. By 1526 his widow had remarried (BB, 4569; G: item 320).

269. *Fernando de Aldama.* (*See fig. 6.10.*) This conqueror does not appear in any of the traditional sources. A Juan de Aldana emigrated from Carmona in the province of Seville for the Indies. He had arrived in Cuba by 1518 and joined the Cortés company. Someone with a very similar name signed the 1520 Segura de la Frontera letter. He probably died in the conquest (BB: item 2998).

270. *Juan de Cáceres.* This conqueror signed the 1520 Segura de la Frontera letter. Díaz del Castillo remembers Juan de Cáceres as a good soldier. In spite of his surname he was not from Cáceres but from nearby Trujillo. Cáceres served as majordomo for Cortés in Havana, before joining the expedition. He benefited later from his close association with Cortés. During the conquest, Cortés entrusted him with several business affairs, and he ended up with the nickname "the rich man" (*el rico*). It is suggested that Cáceres's wife, Mari Hernández, was one of the female members of the company, based on a comment by Díaz del Castillo. When Cortés went to Spain in 1528, Cáceres took over the management of some of his affairs. Cáceres settled in Mexico City and died of natural causes (DdelC, 1:91, 434; 2:66, 269, 344, 349). Because he is listed twice by Díaz del Castillo, some have suggested that there were two men by this name (DdelC, 2:344 and 349). Cáceres arrived in the Indies in 1502 with Governor Ovando. As a settler in Mexico City he was a very active businessman, buying and selling all manner of things, from mules and slaves to houses and stables. He served as a witness for many other conquerors when they testified to their accomplishments in the conquest. He and his wife were patrons of the Dominican church in the city. When his first wife died, he married Catalina González, one of the women who had accompanied the Narváez expedition. He seems to

have received the town of Maravatio in *encomienda* but by 1528 had lost that grant. Cáceres probably died around 1537 (HT, 22–24; G: item 166).

271. *Juan de Torre Quemada.* An Antonio de Quemada signed the 1520 Segura de la Frontera letter. The absence of the conqueror from any of the standard sources indicates that he died in the conquest. A conqueror known as Juan Torres also participated in the conquest. Described by some as an older man with only one eye, he was left in Cempoalla to teach Christianity to the natives. He probably died during the conquest, although other men named Juan Torres do appear in the early historical records for Mexico City, none claimed to be a conqueror (G: item 1050). There was a Juan de Torquemada, from Seville, who immigrated to the Indies in 1517 (BB: item 4049).

272. *Francisco de Lugo.* This conqueror signed the 1520 Segura de la Frontera letter. Díaz del Castillo mentions him many times in his history. He describes him as a captain of several of the expeditions who strived hard. According to Díaz del Castillo, Francisco was the illegitimate son of Alvarado de Lugo the elder, the lord of some towns near Medina del Campo. Francisco died a natural death (DdelC, 2:335). He was from Medina del Campo in the province of Valladolid. Lugo was a staunch supporter of Cortés. He was one of the few conquerors who brought a war dog along. These animals greatly terrorized the natives. He took part in the advance against Narváez. He was one of the leaders of the fore guard during the Noche Triste. After the fall of Tenochtitlan he became one of the lieutenants of the expedition led by Cristóbal de Olid, and then later went with Gonzalo de Sandoval (signature 267) to settle Coatzacoalcos. He was named as one of the court agents for New Spain in 1526, at which time he was a *vecino* of Veracruz. He probably received an *encomienda* in the Coatzacoalcos region. He died sometime around 1532 (HT, 80; G: item 563).

273. *Benito de Vejel.* (See also signature 36.) The name of this conqueror appears twice among the signatories of this letter, yet the two signatures are quite different (*see figs. 6.11 and 6.12*).

274. *Juan de Mancilla.* This conqueror signed the 1520 Segura de la Frontera letter. Mancilla was a member of the group which opposed the power of Cortés following the conquest. He was the author of some derogatory comments painted on the walls of Cortés's home (DdelC, 2:73). During the conquest he was wounded and was still infirm during the Noche Triste. He was named by Cortés to serve as captain of one of the brigantines in the final siege of Tenochtitlan and is credited with capturing the ruler of Texcoco, Cacamatzin. He left for the conquest of Coatzacoalcos and the Chontales with Sandoval and Alvarado, and participated in a few other later expeditions. He settled in Mexico City for a while, becoming a *vecino* in 1525. In the midst of his confrontations with Cortés he sought refuge in the Franciscan monastery. He received several plots of land in the city from the city council, and became a councilman,

regidor, himself in 1532. Six years later he renounced the post in favor of Francisco de Terrazas. He received Tetela and half of the town of Atlatlauca in *encomienda*, which he later sold. Several authors suggest that he left Mexico and returned to Spain in 1538. Some commentators believed that Mancilla was a member of the Narváez expedition (HT, 117–118; Himmerich: item 248; G: item 582). There were also conquerors Juan and Francisco de Manzanilla (see signature 237).

275. *Juan Darias (Juan de Arias); Juan Durán.* No one named Juan de Arias appears in any of the traditional sources. A Juan Durán signed the 1520 Segura de la Frontera letter. Durán was in Cuba by 1519, in time to join the Cortés expedition. Following the conquest he seems to have settled in Puebla. He was listed as a *vecino* of that city in 1542. He owned some mines in the province of Cuzcatlan. He was married to Agueda de Frenesda, and they had at least one daughter. He received the town of Eloxochitlan in *encomienda*. He died in about 1547. Although some believed that he was a member of the Narváez company, in Icaza he clearly indicated that he had arrived with Cortés (G: item 277; HT, 183; Himmerich: item 121; Icaza: item 17).

276. *Domingo de Argüello.* Díaz del Castillo remembers a soldier by this surname who originally was from León in Spain and who died during the conquest (DdelC, 2:343). Other sources indicate that the conqueror's name was Juan, or perhaps Hernando. The man named Argüello was one of the men left in Veracruz when the main body of the expedition pressed inland toward Tenochtitlan. He was young and very vigorous, with a head full of curly, black hair. He was captured and executed by the natives and his head was sent to Moteuczoma (HT, 19; G: item 69).

277. *Martín Nodeo.* This might be the conqueror Martín Oredo who signed the 1520 Segura de la Frontera letter. He left no other trace and so probably died in the conquest (G: item 736).

278. *Alvaro López.* (*See fig. 6.6.*) This is one of six men with the surname López who signed the Veracruz petition. His signature is distinctive in that it has a very complex rubric. One might conclude that either he was a scribe and that was his official mark, or, at the other extreme, he was illiterate and that was his mark. Boyd Bowman lists an Álvaro López, a native of the town of Guadalupe in Cáceres. López testified to having been a member of the company of Cristóbal de Olid and participating in the conquest of Mexico with Cortés. One of his adventures after the conquest was to secure sulfur for the manufacture of gunpowder (Icaza: item 183; see also signature 140). He was a carpenter by training, which came in useful during the conquest. Díaz del Castillo describes López as one of two carpenters who made a cross to be raised at the chapel they built in the island of Cozumel. He was called upon again to construct a similar cross at the Grijalva River (DdelC, 2:100 and 120). López later

testified that he had become suspicious of the natives immediately prior to the Noche Triste when he saw them cleaning pots and pans, and cutting tools, and gathering spices, saying that they were preparing to eat the Spaniards (Thomas, *Conquest*, 384). He had arrived in Cuba in about 1516. He stayed in Tenochtitlan with Alvarado when Cortés left to confront Narváez. López helped to build the first brigantines used along the coast and probably to assemble the ships for the final assault. He settled in Mexico City, becoming a *vecino* in 1525. He received several plots of land from the city council. He was one of the witnesses called by Martín López to testify about the latter's role in the conquest. Alvaro López is credited with being one of the founders of the city of Puebla. In 1531 he was one of the municipal judges, *alcalde*, of that city. He began to develop land near Atlixco. López served as a local magistrate in some native villages. In 1536 he became one of the city councilmen, *regidor*. Not having received an *encomienda*, he sought a pension from the Crown. He married Leonor de Paredes, and they had about four children. He died before 1547 (HT, 75; G: item 536; Icaza: item 183; BB: item 997).

279. *Andrés de Alonso.* Two men named Andrés Alonso signed the 1520 Segura de la Frontera letter. One of these participated in the later conquest of Michoacan with Cristóbal de Olid. After the conquest he settled in Zacatula as a miner. He died by 1527 (G: item 32). The other eventually settled in Puebla after the conquest, where he became a *vecino* in 1534, dying shortly thereafter. He married an Indian woman (G: item 33).

280. *Alonso de Jerez.* This conqueror signed the 1520 Segura de la Frontera letter. He arrived in the Indies in about 1512 and participated in the Hernández de Córdoba expedition. Some list him among the members of the Narváez company. He probably died in the immediate aftermath of the conquest (G: item 500).

281. [*Signature too badly damaged to be read.*]

282. *Francisco de Scarano; Francisco Santos Scarano.* No one going by either of these names appears in any of the traditional sources.

283. [*Signature too badly damaged to be read.*]

FOLIO 8, VERSO

284. *Antonio de Almodóvar.* Díaz del Castillo explained that several members of this family participated in the conquest. The elder member, probably Antonio, his son, Alvaro, and two nephews all were in the company. One nephew died during the conquest, but the others died of natural causes afterward (DdelC, 2:342). Others indicate that he was also known as Antonio Gutiérrez de Almodóvar and that his son was Alvaro Gutiérrez. He may have been captured by pirates immediately after the conquest as he sailed back to

Spain. Nonetheless, he settled in Mexico City after the conquest. In 1528 he signed a power of attorney for his wife to resolve some issues in their home town of Almodóvar del Campo in Spain before she would travel to Mexico to join him. The couple had at least four children. She may have died in Mexico, and Almodóvar then remarried. That same year he received a house plot from the Mexico City council. He received the town of Mizquiahuala in *encomienda*. He died in about 1536 (G: item 28; Himmerich: item 185; HT, 64).

285. *Alonso de Dueñas.* An Alonso de Dueñas left Medina de Rioseco in the province of Valladolid in 1514 for the Indies (BB: item 4545). Two men by this name left the village of Dueñas in the province of Palencia in 1513 and in 1515 to settle in Cuba. At least one of them remained in the city of Santiago de Cuba until 1530 (BB: items, 2448–2449).

286. *Juan de Arriaga.* This conqueror signed the 1520 Segura de la Frontera letter. He was from Berlanga in the province of Soria. He had originally settled on the island of Hispaniola. He participated in the Cortés expedition and in later expeditions, including Guatemala. He eventually received half of the village of Castilblanco and Huajuapan in *encomienda*. He settled in the village of Huajuapan, where he owned a farm and herds of sheep. He served as a local magistrate to other villages in the Oaxaca region. He died before 1564 (G: item 76; HT, 17).

287. *Vasco de Via.* Díaz del Castillo remembers a conqueror with the surname Villa who might be this member of the company (see also signature 133). He was a very strong man of great worth in battle. He had married a kinsman of Cortés's first wife (DdelC, 2:340). The only man named Vasco to sign the 1520 Segura de la Frontera letter was Vasco Porcallo.

288. *García Coral.* No one of this name appears in any of the traditional sources.

289. *Pablo de Guzmán.* Díaz del Castillo tells of two men by this surname, whose given names he could not remember (see also signature 163). One was a locksmith and the other was Cortés's chamberlain. The chamberlain died during the conquest at the hands of the natives (DdelC, 1:91). Cristóbal de Guzmán, who was also a member of the Cortés household, was not the chamberlain remembered by Díaz. The locksmith also built several of the crossbows used by the company (DdelC, 2:248).

290. *Francisco (Fernando?) Trujillo.* Díaz del Castillo recalls three men with this surname (see signature 73). None of the standard sources lists a Francisco Trujillo. The only man by this name known to have immigrated to the Indies settled in Panama in 1514 and became a town councilman and *encomendero* there (BB: item 468).

291. *Juan de Artigas; Juan de Arteaga.* Díaz del Castillo mentions an Artiaga who also went by the name Juan Pérez Malinche: a man who settled in Puebla

and became rich (DdelC, 2:348). He also tells of a scribe by the surname of Artigosa whose son-in-law, Gaspar de Avila, fought in the conquest (DdelC, 2:344). It is possible that this conqueror was the one who Díaz del Castillo called Pérez Malinche, whose real name was Pérez de Arteaga. Several sources indicate that he first went by the name Juan Pérez and only later became Pérez de Arteaga, and finally Pérez de Palencia. His signature here would indicate that he started as Juan de Arteaga. He gained the nickname "Malinche" because he served as a guard to the famous interpreter and translator doña Marina, known as Malintzin or La Malinche. Pérez was very interested in learning Nahuatl, a language he came to speak well. He was an early conqueror of the island of Hispaniola, and then joined the Cortés company. After helping to found the city of Veracruz, he was one of the founders of the city of Puebla. He was active in the commercial life of the city. He was listed as a *vecino* in 1534. He first married an Indian woman, Angelina Pérez, by whom he had six children. Upon her death he married a Spanish woman, Catalina de Santa Cruz, daughter of a conqueror, Francisco de Santa Cruz, with whom he had four more children. He bought and sold land and horses and entered into various contracts. After the conquest he first held Tecali in *encomienda*, although that was taken from him and he ended up with half of the village of Guatinchan (Cuautinchan). He died in about 1558 (HT, 107; G: item 793; Himmerich: item 344).

292. *Juan Ochoa de Elejalde*. Ochoa de Elejalde was a significant member of the company who served in important roles at various points in the conquest. He signed the 1520 Segura de la Frontera letter. Ochoa was from Guipuzcoa, in the Basque country. As such he was considered a noble, *hidalgo*. He arrived in Santo Domingo in 1508 and participated in conquests of Puerto Rico and Cuba, only to return to Santo Domingo. By 1519 he was in Cuba and joined the Cortés company. He distinguished himself in the conquest. He became the sheriff for Cortés, *alguacil*. After Narváez was captured, Cortés ordered Ochoa to scrutinize Narváez's papers. Later Ochoa became the official charged with holding and administering the estates of those who died intestate, *tenedor de bienes de difuntos*. Ochoa participated in several later expeditions, including one to Tehuantepec where he served as royal scribe. Immediately after the conquest he returned to Cuba, where he was a witness to the testament of the governor Diego Velázquez. Upon his subsequent return to Mexico, he received several villages in *encomienda*, including half of Teozacualco, and the villages of Guautla, Tototepetongo, and Tanatepec. He settled first in Mexico City, where he had several pieces of property. He was listed as a *vecino* in 1524. He took on several important posts, both for the royal audiencia and for the Holy Office of the Inquisition. By 1538, he was a *vecino* of Puebla. He received house plots and agricultural land there. He also served in several offices in the municipal government of Puebla, including as assistant sheriff (*teniente de alguacil mayor*),

rural judge (*alcalde de mesta*), city councilman (*regidor*), and holder of the goods of those dying intestate. He married Catalina García Endrino, and they had seven children. In 1546 he received a coat of arms from the king in recognition of his service[24] (HT, 99–100; G: item 720; Villar: item 92; see fig. 6.20).

293. *Fernando de Vargas*. A Francisco de Vargas signed the 1520 Segura de la Frontera letter. Díaz del Castillo writes of two brothers with the surname Vargas from Seville (see signature 168). One of them died in the conquest, and the other died of natural causes later. It is possible that Fernando de Vargas is the brother who died in the conquest. Three men of this name immigrated to the Indies before 1519. Two came from Seville in 1497 and 1512 to Santo Domingo, where one became a postal agent (*correo*) and the other was a nobleman (*espadero*) (BB: items 4068–4069). The third left Toledo for the Indies, along with his sons, Esteban and Juan, in 1511 (BB: item 4430). Francisco de Vargas was a well-known member of the company. He was also from Seville, and was a member of Diego Velázquez's household. He joined the Cortés expedition and served throughout the conquest. He received the towns of Tulancingo, Amatlan, and Xochitepec in *encomienda*. He lost all but Xochitepec soon after the hostilities had ended, and then Xochitepec itself by about 1537. He lived in Mexico City. He served as a local magistrate in several districts, including the mines of Zultepec. He served as a witness for other conquerors' service narratives. His son, Hernando de Vargas, became a page to viceroy don Luis de Velasco (HT, 134–135; G: item 1098; Himmerich: item 472).

294. *Juan de [*. The surname of this conqueror has been made illegible by an ink smear.

295. *Nuño Pérez*. No one of this name appears in any of the traditional sources. This could possibly be Juan Pérez. Two men named Juan Pérez signed the 1520 Segura de la Frontera letter, but, then again, Juan Pérez might well be the most common name in Spanish.

296. *?? de Azedon*. The first name of this conqueror has been lost. A conqueror named Bartolomé de Azedo is listed among the members of the Narváez company (HT, 166).

297. *Pedro Marcos*. Pedro Marco, from Medinaceli in the province of Soria, sailed to Santo Domingo in 1512 (BB: item 4212). An Antón Marco is included in many of the lists of conquerors, but no Pedro.

298. *Hernando Martínez*. Fernando Martínez signed the 1520 Segura de la Frontera letter. Little is known of him. He seems to have joined the company with his brother, possibly Cristóbal. He was killed near Veracruz in 1520 (G: item 618; HT, 87). Another conqueror with a similar name, Hernán Martínez, also signed the Veracruz petition (see signature 244).

299. *Martín*. The surname of this conqueror has been lost. Twenty-one men who signed the 1520 Segura de la Frontera letter had this first name.

Biographies OF THE *Signatories*

300. *Francisco de Valdez*. No one of this name appears in any of the traditional sources. The signature is badly damaged.

301. *Pedro de Ircio*. Ircio, also known as Dircio, and his brother, Martín de Ircio (see signature 43), were well-known members of the company. Both were from Briones in Logroño. Pedro signed the 1520 Segura de la Frontera letter. Díaz del Castillo describes Pedro as being of medium height. He was a passionate man, full of talk about what he would accomplish. He might have been a blowhard, but he became one of the leading captains of the expedition. Díaz del Castillo compares him in a negative manner to Agrajes, a character from the novels of chivalry popular at the time. Agrajes was supposedly a king of Scotland famous for being an expert swordsman. Consequently the reference was meant to imply that Díaz del Castillo felt that Ircio did not live up to his own reputation (DdelC, 2:334). Ircio sailed first on the Grijalva expedition. He became a captain at Veracruz and possibly also joined Montejo on the expedition to Pánuco. He was one of the municipal justices (*alcalde*) at Tepeaca. He was second in command to Gonzalo de Sandoval in the encounter with Narváez. In the final assault on Tenochtitlan he distinguished himself in capturing several of the bridges along the causeways linking the city to the shore. Immediately after the fall of Tenochtitlan Cortés sent him to help govern Veracruz. Pedro joined in a few of the later expeditions. In 1527 he was denounced as a blasphemer to the bishop who was acting as Inquisitor. He died shortly thereafter. He was granted the *encomienda* of Maxcalzingo (HT, 70; G: item 493).

302. *Diego de Godoy, escribano público*. Godoy appears numerous times in Díaz del Castillo's history of the conquest. From the very beginning he is identified as one of the notaries and scribes of the expedition. Although he did not notarize the Veracruz petition, he was named the town clerk (DdelC, 1:108 and 138). Later in the conquest he became one of the leaders. In the expedition to Honduras, Godoy served as second in command under Cortés in establishing the town of Natividad and as a captain in the expedition (DdelC, 2:222). Godoy had also served on the earlier Grijalva expedition, taking the role of clerk. He was particularly active in the later Central American expeditions. He died in Central America, killed by the natives, in about 1526 (G: item 381; HT, 61). Boyd Bowman lists this conqueror twice, once as a native of Pinto, near Madrid, and the other as coming from Extremadura, village unknown (BB: items 4319 and 5100).

303. *Simón de Cuenca*. This might be the same conqueror identified as Benito de Cuenca in the 1520 Segura de la Frontera letter. Cuenca became a minor leader of the expedition. He served as Cortés's steward in Veracruz, and

he imprisoned Narváez in his house in Veracruz after the confrontation with that leader. He was a town councilman, *regidor*, in Veracruz in 1521. Cortés placed him as his lieutenant in the town of Medellín. He died in the Central American region of Xicalanco in a dispute with Francisco de Medina (DdelC, 2:120, 236, 336; HT, 51; G: item 252). Grunberg doubted that he was present in Mexico before 1521.

304. *Pedro de Villafuente; Juan de Villafuerte.* There were no conquerors known by these names. There was a Juan Rodríguez de Villafuerte who played an important role in the conquest. He was a close advisor to Cortés and signed the 1520 Segura de la Frontera letter. He assisted in the construction of the first brigantines and commanded the fleet of brigantines in the final assault. On the first day out on Lake Texcoco, however, he nearly lost his ship and was then replaced by Martín López as captain of the fleet. After the conquest Villafuerte remained in command of the forces in Tenochtitlan while Cortés assaulted Coyoacan. He participated in several later expeditions, including the conquest of Michoacan and Zacatula. He finally settled in the Zacatula area, becoming a *vecino* in 1525. At the request of Cortés he founded the first sanctuary for Nuestra Señora de los Remedios, the patron of the Cortés company. Yet in 1527 he was denounced to the Inquisition for blasphemy. He remained close to Cortés, buying and selling goods on his behalf. He first married a granddaughter of Cacamatzin, one of the last Aztec rulers. When she died he married a Spanish woman, Juana de Zúñiga, a kinswoman of Cortés's first wife. He received a large number of native villages along the south coast of Mexico in *encomienda*. He died sometime before 1547 (HT, 115–116; G: item 898; Himmerich: item 381).

305. *Alonso de la Torre.* Alonso de Torres signed the 1520 Segura de la Frontera letter. He arrived in the New World in 1514, from Madrid, and eventually settled in Cuba. He participated in the conquest of Mexico. In 1528 he was imprisoned in Mexico for failure to pay a fifty-peso debt. He owned a garden outside of Mexico City where he grew produce. He also owned a house in the city. He died sometime in 1529 (G, 1048).

306. *Beltrán de Godoy.* No one of this name appears in any of the traditional sources. He may have been a kinsman of Diego de Godoy, the secretary (see signature 302). A Bernardino de Godoy participated in the conquest (HT, 144).

307. *Cristóbal Corral.* This conqueror signed the 1520 Segura de la Frontera letter. According to Díaz del Castillo, Corral was the first standard-bearer of the company (*alférez*), a role he played on and off throughout the conquest. He was an important, if symbolic, member of the company. Following the conquest he returned to Spain and died there of natural causes (DdelC, 2:336). Corral might have come from the village of Tiemblo in Avila. He was probably a member of Cortés's household before the conquest. On one occasion he

fell during battle, and the banner fell with him. When a group of Indians attempted to kill him, he defended himself with his dagger and was miraculously saved. He held other roles during the conquest, including councilman, *regidor*, in Segura de la Frontera. He was awarded the town of Cuauhtitlan in *encomienda*. He returned to Spain, losing his claim to the grant. He died around 1531 (HT, 30; G: item 243).

308. *Pedro de Toledo*. No one of this name appears in any of the traditional sources. An Alonso de Toledo signed the 1520 Segura de la Frontera letter.

309. *Alonso García*. (See signatures 55 and 147.)

CHAPTER 8

Conclusions

THE FOUNDING OF LA VILLA RICA DE LA VERA CRUZ WAS a unique event in the conquest of Mexico and in the exploration and discovery of the New World up until that point. Certainly other towns had been founded in the Indies prior to 1519, but none became so heavily invested with symbolic meaning. The image of the conquistador—clad in a steel breastplate and *morrión* helmet, striding through the waves to plant the flag of Spain on some American shore—is mythic in its proportions. In just such a way the founding of the town of Veracruz has become imbued with symbolic meaning for Mexicans and for historians. This book has served to look into the events surrounding the founding of the town and to investigate the men who participated, in order to place the event and the actors in a proper context. It is unfortunate that in seeking to lessen the importance of the event by viewing it in a larger context, the book will have the unintended consequence of further reifying this one moment in the conquest of Mexico.

The founding of Veracruz took on its near-mythic status through a confluence of factors. As seen in the chapter on the synopsis of the conquest (chapter 2), and also in the historiography (chapter 3), the founding of Veracruz created a significant break in the narrative of the expedition. In the months following the departure of the expedition from Cuba, Cortés and his men had been content to retrace the route already forged by Hernández de Córdoba and Grijalva. The expedition leaders knew, more or less, where they could safely take on fresh water, which ports had friendly natives, which regions to avoid. The composition of the expedition remained fairly stable. A few men died in battles with the natives, but the expedition acquired a translator, Gerónimo de Aguilar, and then doña Marina and her fellow native women. Other than these women, the expedition had very few native auxiliaries. The expedition would not receive any fresh Spanish reinforcements until early July, with the arrival of the Salcedo expedition. Consequently, the months immediately following the departure from Cuba had a fairly well defined trajectory, a consistent cohort of participants, and what was assumed to be a clear direction.

The landing at Veracruz began to shake up the comfortable consistency of the expedition. The founding of a town was not that unusual. What was unusual was that Cortés had it done in a very legalistic manner. While other conquerors had set up towns for which they eventually sought royal recognition, Cortés set up the town specifically with an eye toward the approval of the Crown. Barely six weeks passed between the landing at Veracruz on April 22 and the legal incorporation of the town, which occurred sometime before June 20. As has been seen in the analysis of the various documents, the purpose of the town was twofold: it provided the conquerors with a base of operations for further exploration and possible conquest, and it provided them with a legal entity under whose auspices they could engage in actions beyond those stipulated in the license from Velázquez. It was in this latter function that the actions of Cortés and his men proved to be innovative, if not revolutionary.

Ever since the town was founded, people have debated the reasons behind its establishment. Even contemporary observers could not entirely agree about whether the impetus came from Cortés or from some cohort in the expedition. Obviously not everyone was in favor, because the sources do agree that there was a group of supporters of Velázquez who opposed the action. Unresolved is whether those men voiced their opposition early in the process, thus pushing Cortés and his followers to act decisively to protect themselves, or whether the Velázquez supporters were merely reacting to what they saw as illegal actions on the part of the majority. Yet, while deep divisions emerged in the company contingent upon the foundation of Veracruz, several men who initially rejected the seeming rebellion against Velázquez came to be strong supporters of Cortés, such as Diego de Ordaz, whose name does not appear in the document under study here.

Among the expeditions and conquests in the New World, the conquest of Mexico stands out largely because of the number of participants, including some 450 Spaniards at Veracruz and possibly upwards of twelve hundred by the fall of Tenochtitlan. It was also a relatively early conquest of the mainland. Only the expeditions to what is now Panama occurred earlier. In many ways the conquests of Peru, Chile, and New Granada drew upon the lessons learned at Veracruz and in the conquest of Mexico in general.[1] While scholars debate the exact degree to which Pizarro, for example, drew on the experiences of Cortés, the exploits of the leader of the expedition to Mexico were well known in Spain and the Americas. There was one veteran of the conquest of Mexico among the men of Cajamarca, along with several others who had seen action in Nicaragua. Moreover, the letters attributed to Cortés were printed in 1530, meaning that Pizarro and his captains certainly had access to that information. Consequently, the conquest of Mexico quickly became the standard whereby other conquests were imagined by the Spaniards of the New World and the Old.

Among the many expeditions of conquest carefully analyzed in recent years by a variety of scholars, the composition of the Cortés company was largely indistinguishable, unlike the Pizarro cohort at Cajamarca, which was exceptional. Looking at the regional origins of the conquerors, most of the expeditions had strong contingents from the realms of Castile and Andalucía, generally accounting for upwards of 70 percent of the men. The men of Cajamarca reflected that pattern to a diminished degree, because the Extremeños made up some 28 percent of the company, whereas in the other expeditions that region usually accounted for only about 16–20 percent of the companies. Similarly, the percentage of nobles at Cajamarca far exceeded that of other expeditions. The men known to be noble at Cajamarca accounted for 22.6 percent of the expedition. Adding in another six men believed to be noble raises the percentage of nobles to 26 percent.[2] The only other area which reflects this level of noble participation is New Granada. Unfortunately, fragmentary data do not allow for a hard and fast conclusion for those at Veracruz, since social origins are available for only a tenth of the men. But of that reduced group, 18 percent were identified as noble.[3] In most of the other expeditions, nobles represented only about 10 percent of the total.

The composition of the Cortés company at Veracruz also reflects a general occupational diversity more in line with other expeditions. Large numbers of men practiced occupations linked in one way or another to either seafaring or war, and many to both. There were thirty-two men who were pilots, seamen, carpenters, or blacksmiths. Another twenty-one were crossbowmen, harquebusiers, or gunners. Thus a total of fifty-three men practiced occupations related to warfare or the sea. At Cajamarca only six men, out of 168, fell into these categories: two sailors, two gunners, and two carpenters.[4]

While data on the other expeditions are fragmentary, the impression is that they were far more like the Cortés expedition than the Pizarro. This can be explained by the background of the Pizarro expedition. Pizarro gained the knowledge he needed to propose an expedition while living in Panama. He then returned to Spain, sought a royal license, and began to mount his expedition while still in Spain, drawing from many members of his extended family and friends from Trujillo. He actively recruited for the expedition but was limited in how many men he could carry. Two groups joined the expedition en route. Once fully constituted, the expedition established a city at Tumbez. Not all the members of the expedition went on to Cajamarca. Thus, the men of Cajamarca were a unique sub-cohort of the larger expedition. Other expeditions were more ad hoc than that. Cortés, for example, actively recruited only on the island of Cuba, although it seems that word of the expedition spread and men arrived from Hispaniola and elsewhere to join. But in many ways the Cortés company was more reflective of the broad cross-section of Spaniards active in the Indies at the time of departure than was the Pizarro expedition.

At this distance, it might seem that the composition of the Cortés company, as compared to the Pizarro company, played a role in events subsequent to the conquest. Following the fall of Tenochtitlan, Cortés and his captains led several additional expeditions to neighboring regions. Certainly there were disputes that broke out among the factions of conquerors, mostly between those men who received *encomiendas* from Cortés and those who did not, allies of the leader and his opponents. These disagreements, while violent from moment to moment, never reached the point of boiling over and engulfing the entire colony. A series of political missteps on the part of the Crown, namely the appointment of the very corrupt First Audiencia, exacerbated these divisions. But again, while there were isolated flare-ups of violence and legal maneuvers, there was no colony-wide rebellion.

In the case of the Pizarro expedition, violence among the conquerors became commonplace. Those members of the company who had not happened to be at Cajamarca felt themselves unfairly excluded from the booty. Divisions also arose among the men of Cajamarca, all of which resulted in years of civil war in Peru after the conquest. Clearly the astounding wealth of Cajamarca put a high contrast between the haves and have-nots of that expedition. Regional differences among the leaders of the factions also played a role. For example, mutual antipathy between men of Extremadura and those of New Castile might have further poisoned relationships.[5] But it is quite possible that the large percentage of nobles in the Pizarro expedition fueled the fires of factionalism. Slights, real and imagined, spurred the *hidalgos* to react strongly against those who insulted them or those who tacitly questioned their honor and social status. The high concentration of nobles exacerbated the problems, creating years of civil strife.

The composition of the Cortés expedition at Veracruz has the most in common with the composition of the Cortés expedition at the time of the fall of Tenochtitlan. Of the men at Veracruz, about half survived the conquest, thus making them two distinct cohorts. The ranks of the company were replenished largely by the Narváez expedition, but ten other expeditions also added men to the body. The snapshot of the whole company at the end of the conquest is quite similar to what has been seen at Veracruz.[6] In both instances, most men were in their twenties and thirties. The regional distribution was nearly identical, although a few more Basques were present at Veracruz than at the end of the conquest. The nobility were better represented at Veracruz, with only 5.7 percent of all conquerors at the end coming from that social stratum. The occupations found at Veracruz were slightly less representative by the time the conquest ended. While thirteen men at Veracruz were carpenters, for instance, only sixteen could be identified as such at the end of the conquest, although the cohort was much larger. Mostly this is due to the difficulty of ascertaining occupations amid the larger cohort. Grunberg was able to find that information for only about 13 percent of the cases he studied.[7] Taken as a whole, the men in the Cortés company at Veracruz accurately represent the cross-section of men in the Indies at that time.

The focus of this study has been on the lives of the men who were present at Veracruz, and not so much on the actions of Cortés. In this regard it seeks to change the way we look at the conquest, in keeping with the New Conquest History. In an absolute sense the foundation of Veracruz was the result of the actions of many, many men, regardless of whether or not Cortés was the instigator. Moreover, each individual conqueror, as seen through the biographies, dealt with the conquest as best he could, given the constraints of the time. Certainly some conquerors of low social status were able to gain prestige and privilege as a result of their actions in the conquest. For example, Benito Bejel, the most humble member of the company, received an *encomienda* and was granted land in Mexico City, set up a dance studio, began teaching music, and became reasonably wealthy.[8] By and large, the elite members of the company also fared well, if they survived.

The document itself embodies the collective mentality of the company. As noted first by Lockhart and later by Restall, the members of the expedition were investors in a common action.[9] Each man brought certain resources to the effort, and expected to be rewarded in proportion. The town council, however it was originally constituted, took seriously the duty of representing the members of the company. The presence of the signatures reinforces the sense of common destiny. These men had embarked on a collective action, founded a city, possibly defied a local governor, and by signing their names manifested their solidarity. As it turns out, the men took common cause with Cortés, whom they felt also was their best option for leadership. One can envision contrary scenarios, and indeed the arrival of the Narváez expedition provided just such a one. Once the small contingent under the leadership of Cortés had successfully ambushed the much larger Narváez force, the members of Narváez's expedition voted with their feet to join Cortés. This was not a foregone conclusion, and opponents of Cortés could have seized the initiative, but did not or could not. At the same time, Cortés did bring a significant number of native auxiliaries to help win the day against the forces of Narváez. While undoubtedly Cortés provided a great deal of leadership, he depended on the support of the rank and file of the expedition and the assistance of the native allies. As such, the presence of the signatures ratifying the actions of the town council speaks volumes about that support, and in all likelihood was meant to do exactly that.

While the petition of the town council provides a great deal of information about the events surrounding the foundation of the town of Veracruz, it has the disadvantage of further reifying the moment of the foundation within the narrative of the conquest of Mexico. This is further complicated by the socio-political world in which the document was forged. As has been explored in depth, the petition represents the sentiments of the "citizens" (*vecinos*) of La Villa Rica de la Vera Cruz. As such it excludes many participants in the conquest who were neither formal members of the company nor legal citizens of the town. There are three groups who in particular are thus excluded: women, native auxiliaries, and slaves.

Recent scholarship has only begun to look into the presence of women on such expeditions. In his work on the entire conquest of Mexico, Grunberg identified only thirteen women, none of whom he believed had sailed in the original expedition. He estimated a total of about twenty accompanied the full expedition, perhaps two of whom were prostitutes.[10] Tangential evidence points to at least one woman within the original cohort, Isabel Rodríguez.[11] But because they were not full members of the company — that is, investors — and neither were they male heads of household, they were not considered citizens of the newly founded town, nor did they enjoy a legal status which would have allowed them to ratify the actions of the town council.

At the time the expedition landed and established Veracruz, it had not yet acquired large numbers of native auxiliaries. As time passed by, and especially after the encounter with the forces of Tlaxcala, the Cortés expedition would come to rely on tens of thousands of natives, but at this point there were very few. The few natives who accompanied the expedition were the native women given to Cortés along with the woman who would serve as his interpreter, doña Marina. Thus there were few natives in the larger expedition in the spring of 1519. Moreover, they would not appear as signatories to the petition of the town council because they both lacked the rights of citizens and, strictly speaking, were not investors in the expedition.

Undoubtedly several of the leading members of the expedition brought slaves with them, although there are very few references to such individuals in the standard narratives of the conquest. Again, lacking the rights to be citizens of the town or to be members of the company, they did not qualify to ratify the petition.

By excluding these members of the expedition, the petition valorizes the participation of those who signed. It creates a skewed vision of the conquest with which only recent scholarship has begun to grapple. Just as the presence or absence of conquerors at Cajamarca meant a life of tremendous wealth or of lost opportunity, so too a person's presence at Veracruz could have created preeminence among the conquerors. Yet because the endeavor was viewed even at the time as being of questionable legality, it did not accord such a status to the participants. In some documents drafted after the conquest these men were referred to as the "first conquerors." More commonly, though, it was membership in the company at the time of the fall of Tenochtitlan that became the hallmark of participation in the conquest, even if the person had only served for a few weeks at the very end. While conquerors would extol their exploits from throughout the conquest, it was the final decisive battle which became the litmus test for membership in the group known as the "conquerors."[12] Nevertheless, the distinctions between these two groups were subtle and by no means consistently applied.

The petition of the town council is extremely important in allowing us to understand the dynamic of the conquest of Mexico. It focuses attention on this crucial moment. It also provides scholars with a point of comparison regarding the composition of the expedition, its goals, and its procedures. A little over a year later, the expedition again mustered out all of its members to sign the papers relative to the foundation of the town of Segura de la Frontera. Unfortunately, the original of that muster does not exist. The copy which has come down to the present was made in the mid-sixteenth century as part of lawsuits involving Cortés. The scribes of the era could not read all of the signatures, and then scholars in the nineteenth century could not read all of the names written by the scribes. In spite of these shortcomings, we do have the names of many of the men. This has served as a check against the signatures on the Veracruz document and was also the basis for much of the work of Thomas and Grunberg. In studying the conquest of Mexico, we are fortunate indeed to have two such documents to allow us to better understand the dynamics of the conquest on individuals.

The petition itself outlines the goals of the expedition, which were to discover and conquer in the name of the Crown. This contrasted with the goals as established by Velázquez. The whole reason for being a town was, in fact, to circumvent the license of Velázquez, regardless of who conceived of the idea.

While the legal procedures used by the Cortés expedition have been subjected to tremendous scrutiny since the very beginning, all we can do is to reflect on what happened, since there simply is no way to know the intentions of the participants. The consensus of legal and historical opinion is that Cortés acted illegally in breaking off his ties to Velázquez and so needed to regularize the expedition by seeking direct royal permission. The establishment of the town was the legal convention through which he could accomplish this. Founding towns was a natural part of the discovery process. But the focus on the legal aspects of town founding seem to have been peculiar to Veracruz, and this came as a result of the unique legal limbo created for which Cortés and his company found themselves in the spring of 1519.

Conclusions

The creation of the town of Veracruz and the transformation of Velázquez from an honored colleague to a reprehensible despot allowed Cortés to take a disparate group of Spanish immigrants and conquerors and create a fairly cohesive company out of them. Cortés manufactured a common enemy for his expedition, which in turn allowed him to ignore or at least paper over the factions which already existed in the company. By cutting ties to Velázquez, he also closed the door to any option other than victory. If the expedition was not successful, the members faced charges of treason should they return to Cuba, or anywhere else in the Hispanic world. The dismantling and burning of the ships, which occurred a few weeks later, was in reality merely an affirmation of this policy, and a reasonable action, since the tropical waters would eventually rot the hulls, making the ships unseaworthy.

By ridding himself of the strongest supporters of Velázquez, and by turning the allegiance of several of the leaders of that faction, Cortés created a company of men who were united. The members of the company invested their energies in a common goal which served their own personal self-interests. To paraphrase Bernal Díaz del Castillo, they sought to "serve God and King" and also to get rich. They passed through a collective experience which set them apart from other men. They flouted the authority of the king, as expressed through Velázquez, only to embrace a direct allegiance to the Crown through the creation of La Villa Rica de la Vera Cruz. Yet it was precisely the legal weight of an incorporated polity that allowed the men of this expedition to support their leader's ambitious and illegal goals while still proclaiming and affirming their loyalty to king and Crown.

Signatories OF THE 1520 Segura DE LA Frontera Letter

AGI, Justicia, leg. 223, I, ff. 34–85.

The document has been published: Joaquín Pacheco and Francisco Cárdenas, eds., *Colección de documentos inéditos relativos al descubrimiento, conquista, y organización de las posesiones españolas en América y Oceania* (Madrid: Sucesores de Ribadeneyra, 1864–1884), 28:480–498; Joaquín García Icazbalceta, *Colección de documentos para la historia de México* (Mexico: Librería de J. M. Andrade, 1858–1866), 1:427–436.

[1] Pedro de Albarado, alcalde
[2] Diego de Ordaz, regidor
[3] Cristobal Dolid
[4] Juan Rodriguez de Villafuerte
[5] Luis de Marin, alcalde
[6] Pedro de Ircio, alcalde
[7] Francisco de Horozco, regidor
[8] Cristoval Martin de Gamboa
[9] Francisco de Solis
[10] Cristoval Corral
[11] Alonso Davila
[12] Rodrigo Alvarez Chico
[13] Diego de Valdenebro
[14] Juan de Salamanca
[15] Bernardio Vazquez de Tapia
[16] Gonzalo de Sandoval
[17] Juan Jaramillo
[18] Juan de Mansilla
[19] Sebastian de Porras
[20] Antonio Quiñones
[21] Martin Perez
[22] Pedro Rodriguez de Escobar
[23] Antonio de Villarroel
[24] Luis de Hoxeda

[25] Francisco de Vargas
[26] Sebastian de Grijalva
[27] Francisco de San Martin
[28] Juan Bono de Quixo
[29] Cristoval de Guzman
[30] Alonso Perez, el bachiller
[31] Gutierre de Badajoz
[32] Geronimo de Aguilar
[33] Alonso de Mendoza
[34] Andres de Tapia
[35] Gomez de Albarado
[36] Vasco Porcallo
[37] Pedro de [*surname missing*]
[38] Alonso del Castillo
[39] Pedro de [*surname missing*]
[40] Fernando de Lerma
[41] Francisco Gutierrez
[42] Alonso de Mora
[43] Fernando Martinez
[44] Pedro de Villalobos
[45] Juan del Valle
[46] Antonio de Villafani
[47] Alonso Romero
[48] Andres de Portillo

[49] Lope de Aviles
[50] Fernando Xerez
[51] Gutierre de Samont
[52] Alonso de Galduñas
[53] Alonso Nortes
[54] Nicolas Gomez
[55] Juanes Cerron
[56] Francisco de Estrada
[57] Lucas Juan Lopez Zaragozano
[58] Pero Sanchez
[59] Martin Garcia
[60] Juan de Leon
[61] Juan Diaz, clerigo
[62] Francisco Daza de Alconchel
[63] Bartolome Franco
[64] Francisco Maldonado
[65] Juan Ruiz de Alaniz
[66] Antonio de Quemada
[67] Mendo Xuarez
[68] Juan Lopez Zaragozano
[69] Pedro Bamba Cabeza de Vaca
[70] Juan Lopez Zaragozano
[71] Juan Navarro
[72] Juan Zamudio
[73] Juan Bueno
[74] Juan Volante
[75] Rodrigo de Salazar
[76] Alsono Gonzalo
[77] Juan Garcia Mendez
[78] Diego de Mola
[79] Francisco Velazquez
[80] Alonso de la Puente
[81] Francisco Montaño
[82] Juan de Vergara
[83] Alonso de Trugillo
[84] Alonso de [surname missing]
[85] Juan Rodrigo
[86] Alonso de Contreras
[87] Cristoval Ortiz
[88] Andres Campos
[89] Alonso Alvarez
[90] Agustino Perez
[91] Martin Velez
[92] Pedro Net[letters missing]

[93] Alonso Quintero
[94] Bautista Ginoves
[95] Francisco Garcia
[96] Clemente Barcelones
[97] Alonso de la Puebla
[98] Juan Rubio
[99] Diego de Naypes
[100] Pedro Romero
[101] Cristoval Rodriguez
[102] Juan de Coxecer
[103] Francisco de Casanova
[104] Alonso Morcillo
[105] Francisco de Alburquerque
[106] Garcia de Vinuesa
[107] Domingo Martinez
[108] Francisco Marquez
[109] Sancho de Barahona
[110] Leonel de Cervantes, el comendador
[111] Miguel de Villasanta
[112] Alonso de Hoxeda
[113] Francisco de Lugo
[114] Francisco de Arevalo
[115] Francisco Garcia
[116] Alonso de [surname missing]
[117] Luis de [surname missing]
[118] Anton de Molina
[119] Francisco Quintero
[120] Cristoval Bernal
[121] Juan de Alcantara
[122] Pedro Lopez Zaragozano
[123] Ramon Ginoves
[124] Luis de Cardenas
[125] Fernando de Olla
[126] Martin Pinto
[127] Luis de Frias
[128] Andres de Valiente
[129] Martin de Jaen
[130] Antonio de Saldaña
[131] Benito de Vejel
[132] Pedro Rodrigo Carmona
[133] Rodrigo de Najara
[134] Francisco Vazquez
[135] Juan de Cardenas
[136] Francisco Marroqui

[137] Rodrigo de Castañeda
[138] Juan de Zamudio
[139] Alonso de Salvatierra
[140] Bartolome Tamayo
[141] Juan Duran
[142] Pedro Romero
[143] Juan de Villacorta
[144] Pedro Zamorano
[145] Alonso de Salamanca
[146] Sebastian Benitez
[147] Pedro Gomez
[148] Juan Batista [Bautista]
[149] Diego de Fernandez
[150] Luis Velazquez
[151] Diego de Sanabria
[152] Gonzalo de Sobrino
[153] Cristoval Martinez
[154] Francisco de Castro
[155] Garcia de Aguilar
[156] Pedro de Sepulveda
[157] Diego Moreno
[158] Nicolas Palanis
[159] Alonso Navarrete
[160] Pedro de Benavente
[161] Velasco Hernandez
[162] Martin de Vergara
[163] Alonso Caballo
[164] Pedro de Villaverde
[165] Pedro Romero
[166] Pedro Moreno
[167] Juan Barrios
[168] Pedro Vizcayno
[169] Alonso del Rio
[170] Juan Ballesteros
[171] Gaspar de Tarifa
[172] Gonzalo de Jaen
[173] Marcos Ginoves
[174] Pedro Gallego
[175] Fernando de Torres
[176] Juan Rodrigo [Rodriquez]
[177] Juan de Leiva
[178] Esteban de Ponte
[179] Francisco Rodriguez
[180] Alonso de Pastrana

[181] Antonio Boria
[182] Juan Tanilo
[183] Pedro Gallar
[184] Sebastian de Lorca
[185] Pedro de [*surname missing*]
[186] Francisco de Utrera Nuñez
[187] Diego Valencia
[188] Fernando de Aguilar
[189] Fernando de Osuna
[190] Alonso Riero
[191] Juan Sedeño
[192] Diego Xuarez
[193] Diego Riero
[194] Pedro Ruiz de Alaniz
[195] Alonso Esturano
[196] Juan de Cabra
[197] Cristoval Gallego
[198] Diego Castellanos
[199] Juan Rico
[200] Juan Perez
[201] Domingo Ginoves
[202] Pedro de Abarca
[203] Juan de Plasencia
[204] Francisco Lopez
[205] Juan de Najara
[206] Alonso de Gibraltar
[207] Martin de Chaves
[208] Juan Ortiz
[209] Juan de Santana
[210] Pedro Fernandez
[211] Rodrigo Dava
[212] Hernan Martin
[213] Andres de Garcia
[214] Francisco de Grijalva
[215] Pedro Sabiote
[216] Pedro Calvo
[217] Rodrigo Hernandez
[218] Martin Soldado
[219] Pedro de Villona
[220] Martin de la Cruz
[221] Alonso Nuñez
[222] Diego Diaz
[223] Andres de Farfan
[224] Francisco Velazquez

[225] Pedro Garcia
[226] Gonzalo de Al[*letters missing*]
[227] Diego Ramirez
[228] Miguel Ximenez
[229] Diego de Santiago
[230] Juan Fernandez Macia
[231] Felipe Napolitano
[232] Nunno Gutierrez
[233] Esteban Consino
[234] Diego de Ayamonte
[235] Diego Montero
[236] Francisco de Gil
[237] Bartolome de Campo
[238] Juan Vizcayno
[239] Aparicio Martin
[240] Miguel Gomez
[241] Juan Flamenco
[242] Antonio de Veyntemilla
[243] Alonso Garcia
[244] Tomas de Rixales
[245] Juan Termeno
[246] Pedro de Rodrigues
[247] Martin de las Casas
[248] Alvaro Gonzalez
[249] Gonzalo Sanchez
[250] Andres Alonso
[251] Nicolas Rodriguez
[252] Bartolome de Villanueva
[253] Jorge de Albarado
[254] Sebastian de Moscoso
[255] Francisco de Albarado
[256] Hernando Lozano
[257] Juan de Arriaga
[258] Juan Ramos de Lares
[259] Pedro de Alanis
[260] Cristoval Pacheco
[261] Alonso de Serna
[262] Bartolome Roman
[263] Francisco de Santa Cruz
[264] Alvaro Becerra
[265] Pedro de Albarca [Abarca]
[266] Andres de Monxaraz [Monjaraz]
[267] Diego Holguin
[268] Gomez Gutierrez

[269] Julian de la Muela
[270] Pedro Gonzalez de Haznalcazar
[271] Alonso Perez
[272] Garcia de Despadola
[273] Andres de Santisteban
[274] Bernaldino de Santiago
[275] Juan Mendez
[276] Juan de Aparicio
[277] Alonso Ximenez de Herrera
[278] Juan Frayle
[279] Juan de [*surname missing*]
[280] Juan Perez de Aquitiano
[281] Juan de Yaxestas
[282] Francisco Morales
[283] [*letters missing*]erros
[284] Garcia del Pilar
[285] Francisco de [*surname missing*]
[286] Juan de [*surname missing*]
[287] Cristoval Hernandez
[288] Diego de Villarreal
[289] Pedro de Guzman
[290] Andres Alonso
[291] Gonzalo Gutierrez
[292] Gonzalo Mexia
[293] Fernando de Frias
[294] Miguel de Ban
[295] Pedro de Cuevas de Sopuerta
[296] Francisco de Oliveros
[297] Alonso de Jerez
[298] Francisco Bonal
[299] Guillen Devalo
[300] Fernando Burguero
[301] Hernando Blanco
[302] Francisco Martin
[303] Hernando de Tobar
[304] Francisco Vazquez
[305] Fray Bartolome [de Olmedo]
[306] Alonso de Villanueva
[307] Francisco Lopez
[308] Francisco Rodriguez
[309] Diego de Porras
[310] Alonso de Herrera
[311] Pedro Gonzalez
[312] Diego Bardales

[313] Juan, Maestre
[314] Cristoval Diaz
[315] Juan Davila
[316] Juan Bellido
[317] Pedro de Solis
[318] Hernando de Roxas
[319] Alonso Bello
[320] Gonzalo Dominguez
[321] Geronimo Salinas
[322] Juan de Cuellar
[323] Juan Ochoa
[324] Diego Alonso de Portillo
[325] Pedro Gutierrez de Valdelomar
[326] Alonso de Basurto
[327] Juan Perez
[328] Francisco de Olmos
[329] Juan de Cuellar
[330] Alonso de Torres
[331] Lorenzo Dava
[332] Hernando de Tapia
[333] Alonso de Ledesma
[334] Juan Moreno
[335] Gregorio Sedeño
[336] Diego de Soto
[337] Bartolome Lopez
[338] Juan Pinzon
[339] Ginex Pinzon
[340] Luis de [surname missing]
[341] Hernando de Robles
[342] Alberto de Cenero
[343] Juan Garcia
[344] Garcilaso Gutierrez
[345] Juan Gomez
[346] Juan Ruiz
[347] Diego Martin
[348] Diego de Llerena
[349] Diego de Salamanca
[350] Juan Alvarez
[351] Pedro Fernandez
[352] Gaspar Aleman
[353] Fernando Trigueros
[354] Gonzalo Ximenez
[355] Gonzalo de Lagos
[356] Juan Carlos de San Remon

[357] Juan del Puerto
[358] Andres Nuñez
[359] Cristoval Garrido
[360] Cristoval Flores
[361] Francisco Flores
[362] Sebastian de Duero
[363] Ochoa de Asno
[364] Tomas de Saona
[365] Esteban Colmenero
[366] Juan Teceliano
[367] Gonzalo Lopez
[368] Martin Lopez
[369] Andres de Truxillo
[370] Francisco del Barco
[371] Geronimo Floriano
[372] Juan Bono
[373] Fernando Priego
[374] Alvaro de Llerena
[375] Pedro de Gibaxa
[376] Alonso de Villanueva
[377] Juan Ximenez
[378] Fernando de Illescas
[379] Pedro, Maestre
[380] Bartolome Sanchez
[381] Sancho de Salzedo
[382] Juan Davila
[383] Pedro de las Asturias
[384] Cristoval Ruiz
[385] Cristoval Farfan
[386] Diego de [surname missing]
[387] Alonso de Cardenas
[388] Pedro Gutierrez
[389] Anton Bravo
[390] Gaspar Gutierrez
[391] Alonso Perez
[392] Martin del Puerto
[393] Domingo Gonzalez
[394] Alvaro Perez
[395] Gomez de Valderrama
[396] Pedro Rodriguez
[397] Ramon Lopez Gabriel
[398] Juan Mayorqui
[399] Rodrigo Juan de Valladolid
[400] Alonso Perez, el bachiller

---

[401] Pedro Lentero
[402] Alonso Gonzalo Najara
[403] Juan de Vallid Vanegas
[404] Juan Muñoz
[405] Pedro Alvarez
[406] Alonso Hidalgo
[407] Martin Dorantes
[408] Pedro Gonzalo Najara
[409] Francisco Garcia
[410] Pedro de Ocaña
[411] Pedro Blanco
[412] Melchor de San Miguel
[413] Rodrigo de Peñas
[414] Juan de Manzanilla
[415] Pedro de Truxillo
[416] Martin Fernandez
[417] Martin Barahona
[418] Pedro Fernandez
[419] Diego de Fonseca
[420] Francisco de Aguilar
[421] Lucas Montañez
[422] Bartolome de Paredes
[423] Lucas de Escalona
[424] Cristoval Martin
[425] Juan de Rivera
[426] Juan Rodriguez
[427] Pedro Calvo
[428] Juan de Carmona
[429] Anton de Rodes
[430] Francisco de Alarcon
[431] Juan Adalama
[432] Gonzalo de Virola
[433] Juan de Caceres
[434] Alonso de Macias
[435] Gonzalo de Medina
[436] Juan Melgarexo
[437] Alonso Hernandez
[438] Andres de Hoces
[439] Anton Gabarro
[440] Gonzalo Martin
[441] Anton de Varelas
[442] Garcia Fernandez de Merida
[443] Lorenzo Payo
[444] Benito Gallego

[445] Alonso de Toledo
[446] Juan Montañez
[447] Bernardino de Oviedo
[448] Juan de Morales
[449] Juan [*surname missing*]
[450] Miguel de Morales
[451] Rodrigo de [Valladolid]
[452] Hernan Garcia
[453] Rodrigo de Prado
[454] Gregorio Muñoz
[455] Alonso de Salamanca
[456] Diego Gomez Cornexo
[457] Lorenzo Ginoves
[458] Juan de Revejo
[459] Pedro del Barco
[460] Alonso de Baena
[461] Pedro de Rulan
[462] Martin Despinosa, el Vizcayno
[463] Gonzalo de Balte
[464] Martin de Segura
[465] Ruy Gonzalez
[466] Rodrigo de Moguer
[467] Bartolome Pardo
[468] Esteban de Carmona
[469] Martin Oredo
[470] Sebastian Rodriguez
[471] Diego Martin
[472] Pedro de Xovirta
[473] Rodrigo Rangel
[474] Antonio de Arevalo
[475] Ramon de Cueva
[476] Pedro de Maluenda
[477] Francisco Solis
[478] Francisco Diaz
[479] Juan de Xerez
[480] Juan Ruiz de Viana
[481] Martin de Ircio
[482] Juan Velez de Cuellar
[483] Pedro Dominguez
[484] Juan de Villar
[485] Benito de Cuenca
[486] Juan de Almodovar
[487] Pedro de Maya
[488] Pedro de Mondragon

[489] Juan Gomez
[490] Gonzalo de Robles
[491] Juan Despunze
[492] Francisco de Vega
[493] Juan Duran
[494] Diego Bermudez
[495] Bartolome de Porras
[496] Juan Alvarez
[497] Rodrigo Davila
[498] Juan de Moguer
[499] Francisco Diaz
[500] Alonso Lucas Vaena
[501] Juan de Salgado
[502] Gonzalo Garcia
[503] Garcia Perez
[504] Juan Garcia Camacho
[505] Juan de [*surname missing*]
[506] Juan Garcia
[507] Francisco de Escobedo
[508] Francisco Ballesteros
[509] Pedro Baez
[510] Juan de Aguidela
[511] Juan Montesino
[512] Gonzalo Reyeto
[513] Andres de Mola
[514] Juan de Tapia
[515] Francisco Miguel de Salamanca
[516] Gaspar Davila
[517] Bartolome Gamite

[518] Juan de Madrigal
[519] Tomas de Roxo
[520] Francisco Galeote
[521] Francisco Morales
[522] Garcia Alonso Galeote
[523] Juan de Solorzano
[524] Diego de Porras
[525] Hernando de Ribera
[526] Fernan Muñoz
[527] Juan de Arcos
[528] Gonzalo de Zamudio
[529] Bartolome Garcia
[530] Fernando Cabrero
[531] Alonso Fernandez
[532] Martin Sanz de Murcia
[533] Fernando de Porras
[534] Alonso Fernandez Pablos
[535] Juan Alvarez Galeote
[536] Alonso Ortiz
[537] Alonso de Moro
[538] Diego Ruiz de Illanes
[539] Cristoval Lobato
[540] Alonso Nortes
[541] Gonzalo de Arcos
[542] [*name missing*] Tervera
[543] Garcia Fernandez
[544] Gonzalo Gordillo
[545] Fernando de Avecilla, escribano
de Su Magestad

Notes

Chapter 1

1. James Lockhart, *The Men of Cajamarca: A Social and Biographical Study of the First Conquerors of Peru* (Austin: University of Texas Press, 1972).

2. See the more fully developed background information in Matthew Restall, *Seven Myths of the Spanish Conquest* (Oxford: Oxford University Press, 2003), 27–43.

3. "Carta del ejército de Cortés al emperador," in Joaquín García Icazbalceta, ed., *Colección de documentos para la historia de México* (Mexico: Librería de J. M. Andrade, 1858–1866), 1:427–436; taken from AGI, Justicia, 222, fols. 12v–23, "Exposición a favor de Cortés." The names are reproduced in the appendix to this book.

4. Matthew Restall, "The New Conquest History," *History Compass* 10 (2012): 151–160.

5. José Ignacio Avellaneda Navas, *Conquerors of the New Kingdom of Granada* (Albuquerque: University of New Mexico Press, 1995).

6. J. Michael Francis, *Invading Colombia: Spanish Accounts of the Gonzalo Jiménez de Quesada Expedition of Conquest* (State College: Penn State Press, 2007).

7. Hugh Thomas, *Who's Who of the Conquistadors* (London: Cassell, 2000); Bernard Grunberg, *Dictionnaire des conquistadores de Mexico* (Paris: L'Harmattan, 2001); Victor M. Alvarez, *Diccionario de conquistadores* (Mexico: INAH, 1975); Robert Himmerich y Valencia, *The Encomenderos of New Spain, 1521–1555* (Austin: University of Texas Press, 1991).

8. Stephanie Wood, *Transcending Conquest: Nahua Views of Spanish Colonial Mexico* (Norman: University of Oklahoma Press, 2003).

9. José Rabasa, *Tell Me the Story of How I Conquered You: Elsewheres and Ethnosuicide in the Colonial Mesoamerican World* (Austin: University of Texas Press, 2011).

10. Florine Asselbergs, *Conquered Conquistadors—The Lienzo de Quauhquechollan: A Nahua Vision of the Conquest of Guatemala* (Boulder: University Press of Colorado, 2004).

11. John F. Schwaller, "Broken Spears or Broken Bones: Evolution of the Most Famous Line in Nahuatl," *The Americas* 66 (2009): 241–252.

12. Laura E. Matthew and Michel R. Oudijk, eds., *Indian Conquistadors: Indigenous Allies and the Conquest of Mesoamerica* (Norman: University of Oklahoma Press, 2007).

13. Camilla Townsend, *Malintzin's Choices: An Indian Woman and the Conquest of Mexico* (Albuquerque: University of New Mexico Press, 2006).

14. Grunberg, *Dictionnaire*; Thomas, *Who's Who*.

1. Pierre Chaunu and Huguette Chaunu, *Séville et l'Atlantique, 1504–1650* (Paris: SEV-PEN, 1955–1960), 2:18–25.

2. The standard survey of this period of exploration is still Samuel Eliot Morison, *The European Discovery of America: The Southern Voyages, 1492–1616* (Oxford: Oxford University Press, 1974).

3. Mario Góngora, *Studies in the Colonial History of Spanish America*, trans. Richard Southern (Cambridge: Cambridge University Press, 1975), 82–88.

4. Carl Ortwin Sauer, *The Early Spanish Main* (Berkeley: University of California Press, 1969), 151–155.

5. Louis André Vigneras, *The Discovery of South America and the Andalusian Voyages* (Chicago: University of Chicago Press, 1976), 23–43.

6. Morison, *Southern Voyages*, 298–299; Sauer, *Early Spanish Main*, 162–177.

7. Morison, *Southern Voyages*, 502–514.

8. Troy Floyd, *The Columbus Dynasty in the Caribbean, 1492–1526* (Albuquerque: University of New Mexico Press, 1973), 194–216; Sauer, *Spanish Main*, 18–37, 204–206.

9. Morison, *Southern Voyages*, 332–350.

10. As will be seen in chapter 3, a considerable number of books have been written about the conquest of Mexico. In general, the best single study written for a general audience is Ross Hassig, *Mexico and the Spanish Conquest* (New York: Longman, 1994). The discussion offered here generally follows the narrative developed by Hassig.

11. Sauer, *Spanish Main*, 174.

12. Sauer, *Spanish Main*, esp. 212–217.

13. Hassig, *Mexico*, 36–41; Bernal Díaz del Castillo, *Historia verdadera de la conquista de la Nueva España* (Mexico: Porrúa, 1977), 1:39–57; Hugh Thomas, *Conquest: Montezuma, Cortés, and the Fall of Old Mexico* (New York: Simon and Schuster, 1993), 85–96.

14. Hassig, *Mexico*, 41–44; Díaz del Castillo, *Historia verdadera*, 1:59–77; Thomas, *Conquest*, 98–115.

15. *Documentos cortesianos*, ed. José Luis Martínez (Mexico: Fondo de Cultura Económica, 1990–1992), 1:47–57.

16. Díaz del Castillo, *Historia verdadera*, 1:81–94; Thomas, *Conquest*, 136–142.

17. The muster taken shortly before the expedition departed Cuba registered 508 men — of whom 109 were seamen, 32 crossbowmen, and 13 musketeers — along with 16 horses, sailing on 11 ships; Bernard Grunberg, "The Origins of the Conquistadores of Mexico City," *Hispanic American Historical Review* 74 (May 1994): 263; Díaz del Castillo, *Historia verdadera*, 1:91–97.

18. Hassig, *Mexico*, 48; Díaz del Castillo, *Historia verdadera*, 1:102–104; Thomas, *Conquest*, 163–164.

19. Hassig, *Mexico*, 51; Díaz del Castillo, *Historia verdadera*, 1:119–121; Thomas, *Conquest*, 172–173. See also the study of doña María and her impact on colonial Mexico: Camilla Townsend, *Malintzin's Choices: An Indian Woman and the Conquest of Mexico* (Albuquerque: University of New Mexico Press, 2006).

20. Hassig, *Mexico*, 53–56; Díaz del Castillo, *Historia verdadera*, 1:151–153; Thomas, *Conquest*, 175–178.

21. Hassig, *Mexico*, 51; Díaz del Castillo, *Historia verdadera*, 1:156–157; Thomas, *Conquest*, 172–173.

22. Díaz del Castillo, *Historia verdadera*, 1:131–133; Thomas, *Conquest*, 196–197.

23. Hassig, *Mexico*, 55–57; Díaz del Castillo, *Historia verdadera*, 1:140–141; Thomas, *Conquest*, 196–197.

24. Hassig, *Mexico*, 57–59; Díaz del Castillo, *Historia verdadera*, 1:144–146; Thomas, *Conquest*, 206–209.

25. Hassig, *Mexico*, 58; Díaz del Castillo, *Historia verdadera*, 1:146–148; Thomas, *Conquest*, 209–210.

26. Cortés, *Cartas*, 28–32; John T. Lanning, "Cortes and His First Official Remission of Treasure to Charles V," *Revista de Historia de América* 2 (June 1938): 5–29.

27. Martínez, *Documentos cortesianos*, 1:77–85. Robert S. Chamberlain, "Two Unpublished Documents of Hernán Cortés and New Spain, 1519 and 1524," *Hispanic American Historical Review* 18 (Nov. 1938): 514–525.

28. Thomas, *Conquest*, 223. There is ample debate as to whether the hulks were actually burned. Thomas, who did extensive research into the question, believes that this detail is a dramatic flourish added to the tale of the conquest in the middle of the sixteenth century.

29. Hassig, *Mexico*, 62; Díaz del Castillo, *Historia verdadera*, 1:175–177; Thomas, *Conquest*, 222–224.

30. Hassig, *Mexico*, 64–74; Díaz del Castillo, *Historia verdadera*, 1:194–199; Thomas, *Conquest*, 243–250.

31. Hassig, *Mexico*, 78–80; Díaz del Castillo, *Historia verdadera*, 1:236–251; Thomas, *Conquest*, 256–264.

32. Hassig, *Mexico*, 81–83.

33. This ruler is commonly known in English as Montezuma. The spelling used here is phonetically closer to the correct pronunciation in Nahuatl. His name means something like "He who scowls in lordly anger."

34. Díaz del Castillo, *Historia verdadera*, 1:262–265; Thomas, *Conquest*, 276–285.

35. Hassig, *Mexico*, 86–88; Díaz del Castillo, *Historia verdadera*, 1:298–300; Thomas, *Conquest*, 314.

36. Richard F. Townsend, *The Aztecs*, 3rd ed. (New York: Thames and Hudson, 2009), 78.

37. *Huey tlahtoani* in Nahuatl means "great speaker," and signified the supreme ruler of the collection of city-states which made up the Triple Alliance.

38. Thomas, *Conquest*, 304–308; Hassig, *Mexico*, 87–88.

39. Hassig, *Mexico*, 89–90.

40. Hassig, *Mexico*, 90–91; Díaz del Castillo, *Historia verdadera*, 1:333–346; Thomas, *Conquest*, 358–363.

41. Díaz del Castillo, *Historia verdadera*, 1:351–363; Thomas, *Conquest*, 369–376.

42. Hassig, *Mexico*, 90–91; Díaz del Castillo, *Historia verdadera*, 1:365–375; Thomas, *Conquest*, 376–382.

43. Hassig, *Mexico*, 91–93; Díaz del Castillo, *Historia verdadera*, 1:381–393; Thomas, *Conquest*, 383–404.

44. Hassig, *Mexico*, 94–97; Díaz del Castillo, *Historia verdadera*, 1:391–404; Thomas, *Conquest*, 407–426.

45. Hassig, *Mexico*, 104–105; Díaz del Castillo, *Historia verdadera*, 1:411–415; Thomas, *Conquest*, 434–441, 447–448.

46. *Documentos cortesianos*, 1:156–163.

47. Thomas, *Conquest*, 447–448; Díaz del Castillo, *Historia verdadera*, 2:104–118.

48. Hassig, *Mexico*, 103–107; Thomas, *Conquest*, 436–450.

49. Hassig, *Mexico*, 108–120; Díaz del Castillo, *Historia verdadera*, 1:444–494; Thomas, *Conquest*, 435–481.

50. Hassig, *Mexico*, 120–141; Díaz del Castillo, *Historia verdadera*, 2:9–53; Thomas, *Conquest*, 485–530.

51. Hassig, *Mexico*, 144–158; Peggy Liss, *Mexico under Spain, 1521–1556: Society and Origins of Nationality* (Chicago: University of Chicago Press, 1975), 48–56.

52. G. Micheal Riley, *Fernando Cortés and the Marquesado in Morelos, 1522–1547* (Albuquerque: University of New Mexico Press, 1973), 28–34.

Chapter 3

1. Henry R. Wagner, *The Rise of Fernando Cortés* (Berkeley: The Cortés Society, 1944), 81. Interestingly, a contemporary observer of the conquest, Bernal Díaz del Castillo, compares the destruction of the ships before the march inland as a "crossing the Rubicon" moment. Bernal Díaz del Castillo, *Historia verdadera de la conquista de la Nueva España*, 7th ed. (Mexico: Porrúa, 1977), 1:175–177.

2. Helen Nader, *Liberty in Absolutist Spain: The Hapsburg Sale of Towns, 1516–1700* (Baltimore: Johns Hopkins University Press, 1990), 72–73.

3. Several scholars have attempted to reconcile the differences between the early histories of the conquest; see Wagner, *The Rise of Fernando Cortés*, and Paul E. Greene, "The Conquest of Mexico: The Views of the Chroniclers," *The Americas* 31 (Oct. 1974): 167–171.

4. Hernán Cortés, *Cartas y documentos* (Mexico: Porrúa, 1963), 3–28.

5. Cortés, *Cartas y documentos*, 28–32; John T. Lanning, "Cortes and His First Official Remission of Treasure to Charles V," *Revista de Historia de América* 2 (June 1938): 5–29.

6. José Luis Martínez, ed., *Documentos cortesianos* (Mexico: Fondo de Cultura Económica, 1990–1992), 1:77–85. Robert S. Chamberlain, "Two Unpublished Documents of Hernán Cortés and New Spain, 1519 and 1524," *Hispanic American Historical Review* 18 (Nov. 1938): 514–525.

7. Marshall H. Saville, "The Earliest Notices Concerning the Conquest of Mexico in 1519," *Indian Notes and Monographs* 10.1 (1920): 5–12, 25–30.

8. All dates here follow the Julian calendar, as the petition was written about sixty years before the Gregorian reform (1582).

9. Francisco López de Gómara, *La conquista de México* (Mexico: Imprenta de I. de Escalante y Cia., 1870).

10. Díaz del Castillo, *Historia verdadera*, 1:39. In the opening pages of his account he does not mention López de Gómara by name, but merely refers to "personas que no lo alcanzaron a saber, ni lo vieron, ni tener noticia verdadera de lo que sobre esta materia propusieron."

11. Several of these are collected in Patricia de Fuentes, *The Conquistadores: First-Person Accounts of the Conquest of Mexico* (New York: Orion, 1963).

12. Known at the time as the Royal and Pontifical University of Mexico.

13. Francisco Cervantes de Salazar, *Crónica de la Nueva España*, ed. A. Millares Carlo (Madrid: Atlas, 1971).

14. Bartolomé de las Casas, *Historia de las Indias*, ed. Juan Pérez de Tudela (Madrid: Atlas, 1961).

15. A creole is a child of European parents who was born in the New World.

16. Juan Suárez de Peralta, *Tratado del descubrimiento de las Indias y su conquista*, ed. Giorgio Perissinotto (Madrid: Alianza, 1990).

17. Antonio de Herrera y Tordesillas, *Historia general de los hechos de los castellanos en las islas y Tierra Firme del mar Océano* (Madrid: Juan Flamenco and Juan de la Cuesta, 1601–1615).

18. Rolena Adorno, "The Discursive Encounter of Spain and America: The Authority of Eyewitness Testimony in the Writing of History," *William and Mary Quarterly* 49 (April 1992): 210–228.

19. This, the so-called First Letter, will be referred to as the "town narrative," to distinguish it from other documents examined here.

20. There could well have been other issues, but Cortés may have chosen to reduce the conflict to these essential arguments to better focus the attention of the company. Beatriz Pastor Bodmer, *The Armature of Conquest: Spanish Accounts of the Discovery of America, 1492–1589*, trans. Lydia Longstreth Hunt (Stanford: Stanford University Press, 1992), 76.

21. In the political philosophy of the era, "justice" (*justicia*) was envisioned as the central function of government and the key power vested in the Crown.

22. Cortés, *Cartas y documentos*, 27: "[S]uplicamos a vuestras majestades que no proveyesen de los dichos cargos ni de alguno de ellos al dicho Diego Velázquez, antes le mandasen tomar residencia y le quitasen el cargo que en la isla Fernandina tiene, pues que lo susodicho, tomándole residencia se sabría que es verdad y muy notorio. Por lo cual vuestra majestad suplicamos manden dar un pesquisidor para que haga la pesquisa de todo esto de que hemos hecho relación a vuestras reales altezas, así para la isla de Cuba como para otras partes, porque le entendemos probar cosas por donde vuestras majestades vean si es justicia ni conciencia que él tenga cargos reales en estas partes ni en las otras donde al presente reside."

23. "[Y] siendo a todos los vecinos y moradores de esta Villa de la Vera Cruz notorio lo susodicho, se juntaron con el procurador de este Consejo y nos pidieron y requirieron por su requerimiento firmado de sus nombres . . ."

24. "Hanos asimismo pedido el procurador y vecinos y moradores de esta villa, en el dicho pedimento, que en su nombre supliquemos a vuestra majestad que provean y manden dar su cédula y provisión real para Fernando Cortés, capitán y justicia major de vuestras reales altezas, para que él nos tenga en justicia y gobernación, hasta tanto que esta tierra

esté conquistada y pacífica, y por el tiempo que más a vuestra majestad pareciere y fuere servido . . ."

25. Martínez, *Documentos cortesianos*, 1:77–84. Chamberlain, "Two Unpublished Documents," 516–523.

26. Cristián A. Roa de la Carrera, *Histories of Infamy: Francisco López de Gómara and the Ethics of Spanish Imperialism* (Boulder: University Press of Colorado, 2005), 1–2.

27. López de Gómara, *La conquista de México*, 95–98.

28. López de Gómara, *La conquista de México*, 98–100.

29. López de Gómara, *La conquista de México*, 134–136.

30. Díaz del Castillo, *Historia verdadera*, 1:131–133.

31. Díaz del Castillo, *Historia verdadera*, 1:134–135.

32. Díaz del Castillo, *Historia verdadera*, 1:135–136.

33. Díaz del Castillo, *Historia verdadera*, 1:136.

34. Díaz del Castillo, *Historia verdadera*, 1:137–138.

35. Díaz del Castillo, *Historia verdadera*, 1:138.

36. Díaz del Castillo, *Historia verdadera*, 1:138–139.

37. Díaz del Castillo, *Historia verdadera*, 1:140–141.

38. Díaz del Castillo, *Historia verdadera*, 1:141–143.

39. Díaz del Castillo, *Historia verdadera*, 1:146, 151–153.

40. Díaz del Castillo, *Historia verdadera*, 1:157–164.

41. Díaz del Castillo, *Historia verdadera*, 1:164–165.

42. Interestingly, Ordaz had been imprisoned along with other supporters of Velázquez, only then to be placed in a position of responsibility by Cortés.

43. Díaz del Castillo, *Historia verdadera*, 1:165–171: "y la firmamos todos los capitanes y soldados que éramos de la parte de Cortés" (168).

44. Díaz del Castillo, *Historia verdadera*, 1:169–174. Some believe that Montejo and Ordaz intentionally stopped, in order to inform Velázquez of the events in Veracruz.

45. Díaz del Castillo, *Historia verdadera*, 1:175–177.

46. Díaz del Castillo, *Historia verdadera*, 1:154. See discussion under signature 222.

47. Christian Duverger, *Crónica de la eternidad: ¿Quién escribió la Historia verdadera de la conquista de la Nueva España?* (Mexico: Taurus, 2012), 55–70.

48. See chapter 6: "Those Who Are Missing."

49. See chapter 7, signature 181: Bernal Díaz.

50. Joaquin García Icazbalceta, *Colección de documentos para la historia de México* (Mexico: Libreria de J. M. Andrade, 1866), 2:554–594; an English translation has been published in Fuentes, *The Conquistadores*, 19–48.

51. "[B]y mutual agreement we wrote a letter to His Majesty the Emperor. It was signed by almost all the marqués's company, and began by giving an account of events to date. . . . [W]e hereby petitioned and would continue to petition until receiving assurances that His Majesty was informed of our account and of how we labored and would yet labor in his service, that nothing be done contrary to what we were writing him, and that His Majesty not grant favors [to Diego Velázquez] without knowing what he was granting" (Fuentes, *The Conquistadores*, 28).

52. "Arriving at the harbor where the ships had been sent, the marqués established the Spanish town he had founded [first] at the port of San Juan" (Fuentes, *Conquistadores*, 25).

53. Another brief account can be found in Suárez de Peralta, *Tratado del descubrimiento de las Indias*, 96–99.

54. Las Casas, *Historia de las Indias*, 4:494–499.

55. Francisco Cervantes de Salazar, *México en 1554: Tres diálogos latinos*, trans. Joaquín García Icazbalceta (Mexico: Universidad Nacional Autónoma de México, 1939).

56. Francisco Cervantes de Salazar, *Crónica de la Nueva España*, ed. Manuel Magallón (Madrid: Atlas, 1971), 1:209–223.

57. Cervantes de Salazar, *Crónica de la Nueva España*, 1:230–236.

58. Herrera y Tordesillas, *Historia general*, 2.5.4–14 and 2.6.1–2; Antonio de Solís y Ribadeneyra, *Historia de la conquista de México* (Barcelona: Thomas Piferrer, 1771), vol. 1, 1.20 and 21; 2.1–14.

59. William H. Prescott, *History of the Conquest of Mexico* (New York: Harper and Brothers, 1843).

60. Hubert H. Bancroft, *History of Mexico*, 1: *1516–1521* (San Francisco: A. L. Bancroft & Co., 1883).

61. Bancroft, *History of Mexico*, 1:169–170.

62. Salvador de Madariaga, *Hernán Cortés* (Buenos Aires: Sudamericana, 1941), 179–183.

63. Madariaga, *Cortés*, 197–201.

64. Wagner, *The Rise of Fernando Cortés*, 117.

65. Wagner, *The Rise of Fernando Cortés*, 113–115. Saville, "The Earliest Notices Concerning the Conquest of Mexico in 1519," 5–12, 25–30.

66. Chamberlain, "Two Unpublished Documents," 514–523.

67. Manuel Giménez Férnandez, *Cortés y su revolución comunera en la Nueva España* (Seville: Consejo Superior de Investigaciones Científicas, Escuela de Estudios Hispanoamericanos, 1948), 97–101. This was issued originally as a supplement to volume 5 of the *Anuario de Estudios Americanos*. Giménez later revised his thinking regarding the actions of Cortés, publishing his definitive view as Manuel Giménez Fernández, "El alzamiento de Fernando Cortés," *Revista de Historia de América* 31 (June 1951): 1–58.

68. Giménez Fernández, "El alzamiento," 3–8.

69. Giménez Fernández, "El alzamiento," 5–6.

70. José Luis Martínez, *Hernán Cortés* (Mexico: Universidad Nacional Autónoma de México and Fondo de Cultura Económica, 1990), 191–193.

71. Martínez, *Hernán Cortés*, 157, 173–178.

72. Víctor Frankl, "Hernán Cortés y la tradición de las Siete Partidas," *Revista de Historia de América* 53/54 (1962): 9–74.

73. Pastor Bodmer, *The Armature*, 63–66.

74. Hugh Thomas, *Conquest: Montezuma, Cortés, and the Fall of Old Mexico* (New York: Simon and Schuster, 1993), 204.

75. Thomas, *Conquest*, 199–200. Christian Duverger, *Cortés* (Paris: Fayard, 2001), esp. 151–167, also rejected Giménez, and believed that Cortés took advantage of the absence

of Montejo and many Velázquez supporters. He does not detail the movements of the expedition, and it is not clear where he believed each act of the process occurred.

76. Nader, *Liberty in Absolutist Spain*, 94–98.

Chapter 4

1. Each of us has traveled to Seville several times to examine the original papers. At one point the document was removed for conservation purposes, but was subsequently returned to the bundle.

2. "[E]n presencia de mi Pedro Hernandez escrivano de la rreyna doña Juana e del rrey don Carlos su hijo nuestros señores e su notario publico en la su corte e en todos los sus rreynos e señorios e escribano publico de la dicha villa . . ." (folio 1, recto, lines 11–14).

3. Filemón Arribas Arranz, *Los escribanos públicos en Castilla durante el siglo XV* (Madrid: Junta de Decanos de los Colegios Notariales de España, 1964); John H. Parry, *The Sale of Public Office in the Spanish Indies under the Hapsburgs* (Berkeley: University of California Press, 1953), 6–11.

4. "Suplicareys de nra parte a sus Reales altezas que en ninguna manera provean ni hagan md a Diego Velazquez del adelantamiento ni de governacion ni de otro oficio ninguno en estas partes" (José Luis Martínez, *Documentos cortesianos* [Mexico: Fondo de Cultura Económica, 1990], 1:78–79). English translation by Schwaller.

5. "[S]uplican que a Diego Velazquez no haga merced de le encargar ni probeer cosa ninguna en estas partes ni le hacer merced della . . ." (folio 2, verso, lines 2–4).

6. "[E] los cargos e oficios Reales que en estas yslas a tenido y en estas partes aver dado muy Buena quenta y servido a sus Reales altezas en ellos e ser muy bien quisto e demas aver gastado qto tenia en la dha armada e q de server a la dha corona real" (Martínez, *Documentos cortesianos*, 1:77–78). English translation by Schwaller.

7. "[Q]ue el señor Hernando Cortes a venido a estas partes en servicio de sus altesas para las conquistar e gastado muchas sumas de maravedis e dexado la conpania que el dicho Diego Velazquez con el avia hecho de que se pudiera bien aprovechar e como vasallo e leal servidor de sus altezas procuro que para que su rreal corona fuese aumentada se poblase esta tierra e con su yndustria y trabajo todo o la mayor parte ya conquistada e debaxo de la servidumbre de sus altesas que asi por esto como que por otras muchas cosas contenidas en el capitulo señaladamente para esto en la ynstrucion contenido que su magestad sea servido de le encargar el dicho cargo de conquistador e capitan general e Justicia mayor de estas partes . . ." (folio 3, recto, lines 4–16).

8. "Nos hagan merced que los yndios destas partes sean perpetuos e para ello manden dar provisyones Reales par el dho Fernando certes Para que nos los reparta y encomiende perpetuamente por los primeros conquistadores e pobladores" (Martínez, *Documentos cortesianos*, 1:79–80). English translation by Schwaller.

9. "[Q]ue pueda rrepartir los yndios della perpetuamente" (folio 3, recto, lines 17–18).

10. Díaz del Castillo, *Historia verdadera*, 1:167.

———

Chapter 5

1. My thanks to my son, Robert C. Schwaller, for his assistance with this paragraph. Only late in the editing process did I realize that we had failed to transcribe and translate this important component of the petition.

Chapter 6

1. Portions of the biographical sketches of individual conquerors will be presented in this chapter. The full citations and scholarly apparatus for these biographies can be found in each entry in chapter 7.

2. Tomás Thayer Ojeda and Carlos J. Larraín, *Valdivia y sus compañeros* (Santiago de Chile: Imprenta universitaria, 1950).

3. Mario Góngora, *Los grupos de conquistadores en Tierra Firme (1509–1530)* (Santiago de Chile: Universidad de Chile, 1962).

4. James Lockhart, *Men of Cajamarca: A Social and Biographical Study of the First Conquerors of Peru* (Austin: University of Texas Press, 1972).

5. José Ignacio Avellaneda Navas, *Conquerors of the New Kingdom of Granada* (Albuquerque: University of New Mexico Press, 1995). J. Michael Francis, *Invading Colombia: Spanish Accounts of the Gonzalo Jiménez de Quesada Expedition of Conquest* (State College: Penn State Press, 2007).

6. In the published edition there are 420 signatures. In the analysis done by Nader, which we include as an appendix, there are 545.

7. By and large Bernard Grunberg, *Dictionnaire des conquistadores de Mexico* (Paris: L'Harmattan, 2001), provides the most extensive record of birth and death dates from which these values are calculated. All of these data are rough estimates. In the sixteenth century, people tended to be flexible about their age, usually rounding up or down to the nearest year divisible by five. Consequently a large number of the men reportedly were born in either 1495 or 1500 (twenty-one and twenty-four, respectively).

8. Lockhart, *Cajamarca*, 26.

9. Avellaneda Navas, *Conquerors*, 62.

10. Francis, *Invading Colombia*, 7.

11. Thayer Ojeda and Larraín, *Valdivia*, 68.

12. Lockhart, *Cajamarca*, 60; Francis, *Invading Colombia*, 8.

13. J. H. Elliott, *Imperial Spain, 1469–1716* (New York: Mentor Books, 1963), 17–43.

14. Bernard Grunberg, "Origins of the Conquistadores of Mexico City," *Hispanic American Historical Review* 74 (May 1994): 268.

15. Lockhart, *Cajamarca*, 28–29.

16. Avellaneda Navas, *Conquerors*, 60. Obviously Old and New Castile taken together provided nearly as many men as did Andalucía.

17. Góngora, *Grupos sociales*, 77.

18. Thayer Ojeda and Larraín, *Valdivia*, 73–74. Old and New Castile together provided twenty-one men, more than Extremadura but less than Andalucía.

19. Grunberg, *Dictionnaire*, item 573.

20. Díaz del Castillo, *Historia verdadera*, 2:347: Juan García, Hernán Martín, and one unknown.

21. Díaz del Castillo, *Historia verdadera*, 1:96.

22. Lockhart, *Cajamarca*, 38.

23. Góngora, *Grupos sociales*, 81.

24. Díaz del Castillo, *Historia verdadera*, 1:92–93.

25. Lockhart, *Cajamarca*, 96–102.

26. Grunberg, "Origins," 277.

27. Lockhart, *Cajamarca*, 32.

28. Góngora, *Grupos sociales*, 79.

29. C. Harvey Gardiner, *The Constant Captain: Gonzalo de Sandoval* (Carbondale: Southern Illinois University Press, 1961), 194–196.

30. This is an odd pairing of villages, since they are so far distant from one another. The villages of Atlalaucan and Tetela are side-by-side in the southeastern corner of the Valley of Mexico, but seem to have been assigned to others or retained by Cortés for his own estates. Peter Gerhard, *A Guide to the Historical Geography of New Spain*, rev. ed. (Norman: University of Oklahoma Press, 1993), 103 and 294.

31. The original royal decree granting the coat of arms to Ochoa is held in the Gilcrease Museum in Tulsa, OK.

32. AGI, Indiferente General, 1220, Información de parte y de oficio de Pero Rodríguez, 1568. My thanks to Robert C. Schwaller for bringing this other conqueror to my attention. Thomas, *Who's Who*, 401.

33. Thomas, *Who's Who*, 30; Grunberg, *Dictionnaire*, item 240.

34. Guillermo Porras Muñoz, *El gobierno de la ciudad de México en el siglo XVI* (Mexico: Universidad Nacional Autónoma de México, 1982), 92, 144, et passim; Thomas, *Who's Who*, 140–141; Grunberg, *Dictionnaire*, item 1148.

35. Quoted in Thomas, *Who's Who*, 102.

36. Díaz del Castillo, *Historia verdadera*, 2:353.

37. Thomas, *Who's Who*, 102–105; Porras Muñoz, *El gobierno*, 377; Grunberg, *Dictionnaire*, item 731. John Hemming, *The Search for El Dorado* (New York: Dutton, 1978), 9–16.

38. Patricia de Fuentes, *The Conquistadors: First-Person Accounts of the Conquest of Mexico* (New York: Orion, 1963), 17–48.

39. Fuentes, *The Conquistadors*, 28.

40. Thomas, *Who's Who*, 124–130; Grunberg, *Dictionnaire*, item 1031.

41. Thomas, *Who's Who*, 55; Grunberg, *Dictionnaire*, item 293.

42. Thomas, *Who's Who*, 95; Grunberg, *Dictionnaire*, item 684.

43. Thomas, *Who's Who*, 1–3; Grunberg, *Dictionnaire*, item 10.

44. Thomas, *Who's Who*, 71–72; Grunberg, *Dictionnaire*, item 499; Porras Muñoz, *El gobierno*, 324–330.

45. Thomas, *Who's Who*, 60–61; Grunberg, *Dictionnaire*, item 368. Ricardo E. Alegría, *Juan Garrido: El conquistador negro en las Antillas, Florida, México y California*, 2nd ed. (San Juan: Centro de Estudios Avanzados de Puerto Rico y el Caribe, 2004).

46. Thomas, *Who's Who*, 134; Grunberg, *Dictionnaire*, item 343.

47. Lockhart, *Cajamarca*, 59–60.

48. Francis, *Invading Colombia*, 7–8.

Chapter 7

1. Montejo has warranted his own biography: J. Ignacio Rubio Mañé, *Monografía de los Montejos* (Mérida: Liga de acción social, 1930).

2. Donald E. Chipman, *Moctezuma's Children: Aztec Royalty under Spanish Rule, 1520–1700* (Austin: University of Texas Press, 2005), 49–50.

3. Francisco López de Gómara, *Historia de la conquista de México* (Mexico: I. Escalante, 1870), 1:152.

4. Notice that many of the men whose signatures appear in this part of the folio are described by Díaz del Castillo in a single section (DdelC, 2:338). This could imply that they formed part of a company within the expedition and that Díaz del Castillo remembered people according to the company in which they served.

5. It is also curious that these three conquerors — Gallego, Castañeda, and Granada — who appear on the Veracruz petition in close proximity, all received coats of arms from the Crown.

6. Peter Gerhard, *The North Frontier of New Spain* (Norman: University of Oklahoma Press, 1982), 140–141.

7. He is the first person to use the term "New Mexico" in referring to the northern territories of New Spain. John L. Kessell, *Spain in the Southwest: A Narrative History of Colonial New Mexico, Arizona, Texas, and California* (Norman: University of Oklahoma Press, 2002), 65–66.

8. It is interesting that the signatures of (possibly) three men who owned horses appear near one another in the Veracruz petition: Donal, Ortiz, and Vázquez de Tapia (on whom see signature 125).

9. Guillermo Porras Muñoz, *El gobierno de la ciudad de México en el siglo XVI* (Mexico: Universidad Nacional Autónoma de México, 1982), 288–291.

10. Jorge Gurría Lacroix, *Relación de méritos y servicios del conquistador Bernardino Vázquez de Tapia* (Mexico: Universidad Nacional Autónoma de México, 1972).

11. Signatures 125–134 seem to have been executed by the same person.

12. López is the subject of at least two biographies: C. Harvey Gardiner, *Martín López: Conquistador, Citizen of Mexico* (Lexington: University of Kentucky Press, 1958), and Guillermo Porras Muñoz, "Martín López, carpintero de ribera," *Revista de Indias* 31–32 (1948): 307–239. Gardiner also wrote *Naval Power in the Conquest of Mexico* (Austin: University of Texas Press, 1956), which focused on López and the final assault.

13. AGI, Indiferente General, 1220, Información de parte y de oficio de Pero Rodríguez, 1568. My thanks again to Robert C. Schwaller for pointing out this individual.

14. Probably don Alonso de Cárdenas, the last master of the military-religious Order of Santiago before the Crown took over direct administration of the organization.

15. Porras Muñoz, *El gobierno*, 438–441.

16. At least two men who signed the Veracruz petition in this spot are described as more mature members of the company: Paredes and Hernández. Just below them, signature 179, is Lorenzo Suárez, also described as older.

17. G. R. G. Conway, "Hernando Alonso: A Jewish Conquistador with Cortés in Mexico," *Publications of the American Jewish Historical Society* 31 (1928). This article holds that Alonso was a member of the Narváez expedition. It is possible that Conway did not understand the nuance of the testimony and that he only assumed Alonso was in the Narváez company. The facsimile signature supplied in the article does not resemble the signature on the Veracruz petition.

18. Note again that two other men cited just above this individual's name were also described as mature: signatures 170 and 172.

19. The next four signatures and that of Luis de Frias (signature 210) seem to all be in the same hand.

20. Díaz del Castillo mentions another conqueror from Las Garrovillas, a fellow named Hurones (DdelC, 2:349).

21. Several men in this section participated in the Montejo expedition up the coast, including Juan de Limpias (signature 236), Antón de Alaminos (signature 244), and Alvarez Chico.

22. Porras Muñoz, *El gobierno*, 145 and 152.

23. Sandoval warranted his own biography: C. Harvey Gardiner, *The Constant Captain: Gonzalo de Sandoval* (Carbondale: Southern Illinois University Press, 1961).

24. John F. Schwaller, "Tres familias mexicanas del siglo XVI," *Historia Mexicana* 31:122 (Oct.–Dec. 1981): 171–196.

Chapter 8

1. Matthew Restall, *Seven Myths of the Spanish Conquest* (Oxford: Oxford University Press, 2003), 18–26. Whether consciously or not, Pizarro drew upon the experience of Cortés, and patterns developed in both the Reconquest of Spain and earlier conquests in the Indies.

2. James Lockhart, *Men of Cajamarca: A Social and Biographical Study of the First Conquerors of Peru* (Austin: University of Texas Press, 1972), 32.

3. José Ignacio Avellaneda Navas, *Conquerors of the New Kingdom of Granada* (Albuquerque: University of New Mexico Press, 1995), 89–90.

4. Lockhart, *Cajamarca*, 38.

5. Lockhart, *Cajamarca*, 82–89.

6. Bernard Grunberg, "The Origins of the Conquistadores of Mexico City," *Hispanic American Historical Review* 74 (May 1994): 259–283.

7. Grunberg, "Origins," 267–280.

8. Bernard Grunberg, *Dictionnaire des conquistadores de Mexico* (Paris: L'Harmattan, 2001), item 1111.

9. Lockhart, *Cajamarca*, 17–22; Restall, *Seven Myths*, 27–43.

10. Grunberg, "Origins," 277–278.

11. See signature 161: Sebastián Rodrigo.

12. Robert Himmerich y Valencia, *The Encomenderos of New Spain, 1521–1555* (Austin: University of Texas Press, 1991), 6.

Bibliography

Adorno, Rolena. "The Discursive Encounter of Spain and America: The Authority of Eye-witness Testimony in the Writing of History." *William and Mary Quarterly* 49 (April 1992): 210–228.

Alegría, Ricardo E. *Juan Garrido: El conquistador negro en las Antillas, Florida, México y California.* 2nd ed. San Juan: Centro de Estudios Avanzados de Puerto Rico y el Caribe, 2004.

Alvarez, Victor M. *Diccionario de conquistadores.* 2 vols. Mexico: INAH, 1975.

Arribas Arranz, Filemón. *Los escribanos públicos en Castilla durante el siglo XV.* Madrid: Junta de Decanos de los Colegios Notariales de España, 1964.

Asselbergs, Florine. *Conquered Conquistadors—The Lienzo de Quauhquechollan: A Nahua Vision of the Conquest of Guatemala.* Boulder: University Press of Colorado, 2004.

Avellaneda Navas, José Ignacio. *Conquerors of the New Kingdom of Granada.* Albuquerque: University of New Mexico Press, 1995.

Bosch García, Carlos. *Sueño y ensueño de los conquistadores.* Mexico: Universidad Nacional Autónoma de México, 1987.

Boyd-Bowman, Peter. *Indice geobiográfico de cuarenta mil pobladores españoles de América en el siglo XVI,* 1: *1493–1519.* Bogota: Instituto Caro y Cuervo, 1964.

Breinen, Rebecca P., and Margaret A. Jackson, eds. *Invasion and Transformation: Interdisciplinary Perspectives on the Conquest of Mexico.* Boulder: University of Colorado Press, 2008.

Brooks, Francis J. "Motecuzoma Xocoyotl, Hernán Cortés, and Bernal Díaz del Castillo: The Construction of an Arrest." *Hispanic American Historical Review* 75 (May 1995): 149–183.

Cervantes de Salazar, Francisco. *Crónica de la Nueva España.* Ed. A. Millares Carlo. 2 vols. Madrid: Atlas, 1971.

———. *México en 1554: Tres diálogos latinos.* Trans. Joaquín García Icazbalceta. Mexico: Universidad Nacional Autónoma de México, 1939.

Chamberlain, Robert S. "Two Unpublished Documents of Hernán Cortés and New Spain, 1519 and 1524." *Hispanic American Historical Review* 18 (Nov. 1938): 514–525.

Chaunu, Pierre, and Huguette Chaunu. *Séville et l'Atlantique, 1504–1650.* 8 vols. Paris: SEVPEN, 1955–1960.

Chipman, Donald E. *Moctezuma's Children: Aztec Royalty under Spanish Rule, 1520–1700*. Austin: University of Texas Press, 2005.

Clendinnen, Inga. "'Fierce and Unnatural Cruelty': Cortés and the Conquest of Mexico." *Representations* 33 (Winter 1991): 65–100.

Conway, G. R. G. "Hernando Alonso: A Jewish Conquistador with Cortés in Mexico." *Publications of the American Jewish Historical Society* 31 (1928).

Cortés, Hernán. *Cartas y documentos*. Mexico: Porrúa, 1963.

Díaz del Castillo, Bernal. *Historia verdadera de la conquista de la Nueva España*. 2 vols. 7th ed. Mexico: Porrúa, 1977.

Dorantes de Carranza, Baltasar. *Sumaria relación de las cosas de la Nueva España*. Mexico: Porrúa, 1987. Includes "Conquistadores de México," by Manuel Orozco y Berra, 279–419.

Duverger, Christian. *Cortés*. Paris: Fayard, 2001.

———. *Crónica de la eternidad: ¿Quién escribió la Historia verdadera de la conquista de la Nueva España?* Mexico: Taurus, 2012.

Elliott, J. H. *Imperial Spain, 1469–1716*. New York: Mentor Books, 1963.

Ezquerra, Ramón. "Los compañeros de Cortés." *Estudios Cortesianos: Recopilados con el motivo del IV Centenario de la muerte de Hernán Cortés (1547–1947)*, 37–95. Madrid: Instituto Gonzalo Fernández de Oviedo, Consejo Superior de Investigaciones Científicas, 1948.

Floyd, Troy. *The Columbus Dynasty in the Caribbean, 1492–1526*. Albuquerque: University of New Mexico Press, 1973.

Francis, J. Michael. *Invading Colombia: Spanish Accounts of the Gonzalo Jiménez de Quesada Expedition of Conquest*. State College: Penn State Press, 2007.

Frankl, Víctor. "Hernán Cortés y la tradición de las Siete Partidas." *Revista de Historia de América* 53/54 (1962): 9–74.

Fuentes, Patricia de. *The Conquistadores: First-Person Accounts of the Conquest of Mexico*. New York: Orion, 1963.

García, Casiano. *Vida del comendador Diego de Ordaz, descubridor del Orinoco*. Mexico: Jus, 1952.

García Icazbalceta, Joaquín. *Colección de documentos para la historia de México*. 3 vols. Mexico: Librería de J. M. Andrade, 1858–1866.

Gardiner, C. Harvey. *The Constant Captain: Gonzalo de Sandoval*. Carbondale: Southern Illinois University Press, 1961.

———. *Martín López: Conquistador, Citizen of Mexico*. Lexington: University of Kentucky Press, 1958.

———. *Naval Power in the Conquest of Mexico*. Austin: University of Texas Press, 1956.

Gerhard, Peter. *A Guide to the Historical Geography of New Spain*. Rev. ed. Norman: University of Oklahoma Press, 1993.

———. *The North Frontier of New Spain*. Norman: University of Oklahoma Press, 1982.

Gímenez Férnandez, Manuel. "El alzamiento de Fernando Cortés." *Revista de Historia de América* 31 (June 1951): 1–58.

———. *Cortés y su revolución comunera en la Nueva España*. Seville: Consejo Superior de Investigaciones Científicas, Escuela de Estudios Hispanoamericanos, 1948.

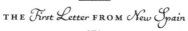

Góngora, Mario. *Los grupos de conquistadores en Tierra Firme (1509–1530)*. Santiago de Chile: Universidad de Chile, 1962.

———. *Studies in the Colonial History of Spanish America*. Trans. Richard Southern. Cambridge: Cambridge University Press, 1975.

González Leal, Mariano. *Relación secreta de conquistadores*. Guanajuato: Universidad de Guanajuato, 1979.

Greene, Paul E. "The Conquest of Mexico: The Views of the Chroniclers." *The Americas* 31 (Oct. 1974): 167–171.

Grunberg, Bernard. *Dictionnaire des conquistadores de Mexico*. Paris: L'Harmattan, 2001.

———. *Histoire de la conquête du Mexique*. Paris: L'Harmattan, 1995.

———. "The Origins of the Conquistadores of Mexico City." *Hispanic American Historical Review* 74 (May 1994): 259–283.

Gurría Lacroix, Jorge. *Relación de méritos y servicios del conquistador Bernardino Vázquez de Tapia*. Mexico: Universidad Nacional Autónoma de México, 1972.

Hassig, Ross. *Mexico and the Spanish Conquest*. New York: Longman, 1994.

Hemming, John. *The Search for El Dorado*. New York: Dutton, 1978.

Herrera y Tordesillas, Antonio de. *Historia general de los hechos de los castellanos en las islas y Tierra Firme del mar Océano*. Madrid: Juan Flamenco and Juan de la Cuesta, 1601–1615.

Himmerich y Valencia, Robert. *The Encomenderos of New Spain, 1521–1555*. Austin: University of Texas Press, 1991.

Icaza, Francisco de. *Diccionario de conquistadores de la Nueva España*. 2 vols. Madrid: Imprenta "El adelantado de Segovia," 1923.

Kessell, John L. *Spain in the Southwest: A Narrative History of Colonial New Mexico, Arizona, Texas, and California*. Norman: University of Oklahoma Press, 2002.

Lanning, John T. "Cortes and His First Official Remission of Treasure to Charles V." *Revista de Historia de América* 2 (June 1938): 5–29.

Las Casas, Bartolomé de. *Historia de las Indias*. Ed. Juan Pérez de Tudela. 2 vols. Madrid: Atlas, 1961.

Liss, Peggy. *Mexico under Spain, 1521–1556: Society and Origins of Nationality*. Chicago: University of Chicago Press, 1975.

Lockhart, James. *Men of Cajamarca: A Social and Biographical Study of the First Conquerors of Peru*. Austin: University of Texas Press, 1972.

López de Gómara, Francisco. *La conquista de México*. Mexico: Imprenta de I. de Escalante y Cia., 1870.

Madariaga, Salvador de. *Hernán Cortés*. Buenos Aires: Sudamericana, 1941.

Martínez, José Luis, ed. *Documentos cortesianos*. 4 vols. Mexico: Fondo de Cultura Económica, 1990–1992.

———. *Hernán Cortés*. Mexico: Universidad Nacional Autónoma de México and Fondo de Cultura Económica, 1990.

Matthew, Laura E., and Michel R. Oudijk, eds. *Indian Conquistadors: Indigenous Allies and the Conquest of Mesoamerica*. Norman: University of Oklahoma Press, 2007.

Morison, Samuel Eliot. *The European Discovery of America: The Southern Voyages, 1492–1616*. Oxford: Oxford University Press, 1974.

Nader, Helen. *Liberty in Absolutist Spain: The Hapsburg Sale of Towns, 1516–1700*. Baltimore: Johns Hopkins University Press, 1990.

Pacheco, Joaquín, and Francisco Cárdenas, eds. *Colección de documentos inéditos relativos al descubrimiento, conquista, y organización de las antiguas posesiones españolas de América y Oceanía*. 42 vols. Madrid: Sucesores de Ribadeneyra, 1864–1884.

Parry, John H. *The Sale of Public Office in the Spanish Indies under the Hapsburgs*. Berkeley: University of California Press, 1953.

Pastor Bodmer, Beatriz. *The Armature of Conquest: Spanish Accounts of the Discovery of America, 1492–1589*. Trans. Lydia Longstreth Hunt. Stanford: Stanford University Press, 1992.

Porras Muñoz, Guillermo. *El gobierno de la ciudad de México en el siglo XVI*. Mexico: Universidad Nacional Autónoma de México, 1982.

———. "Martín López, carpintero de ribera." *Revista de Indias* 31–32 (1948): 307–239.

Prescott, William H. *History of the Conquest of Mexico*. New York: Random House, 2001.

Rabasa, José. *Tell Me the Story of How I Conquered You: Elsewheres and Ethnosuicide in the Colonial Mesoamerican World*. Austin: University of Texas Press, 2011.

Restall, Matthew. "The New Conquest History." *History Compass* 10 (2012): 151–160.

———. *Seven Myths of the Spanish Conquest*. Oxford: Oxford University Press, 2003.

Riley, G. Micheal. *Fernando Cortés and the Marquesado in Morelos, 1522–1547*. Albuquerque: University of New Mexico Press, 1973.

Roa de la Carrera, Cristián A. *Histories of Infamy: Francisco López de Gómara and the Ethics of Spanish Imperialism*. Boulder: University Press of Colorado, 2005.

Rubio Mañé, J. Ignacio. *Monografía de los Montejos*. Mérida: Liga de acción social, 1930.

Sauer, Carl Ortwin. *The Early Spanish Main*. Berkeley: University of California Press, 1969.

Saville, Marshall H. "The Earliest Notices Concerning the Conquest of Mexico in 1519." *Indian Notes and Monographs* 10.1 (1920): 5–54.

Schwaller, John F. "Broken Spears or Broken Bones: Evolution of the Most Famous Line in Nahuatl." *The Americas* 66 (2009): 241–252.

———. "Tres familias mexicanas del siglo XVI." *Historia Mexicana* 31:122 (Oct.–Dec. 1981): 171–196.

Solís y Ribadeneyra, Antonio de. *Historia de la conquista de México*. Barcelona: Thomas Piferrer, 1771.

Suárez de Peralta, Juan. *Tratado del descubrimiento de las Indias y su conquista*. Ed. Giorgio Perissinotto. Madrid: Alianza, 1990.

Thayer Ojeda, Tomás, and Carlos J. Larraín. *Valdivia y sus compañeros*. Santiago de Chile: Imprenta universitaria, 1950.

Thomas, Hugh. *Conquest: Montezuma, Cortés, and the Fall of Old Mexico*. New York: Simon and Schuster, 1993.

———. *Who's Who of the Conquistadors*. London: Cassell, 2000.

Todorov, Tzvetan. *The Conquest of America: The Question of the Other*. Norman: University of Oklahoma Press, 1999.

Townsend, Camila. "Burying the White Gods: New Perspectives on the Conquest of Mexico." *American Historical Review* 108 (June 2003): 659–687.

———. *Malintzin's Choices: An Indian Woman and the Conquest of Mexico*. Albuquerque: University of New Mexico Press, 2006.

Townsend, Richard F. *The Aztecs*. 3rd ed. New York: Thames and Hudson, 2009.

Vigneras, Louis André. *The Discovery of South America and the Andalusian Voyages*. Chicago: University of Chicago Press, 1976.

Villar Villamil, Ignacio de. *Cedulario heráldico de conquistadores de Nueva España*. Mexico: Museo Nacional, 1933.

Wagner, Henry R. *The Rise of Fernando Cortés*. Berkeley: The Cortés Society, 1944.

Wood, Stephanie. *Transcending Conquest: Nahua Views of Spanish Colonial Mexico*. Norman: University of Oklahoma Press, 2003.

Index

Alonso, Rodrigo, 215

Alonso de . . . (sig. 186), 85, 212

Alva, Arriego de (sig. 262), 91, 229

Alva Ixtlilxochitl, Fernando de, 45

Alvarado, Gómez de, 36, 155

Alvarado, Gonzalo de (sig. A), 75, 105, 134, 137–138, 155, 160

Alvarado, Jorge de, 36, 155

Alvarado, Juan de, 36

Alvarado, Pedro de (sig. D), 20, 23, 36–37, 52, 65, 99, 102, 105, 134, 137–138, 142–143, 145, 155, 160–162, 168, 170, 172, 188, 202, 207–208, 210, 213, 223, 225, 231–232, 234

Alvarez, Alonso, *maestre* (sig. 104), 81, 127, 193

Alvarez, Francisco (sig. 260), 91, 125, 229

Alvarez, Hernando, 125

Alvarez, Juan (sig. 28), 77, 125, 172

Alvarez, Juan, *maestro, el manquillo* (sig. 37), 34, 77, 111, 114, 125, 127–128, 164, 173–174

Alvarez, Victor, 4, 159

Alvarez Chico, Fernando, 164

Alvarez Chico, Francisco (sig. H), 56–57, 65, 67, 69, 99, 102, 105, 125, 162, 164, 225, 229

Alvarez Chico, Juan, 155, 164, 172

Alvarez Chico, Rodrigo (sig. 246), 91, 114, 155, 164–165, 225–226

Alvarez de Espinosa, Alonso, 193

Alvarez Rubazo, Juan, 172

Amatlan, 237

Amaya, Antonio de, 185

Amaya, Pedro de, 185. *See also* Maya, Pedro de

Amecameca, 18, 22

Anaya, Diego de (sig. 80), 79, 184–185

Andalucía, 119–121, 125, 132, 156, 167, 243

Andrade, doña Beatriz de, 155

Anos, Miguel de (sig. 199), 87, 215

Antilles, 140

Aracena (Huelva), 180

Aragón, 119–123, 133–134

Arce, Ochoa de (sig. 17), 77, 168

Archives of the Indies, 1, 47

Arcía, Ochoa de (sig. 17), 77, 168

Arcos, Ana de, 187

Arcos, Cervera, 167

Arcos, Gonzalo de (sig. 10), 77, 167, 201

Arcos, Hernán de (sig. 141), 83, 201

Arcos, Juan de. *See* Darcos, Juan

Arcos, Ochoa de (sig. 17), 77, 168

Arcos de la Frontera (Cádiz), 167

Argüello, Alonso de (sig. 188), 87, 212

Argüello, Domingo de (sig. 276), 96, 212, 233

Argüello, Hernando (or Juan) de, 212, 233

Arias, Juan de (sig. 275), 95, 110, 233

Arias Dávila. *See* Dávila, Pedrarias

Arias de Sopuerta, Pedro (sig. 117), 81, 122, 127, 195, 196

Arimao, 194

Arriaga, Juan de (sig. 286), 93, 235

Arteaga, Juan de (sig. 291), 93, 236

Artigas (sig. 291), 93, 235–236

Artigosa, 236

artillery, 132–134, 160, 183, 194, 224, 228. *See also* cannon

artisan, 134

Asia, route to, 9–10

Asno, Ochoa de, 168

Asselbergs, Florine, 4–5

Asturias, 119–121

Atahualpa, 107–108

Atengo, 212

Atitalaquia, 180, 228

Atlatlauca, 142–143, 176, 192, 233

Atlixco, 133, 206, 234

audiencia, 10, 236; First Audiencia, 24, 31, 141–142, 228, 249; Second Audiencia, 24, 142, 173, 184, 188, 194

Avellaneda Navas, José Ignacio, 4, 108, 117

Ave María, 35

Avila (Avila), 210, 216–217

Avila, Alonso de (sig. E), 36–37, 99, 105, 137–138, 162–163, 171

Avila, Gaspar de, 183, 236

Index

Martín Muñoz (Segovia), 142, 176

Martín Narices, Juan, 202

Martín Parra (de Porres), Pedro (sig. 51), 79, 177

master. *See* ship's master

Matlactlan, 161

Matthew, Laura, 5

Maundy Thursday (1519), 43

Maxcalzingo, 238

Maya, Antonio de, 172–173

Maya, Pedro de (sig. 32), 77, 172–173

Maya Indians, 14, 155

Meco, Juan de (sig. 35), 77, 173

Medellín (Badajoz), 121, 153, 230

Medellín (Mexico), 177, 219, 222, 239

Medellín, counts of, 138, 160

Medellín, Rodrigo de (sig. 205), 87, 121, 216

Medina, Francisco de (sig. 64), 79, 180, 239

Medina, Juan de (sig. 96), 81, 126, 190

Medinaceli (Soria), 237

Medina del Campo (Valladolid), 144, 180, 201, 232

Medina de Ríoseco (Valladolid), 212, 235

Melgarejo, Juan (sig. 58), 79, 179

Méndez, Juan (sig. 196), 87, 121, 214–215

Méndez de Alcántara, Juan, 215

Mendoza, doña María de, 175

Mendoza, don Antonio de, viceroy, 175

merchant, 9, 11, 16, 24, 129, 164, 179, 202, 207, 213, 215, 229

Mérida (Mexico), 145

Merino, Gómez (sig. 109), 81, 194

Mesa, Francisco de, 152

Mexía, Gonzalo de, 37

Mexica, 7, 55, 126. *See also* Aztecs

Mexico, Gulf of, 10–12, 19, 196, 203, 225

Mexico, Valley of, 18, 21–24, 115, 130

Mexico City, 23–24, 27, 129, 131, 133, 140, 142–144, 149, 151–155, 160–162, 165, 167, 171–172, 174, 176–177, 179–180, 182, 184, 186, 188–190, 195–199, 201–203, 206–208, 210–211, 213–214, 216–220, 222–223, 225–228, 230–232, 234–235, 239

Mexquita, Martín de la, 225

Mi . . . , Alonso (sig. 78), 79, 184

Miaguatlan, 222

Michoacan, 23, 133, 143–144, 164, 182, 186, 193–195, 208–209, 221, 226, 234, 239

military-religious orders, 25, 153. *See also* Calatrava; Santiago, military-religious order of

Milpa, 192

miner, 140, 142–143, 147, 166, 179, 195, 213, 216, 228, 233–234

Mistla, 145, 176

Mixteca, 187

Mixtepec, 142, 177

Mixton War, 162

Mizquiahuala, 214, 235

Mochitlan, 175

Moctezuma, doña Isabel, 163, 182

Moguer (Huelva), 121, 175, 183, 187, 196, 200, 209

Moguer, Rodrigo de (sig. 134), 81, 200

Mola, Andrés de (sig. 158), 83, 205

Mombeltran (Avila), 211

Monjaraz, Andrés de (sig. 230), 89, 124, 143, 218, 221–222

Monjaraz, Gregorio de (sig. 233), 89, 124, 143, 218, 222

Monjaraz, Martín de (sig. 213), 87, 122, 124, 218, 222

Monroy, Alonso de (sig. 195), 87, 126–127, 137, 214

Montaño, Francisco, 194, 201

Montefrio, Pedro (sig. 252), 91, 227

Montejo, Francisco de (sig. C), 30, 32, 34–35, 38, 43, 45–47, 50–52, 58, 65, 69, 99, 102–103, 105, 114, 124, 145–146, 162, 163, 174, 194, 223, 225, 238

Montes de Oca, Marina, 166

Montezuma. *See* Moteuczoma

Montoya, Francisco (sig. 110), 81, 194

Mora, Alonso, 189

Mora, Juan de (sig. 95), 81, 189–190

Morales, Ana de, 231

Morales, Juan de, 189

CPSIA information can be obtained
at www.ICGtesting.com
Printed in the USA
LVHW012312161121
703493LV00001B/148

9 781477 307632